T0355177

OXFORD TECHNOLOGY LAW AND POLICY

Series Editors

FRANK PASQUALE

Professor of Law, Cornell Tech and Cornell Law School

JULIA POWLES

Associate Professor of Law and Technology, The University of Western Australia

Ethical Data Science:
Prediction in the Public Interest

OXFORD TECHNOLOGY LAW AND POLICY

Series Editors
Frank Pasquale, Cornell University and
Julia Powles, University of Western Australia

The Oxford Technology Law and Policy series aims to publish scholarly works of the highest quality, focusing on research that combines rigorous social, political, and ethical theory with a practical sense of the policy implications of critical thought. The series welcomes works exploring contemporary controversies over technology (including automation, robotics, artificial intelligence, data policy, privacy, digital rights, and platform capitalism), as well as those that develop historical methods to reinterpret technological advancements, focused on the role of law and policy in channeling the development of technology. The series does not favor any single approach and invites works rooted in both long-standing and emerging traditions of critical technology studies, from both established and new voices. The Series Editors welcome innovative and interdisciplinary approaches that advance the discussion on technology law and policy.

Ethical Data Science

Prediction in the Public Interest

ANNE L. WASHINGTON, PHD

OXFORD
UNIVERSITY PRESS

OXFORD
UNIVERSITY PRESS

Oxford University Press is a department of the University of Oxford. It furthers the University's objective of excellence in research, scholarship, and education by publishing worldwide. Oxford is a registered trade mark of Oxford University Press in the UK and certain other countries.

Published in the United States of America by Oxford University Press
198 Madison Avenue, New York, NY 10016, United States of America.

© Oxford University Press 2023

Library of Congress Cataloging-in-Publication Data
Names: Washington, Anne L., author.
Title: Ethical data science : prediction in the public interest / Anne L. Washington.
Description: New York, NY : Oxford University Press, [2023] |
Series: Oxford technology law and policy |
Includes bibliographical references and index.
Identifiers: LCCN 2023032900 | ISBN 9780197693025 (hardback) | ISBN 9780197693056 (epub) |
ISBN 9780197693049 (updf) | ISBN 9780197693063 (online)
Subjects: LCSH: Data mining—Moral and ethical aspects. | Predictive analytics—
Moral and ethical aspects. | Machine learning—Moral and ethical aspects.
Classification: LCC QA76.9.D343 W375 2023 | DDC 006.3/12—dc23/eng/20230810
LC record available at https://lccn.loc.gov/2023032900

DOI: 10.1093/oso/9780197693025.001.0001

Printed by Integrated Books International, United States of America

Note to Readers

This publication is designed to provide accurate and authoritative information in regard to the subject matter covered. It is based upon sources believed to be accurate and reliable and is intended to be current as of the time it was written. It is sold with the understanding that the publisher is not engaged in rendering legal, accounting, or other professional services. If legal advice or other expert assistance is required, the services of a competent professional person should be sought. Also, to confirm that the information has not been affected or changed by recent developments, traditional legal research techniques should be used, including checking primary sources where appropriate.

*(Based on the Declaration of Principles jointly adopted by a Committee of the
American Bar Association and a Committee of Publishers and Associations.)*

You may order this or any other Oxford University Press publication
by visiting the Oxford University Press website at www.oup.com.

Contents

Introduction

Ethical Data Science

1. ETHICAL DATA SCIENCE

Order a smoothie, and it is likely the juice shop will make it in front of you. A "Very Berry" smoothie is evocative of something sweet and red, but it is hard to know exactly what will be in it. Without seeing strawberries, cherries, and raspberries tossed in the mixer, who would know if a beet slipped in by mistake? It may be difficult to guess the ratio of ingredients in a blended drink and impossible to determine which were locally grown.

Data science is like a smoothie. But it is rarely prepared in an open kitchen.

Predictive data science is obscure for most people. How does a streaming service guess what to play next? Why does the search engine know where I vote? Why am I getting emails from the brand I mentioned in a text? How do social media sites prioritize posts? A deeply opaque computational process anticipates and then shapes routine interpersonal, civic, community, financial, professional, and cultural experiences. While many of us might blame the algorithm, only those with specialized knowledge know exactly what happens behind the scenes.

Harm caused by predictive systems sometimes makes the news. Proctoring software accuses students of cheating when the room has low lighting. An identity verification model blocks legitimate unemployment claims. Fraud detection programs automatically initiate legal action against welfare recipients. These consequential actions happen all the time and might garner media attention or public ire. Yet few people know how predictions function.

Ethical Data Science. Anne L. Washington, Oxford University Press. © Oxford University Press 2023.
DOI: 10.1093/oso/9780197693025.003.0001

Even when data science predictions run smoothly, it is always outside the control of individuals experiencing them. Predictions can sometimes be beyond the control of the technologists, statisticians, and computer scientists who design the predictive systems. Only a few executives understand the business models and fiscal priorities determining the choices data scientists can make. Predictive data science is a wholesale business.

To understand how and why predictions impact society, they must first be seen as bureaucratic artifacts. Data science capacity is not universally available. The technology that influences our behaviors, determines our beliefs, and anticipates our actions is predominantly in the hands of a few massive infrastructures.

Governments, corporations, associations, universities—in short, organizations—control predictive technology. Few independent data scientists have access to the necessary resources to be so powerful. And one person rarely has the authority to instantaneously propagate influential predictions to large populations. Predictive data technology is subject to the strategic, fiscal, contractual, and trade secret conditions imposed by the organization that paid for it. Instead of predictions being public goods, data science primarily extends internal analytics and supports existing management information systems.

The needs of society are secondary to the interests of organizations able to mass-produce predictions and control huge digital infrastructures. Businesses prioritize their financial and market interests by targeting and catering to ideal customers. Digital government and open-data initiatives lay the foundation for algorithmic predictions while also presenting new challenges to the administrative state. Governments prioritize partisan interests and fiscal responsibilities that could result in uneven access to services. Who, then, advocates for people outside these priorities who have no choice but to interact with digital ecosystems that ignore or harm them?

A public interest technology approach recognizes that the digital revolution is not a luxury service for elite consumers but is an enforced global standard on absolutely everybody. We must approach data science less like a machine and more like a complex policy decision. Ideally, public policy maximizes positive benefits and minimizes negative impact. Multiple forms of expertise are necessary to meet this goal as well as prepare for the rare situations, forgotten populations, and unexpected patterns. Acknowledging human values will be as vital as correct calculations for prediction in the public interest.

Ethical Data Science empowers technologists and others who want to systematically intervene to address the societal consequences of predictive technology. Data science predictions could be held to a higher standard by tracing a production process that often pits expediency against accountability. Unpacking predictions will boost anyone already technically proficient while, for everyone else, it demystifies the intellectual core of data science. Ethical data science centers appropriate social contexts for action and invites multiple well-reasoned directions for action.

1.1 Thinking Like a Data Scientist

Data science thinking has revolutionized society. Digital measurements make it possible to seamlessly track progress and make changes. See a problem? Get data, run an experiment, identify an optimal solution, and implement it. Being able to measure the world to understand it is at the heart of all scientific advancement. Improved engineering and newer quantitative approaches steadily increase data science capacity. Computational thinking expands this ability to include formulating problems through logic and representations. Statistical thinking analyzes variance across observations, taking into account rare events, patterns, and missing information. All this mathematical elegance creates a strong evidence-based understanding of the world that can be verified and tested. Yet evaluating the rightness or wrongness of prediction is not always about solving an equation.

Purely technical solutions to health care, education, workforce, or other matters of public policy often fail because they do not realistically anticipate societal responses or reflect moral expectations. It remains elusive how predictive data science changes elections, creative industries, or the economy. What is more readily apparent is that math cannot solve all social problems. The optimal distribution of school buses in Boston utterly failed in the court of public opinion and was never implemented. COVID-19 phone apps did not reduce the spread of the virus. These cases and others show that the best mathematics and models do not have a material force for change in social systems. Computer science that shapes society must confront questions about how humanity is expressed through and within digital infrastructures.

People are hard to compare. We contain multitudes.

Sociologist Wendy Espeland defines the process of representing and comparing items with a common metric, commensuration. It is commensuration that makes it possible to have a single currency for buying sandwiches or buying houses. Incommensurable items, such as friendships, have unique intrinsic values that are hard to standardize and match. Social scientists have long been aware of this and take precaution when analyzing large data sets. Even if done correctly, identifying groups based on similar behavioral trends will always have a social consequence because differences can be used as a coercive tool of power.

Society is debating the appropriate ways to leverage industrial-scale mathematics that encodes differences between people based on traits or activities. Advocates believe that a better society is possible with faster computation and more digital material. Delivery of digital services is simply faster and wastes fewer resources. Opponents note that data collection inevitably leads to surveillance of low-status populations. Furthermore, some argue that the socially powerful inexpertly wield data science as a blunt tool of oppression and that ultimately the agenda behind efficiency goals is wide-scale exploitation.

Control of the many by the few is the opposite of ideal governance and ethical norms. Calculations that function seamlessly for the majority may be completely useless for everyone else. Worse, many organizations enforce majority preferences for no other reason than simple expediency of operations. Without intervention, predictions could remain solely a technocratic instrument of domination. Data science must begin to ask fundamental questions about power and politics within institutional contexts.

Yet organizations have no urgency to democratize predictions because the governments and businesses that control predictive data science are driven by their own incentive structures. Governments cannot act outside of their statutory authority. Businesses stay true to their clients, industry, and shareholders. None of these organizations have a moral or ethical obligation to provide a social good, especially one beyond their core mandate.

The current digital ecosystem makes it all too easy to simply source readily available material, model what's already popular, compare what is easy, and optimize for the most powerful. Predictive analytics incorporates many aspects of social science yet often without the rigorous methodological training in statistics, causation, and ethical treatment of human subjects. Yet data science for the public good is not just about seemingly neutral scientific rigor. Too many ignore the humanistic endeavor that predictive science evokes. This book grounds predictive data science tasks alongside arts and humanities methodology to unleash creative expression for technical excellence.

Given all this, can prediction ever serve the public interest?

Yes, it can. But thinking like a data scientist cannot be limited to running experiments when so many other interests are at play. A deeper conversation awaits.

1.2 Unpacking Prediction

Predictions are as old as time. From the I Ching and the Minoan Snake Goddess to a contemporary database company, oracles have responded to questions about what would happen next. The human desire to know the future has remained constant over millennia. What is new is that digital predictions anticipate the future while simultaneously restricting the conditions for contemporaneous action. If the prediction determines that the shopper prefers yellow shirts, no other color is ever suggested. Data-driven predictions anticipate and then shape everyday interpersonal, civic, community, financial, professional, and cultural experience.

Behind each of these predictions is an algorithm, a computer routine that produces consistent results by following a set of rules. Algorithms make it possible to enforce policies uniformly or repeat actions without deviation. Data scientists build algorithms to generate predictions. Predictive algorithms process large amounts of data about the past to assess the probability of future occurrences.

Daily interactions are technologically structured through banal and somewhat convenient low-risk predictive algorithms. A spellchecker autocompletes sentences. A search engine anticipates the next word in the query. The software recommends a similar photo. Predictive patterns can be as trivial as asking everyone who orders the burger if they want fries with that. Basically, predictive algorithms can be applied to anything, but this book considers how they anticipate moods and human action. And, understanding prediction is urgent.

Decisions made with predictive algorithms have since expanded far beyond selling products and guessing default settings. Today, a facial expression might disqualify a job candidate, and failure to match a selfie to a driver's license could mean eviction. Data collected for one purpose can determine consequential decisions in another arena because predictive algorithms are the byproduct of incremental transformations.

Data science is similar to any product manufactured by an organization given that it follows through a broad chain of custody. Digital material is moved from one site of expertise to another until a prediction is implemented. Importantly, each step may be performed by different groups and therefore influenced by them. Data science, even in the hands of one person, still must navigate layers of standards, choice architecture, curation decisions, trends, and statistical assumptions.

Algorithms are highly processed derivative products. A proven approach to accountability in derivative products is traceability.

Traceability tracks the history and sources for each constituent part, such as in manufacturing, which follows the path of harvesting, processing, and distribution. For example, labor violations for athletic clothing were discovered after buyers demanded that subcontractors reveal the names of their suppliers. A traceable process can locate success, failure, regulatory remedy, and ethical practice before products are released to the public. A traceable approach to data science would delineate each activity necessary to create a prediction, from gathering data through learning new patterns. An ethical strategy for data science traceability examines tasks and component parts for accountability.

A traceable sequence for data science organizes the book and is called the *prediction supply chain*.

Prediction supply chains manufacture data-driven insights.

Everyday life serves as the raw material for the transformation of digital sources into meaningful patterns. A sequence of partnerships makes predictive products available for distribution. This process is at the heart of data science, evidence-based policy, artificial intelligence, automated decision-making, and other data technologies. Some call this the data life cycle or the machine learning pipeline to emphasize a technical sequence of steps. Yet a supply chain perspective calls greater attention to predictions as human-made manufactured products and shifts our focus from computing to the surrounding business operations, social hierarchy, and economic systems. Supply chains establish standards of business conduct that lay the foundations for traceability and transparency.

Predictive algorithms differentiate people to make sales, influence behaviors, categorize beliefs, ascertain character, or distribute resources. Predictions can also connect people to encourage community, champion mutual aid, or inform with viable alternatives. Predictive algorithms are only obscure because the process creating them remains obscure. If prediction is a team sport, more of us need to be part of the team and understand the game. Without ethical approaches, the prediction supply chain can devolve into merely a speculation supply chain. It is time to better understand how predictive algorithms function and how to make them work for more people.

1.3 Why This Book

Many technologists want to use their scientific expertise for positive change. They do so amidst a growing public critique of the harmful effects of predictive technologies. This would be one of the first books to meet the needs of those striving to create data science that contributes to the public good.

Ethical Data Science is a pragmatic invitation to create predictive data technologies that benefit more people through consideration of past wrongs to imagine new futures. Data scientists will be able to better conceptualize the myriad of decisions they make in order to share strategy with other experts.

Algorithmic accusations can devastate those with least social power. Predictive systems that cannot handle unexpected situations may levy heavy burdens and penalties on forgotten populations. For data science to serve humanity, it would need to enhance its ability to serve outliers, the vulnerable, the least profitable, and the least likely of situations. Predictions that work for only the most powerful do not trickle down necessarily to support the common good.

As one of the first books on public interest technology, *Ethical Data Science* joins the growing multidisciplinary movement that wants human values to counterbalance the institutional incentives that drive computational prediction. Similar to public interest lawyers, public interest technologists direct their professional skills against powerful interests in collaboration with marginalized groups, underserved communities, low-rights populations, or people without a political voice. The book argues that data science prediction embeds administrative preferences that often ignore the disenfranchised.

A unique contribution of the book is that it challenges data science by demonstrating where and how it could improve. The problems and failures of data science are well chronicled in scholarly literature through empirical evidence, critical assessments, and philosophical treatises. While there is substantial material for proving, arguing, and theorizing why predictive algorithms fail, responses for making things better are still emerging. Other computer ethics books explain legal vulnerabilities of software engineering but do not handle the unique problems of data technology. Few texts reflect on how technology-informed public policy could make a difference. This accessible guide builds on established research practices for respectfully handling aggregate data that describes people. The book also serves as a companion for the movement on fairness, accuracy, and transparency in machine learning technology.

On a scholarly level, the book explores the intellectual foundations of data science. Essential social science concepts demonstrate the trade-offs inherent in analyzing data about human behavior and introduce statistical practices for ethically analyzing data sets. At each step in the process, the text reminds us that digital material is an expression of human culture and personal identity. Data science in the public interest takes imagination typically available in humanistic inquiry though rarely found in science, technology, engineering, and math (STEM) curricula. The arts and humanities offers interdisciplinary inquiry that can propel predictive science to its full human potential. Trained as a computer scientist with a background in libraries, I consider data science as a continuation of human recordkeeping that structures the social order.

On a practical level, the book empowers a wider community to participate in informed debates about predictive technologies and their human impact. Equally highlighting technical choices and every day concepts, its step-by-step process grounds conversations about data science across a variety of expertise. The predictive supply chain approach will enhance communication between subject matter experts and technologists. Practitioners, academics, students, policymakers, and legislators will learn how to identify social dynamics in data trends, reflect on ethical questions, and deliberate over solutions. Situating data science within multiple layers of effort exposes dependencies while also pinpointing opportunities for research ethics and policy intervention.

1.4 Organization of This Book

Ethical Data Science combines deliberative assessments with positive action. Challenges to assumptions serve as the intellectual foundation for later refining technical actions. The book closes with advice and policy solutions for implementing and deploying data science in society.

The potential for principled action unfolds over six chapters that trace the prediction supply chain. Finding resources, making abstractions, determining similarities, prioritizing actions, sharing new knowledge, and monitoring progress are things everyone encounters daily but are also aligned with steps in making data-driven predictions. The structure of the book intentionally formalizes data science into discrete stages to trace multiple fault points where technical choices have social ramifications. Each chapter explains the activity's technically necessity, historical perspectives, and related ethical concepts for regulated research. As an alternative to thinking like a data scientist, each chapter introduces the thought processing of an arts or humanities discipline. Readers are invited to think like chefs, painters, historians, librarians, philosophers, and architects to refine data analysis.

The introduction, "Ethical Data Science," poses the book's primary argument, explains predictive algorithms, and defines the prediction supply chain. The prologue presents the core contribution of this text, which is a process approach to data science ethics called the "prediction supply chain." A focus on process recognizes that a different series of choices could produce alternate viable results. Data scientists are invited to think like culinary artists who make healthy creative meals without poisoning anyone.

Chapter 1, "Source," demonstrates how data processing lays the intellectual foundations for prediction credibility. Data scientists who can think like a painter intentionally assemble available material to compose strong evidence for prediction. The "Source" chapter considers how data scientists find appropriate sources and common problems to avoid.

Chapter 2, "Model," questions the plausibility of predictive goals and their normative ideals. Ethical data modeling considers assumptions that compromise the validity of predictions. Thinking like a historian is to establish credible narratives with available fragmentary evidence. The "Model" chapter considers how data scientists conceptualize predictive goals through abstractions.

Chapter 3, "Compare," recognizes that the core activity of data science, contrasting populations, exerts social power. Thinking like a librarian means creating a consistent intellectual order while accommodating the fact that knowledge is always being revised. The "Compare" chapter asks how data scientists determine similarity and difference.

Chapter 4, "Optimize," examines necessary trade-offs for efficiency in data science. Ethical optimization explains the balance of risks and rewards. Thinking like a philosopher invites data science projects to justify priorities with a comprehensive interpretation of alternatives. The "Optimize" chapter asks how data scientists determine what priorities and precedents are set in algorithms.

Chapter 5, "Learn," determines how benefits are distributed. A logic of aggregation explains how and where to apply the inferences generated from combining sources. Thinking like an architect asks data scientists to not build just one building but to contribute to the shape of the city. The "Learn" chapter asks how data scientists determine who benefits from aggregated insights.

Chapter 6, "Show Us Your Work or Someone Gets Hurt," argues that efficiency should be defined broadly to include administrative burdens placed on the public to correct systems once implemented. This chapter asks how to generate feedback into predictive systems so they can incrementally make necessary improvements. Efficiency can fail for unexpected cases, often shifting the responsibility for corrections to people experiencing predictive systems. The policy equivalent of a Paperwork Reduction Act for algorithms may help regulators and advocates to better check efficiency claims by tracking feedback that could prove the contrary.

Chapter 7, "Prediction in the Public Interest," imagines an alternative track for data science. While previous chapters sought to incrementally improve existing systems, this chapter considers the possibility of liberation through prediction done differently. Just as publishers and libraries found ways to coexist, data science can exist without conflicts of interest, ushering in nonmarket or even deviant data science. The conclusion reviews data science outside the control of large organizations and asks how data science could become more inclusive.

1.5 Introduction Summary

To say that data predictions influence society is almost an understatement. Algorithms weave together our social fabric by comparing digital information about people across time and between populations. Solutions to complex social issues that fail to take into account the inherent political and commercial aspects of data science set the stage for harm and distrust. More people need to understand predictive systems so they can advocate for themselves or for the autonomy and personal privacy of everyone. Organizational motives currently tip the data science scales. Advocates and opponents of data science need to come together to counterbalance institutional forces and advocate for prediction in the public interest. *Ethical Data Science* argues that it is possible to blend digital materials to create new knowledge from an ethical standpoint if the production of data science broadens to include multiple forms of expertise.

Prologue

Tracing Ethics in the Prediction Supply Chain

1. TRACING ETHICS IN THE PREDICTION SUPPLY CHAIN

A paramount question of our time is whether data science will ever truly serve the public interest under the current conditions of prediction. Predictive algorithms incrementally increase value by moving between sites of labor and capital investments. Data reused outside their original context is the hallmark of predictive data science (Dhar 2013; Ginsberg et al. 2009; Halevy, Norvig, and Pereira 2009; Lazer et al. 2009; Provost and Fawcett 2013). Data science is possible because data serve as commercial commodities traded between organizations.

The exchange and transformation of digital material is the foundation of building complex data intelligence products. Although most digital insights are far more complex, consider a free mail service. It aggregates email word frequencies to sell ads to marketers interested in those keywords. Words, behaviors, or activities serve as proxies for desired customers and determine who sees which advertisement. Companies pay to promote a targeted advertisement to a select population.

Data science may seem like a magic box that generates inevitable answers, but it is actually a highly processed product. Behind every prediction stands a

Ethical Data Science. Anne L. Washington, Oxford University Press. © Oxford University Press 2023.
DOI: 10.1093/oso/9780197693025.003.0002

cross-section of people, groups, expertise, artifacts, technologies, standards, and practices.

A hot dog might seem like a magic box if we do not know what's really inside the casing and why the market produces meat scraps in the first place. The further from expertise, the more room for deception, which is why governments began to inspect factories when people stopped buying sausage from neighborhood butchers. Safety initiatives rid markets of harmful food while still allowing innovation and scale. Prediction is in a similar transition from artisanal craft to factory production as digital resources proliferate throughout our worlds.

Data science operates within a prediction supply chain, which is a suite of legal, social, and, most importantly, commercial interests. Activities within a prediction's chain of custody are traceable and therefore become sites of accountability.

1.1 Supply Chain Ethics

A supply chain perspective recognizes that in contemporary markets few organizations operate alone. Instead, firms are deeply entwined with others through a series of formal and informal relationships. A supply chain is a string of partnerships that optimize the production and delivery of goods or services to a market.

As a strategy of war, supply chains originally depicted the movement of food and ammunition to provision troops during battle. Today, supply chains represent the manufacture and movement of consumer goods in operations management (Beamon 1998) and logistics (Bowersox 2013). Each location in a supply chain adds value, which accumulates toward the quality and cost of the final product that is delivered.

At its simplest, a supply chain is a production and distribution process in which experts with unique skills transform materials into merchandise (Vidal and Goetschalckx 1997). It starts with a material supplier who locates, gathers, processes, and secures rights to move materials from their original location. A parts supplier transforms the processed material into units for manufacturing. A manufacturer assembles items with supplier parts and packages them for distribution. A wholesale distributor transports packaged products at the pace dictated by the market to maximize consumer sales. Each stage in the supply chain is an opportunity to impact quality, timing, or cost.

Activists leverage supply chains to attract attention to social causes. For instance, universities faced student protests because of questionable labor practices in the production of university logo clothing (Wright, Smith, and Wright 2007). Recognizing that corporations in many countries were struggling with how to source minerals in conflict zones, the Organisation for Economic Co-operation and Development offered guidelines for reducing supply chain risks (OECD 2013). The politics of supply chains has prompted wage reform and environmental sustainability across interconnected businesses (O'Rourke 2014).

From its early military origins to its more recent incarnation in socially responsible retail, the notion of a supply chain has provided a sturdy framework for conceptualizing a network of people, organizations, activities, and artifacts. The prediction supply chain promises avenues for improvement like the environmental (Wible, Mervis, and Wigginton 2014), public health (Maloni and Brown 2006), and blood diamonds (OECD 2013) protests advanced ethical outcomes in the production of tangible objects.

1.2 The Prediction Supply Chain

Encapsulating my philosophy of data science in the public interest, the prediction supply chain is not a metaphor. Optimization or the ideal efficient use of resources drives both logistics and predictive data science. The prediction supply chain creates the material, operational, economic, and intellectual conditions for interpreting data-driven insights. Each technical transformation adds value for later exchange.

The reuse of data to create shopper profiles by the insurance industry illustrates how information moves between organizations to create a prediction. Once requiring blood tests to predict the likelihood of disease, insurance companies now rely on credit card transactions (Maremont et al., 2010). A shopper searches for gym equipment, which alerts the search engine of a potential purchase. When the shopper purchases a stationary bike, the retailer builds a consumer profile. The bank bundles the purchase with other transactions to profile buying habits. A data broker, who buys from multiple sources, aggregates profiles from the search engine, the bank, and the store. The insurance company purchases from the data broker profiles of shoppers who exercise. The data science team integrates these profiles with their own detailed information to predict client health. The purchase of exercise equipment was an indicator of a health risk for someone with a long commute. Shoppers who did not purchase gym equipment were deemed healthier if they lived and worked in the same zip code.

Data are commodities exchanged in what are now unregulated and unmonitored markets. Prediction supply chains find or generate digital sources, identify patterns from aggregate data, and apply new insights in an ongoing cycle. Each partnership bundles business decisions that are dependent on economic patterns of supply and demand.

The exchange of digital material is not always a commercial transaction. Since 2009, governments worldwide have championed the release of information paid for by the public sector. Governments regularly release information as open data, making it free for download on the internet with little or no licensing requirements.

Open government data are also exchanged to create predictive value. For example, campaign finance laws require members of Congress to submit the names of donors. A government agency makes it available as open data free to reuse. Imagine that each year nonprofits download the donor list for all politicians who voted favorably on their legislative agendas. By combining this list with their own, the nonprofits predict the characteristics of potential donors for their cause.

Predictive data science has its roots in marketing. Bulk mailers wanted to reduce the expense of sending advertisements and to increase the probability that a promotion would be successful. Direct marketers soliciting additional sales would associate postal codes with, for instance, magazine subscriptions. A computational turn shifted from demographics to patterns within markets (Cespedes and Smith 1993). Data science could refine the "soccer mom" marketing demographic to "35-year-old north-eastern female fans of Manchester United." Given certain characteristics, advertisers leverage predictions to estimate who might buy what and when.

Few outside marketing needed to understand the mathematical logic behind what week to start pumpkin spice season. Some Starbucks executives know why the sale of sweet items flavored with cinnamon, clove, and fragrant spices found in pumpkin pie has steadily moved from mid-autumn in 2003 to the last Tuesday in August in 2021. Originally designed to automate customer discovery, data science quietly seeped from advertisements into aspects of society where we expect fair and balanced solutions. Mundane information now predicts decisions in finance, medicine, government, and insurance.

The core activities within the prediction supply chain and addressed in the following chapters are source, model, compare, optimize, and learn. Each chapter matches these technical activities with a way of thinking from a humanities discipline. Sourcing appropriate observations with concepts of informed consent and with the nuance of an artist will make stronger predictions. Modeling valid dependencies establishes a strategic direction much like a historian building a narrative. Comparisons match relevant patterns and maintain autonomy while building a coherent intellectual infrastructure, like a library catalog. Optimization justifies the trade-offs of efficiency by providing philosophical reasoning. Learning creates insights like an architect who builds one building but with an awareness that over time, it will house others.

A focus on process exposes multiple points of intervention and risk. This also models how the greater research community has handled the ethics of experimental human studies.

1.3 Research Ethics

Research ethics regulation stands in stark contrast to the prediction supply chain. Supply chains openly trade information, while research studies curate limited access to carefully designed data sets (Borgman 2020). Contemporary regulators impose a strict standard before experimental studies can proceed.

Biomedical, social, and behavioral scientists have close associations with the participants in their research studies. Human subjects research studies must be reviewed in advance to identify potential ethical problems. In the least, researchers must explain how the knowledge does not harm participants. Some populations, such as people who are incarcerated, are considered vulnerable because they have limited or no power in relationship to the large institutional forces controlling their lives.

Human subjects boards exist around the world at the national level and at universities. These boards establish boundaries of what constitutes human subjects research and also take into account how to mitigate potential harms within their national legal context. The Institutional Review Board (IRB) is the regulatory mechanism in the United States to evaluate research proposals. All funded research must go through the IRB approval process, especially biomedical and behavioral research involving people.

Governments established these systems in the face of a string of ethical violations. The drug thalidomide, given to pregnant women to relieve nausea, caused severe physical birth defects. The US federal government conducted a forty-year biomedical study that merely tracked how Black men died of syphilis without offering treatment, even after a medical cure became available. The US Public Health Scandal in 1972 revealed a total failure to respect the community in which the research took place and the individuals who were suffering from illness ("Former Director for Tuskegee Syphilis Study Believes Work Was 'Completely Ethical'" 1972). John H. Heller and the physicians he led exploited sick men in Tuskegee, Alabama, in ways that are legally and professionally prohibited in a traditional clinical setting where patient care is expected (Heller 1972).

The US Congress formed the National Commission for the Protection of Human Subjects of Biomedical and Behavioral Research in the aftermath of Heller's dismissal as the top US public health official. The scholars and community leaders convened in Belmont, California, and issued a report that established human subjects research guidelines for any federally funded study (U.S. Department of Health, Education, and Welfare and National Commission for the Protection of Human Subjects of Biomedical and Behavioral Research 1979). The Belmont Report championed three main principles: respect for persons, justice, and beneficence, in addition to practices of informed consent and assessment of risks and benefits.

A few miles away from Belmont, in Menlo Park, California, another group convened in 1993, this time to consider how ethical research principles should be applied to information technology research (U.S. Department of Homeland Security et al. 2012). The Menlo Report built on Belmont's three principles and also included stakeholder perspectives, respect for law, mitigating harms, and accountability.

Principles of consent, dignity, justice, and selection of participants, which are core to the Belmont Principles, are harder to ascertain when it comes to data science. Digital material is used and reused over time by several organizations and individuals crossing languages, legal jurisdictions, and cultures. There is no standard way to track and explain why a project reduced three million observations to thirty thousand. Data sets of this size do not allow any meaningful interaction with individual preferences. There exist few professional standards for documenting patterns of reuse, data cleaning, and other crucial decisions. Ethics regulation is configured to monitor biomedical and behavioral investigators associated with an institution. Predictive data science studies outside that context are difficult to hold to the same standard. However, many of the core ideas of research ethics remain aspirational for data science.

Concepts from research ethics regulation serve as important steppingstones as adequate tech policy develops for data science. As we proceed, the prediction supply chain is matched with concepts from research ethics to indicate opportunities for further reflection and connection: informed consent–source, justice–model, autonomy–compare, trade-offs–optimize, beneficence–learn.. Finally, in the final chapter on implementation, we apply the principles of accountability from the Menlo Report.

1.4 Manufacturing Risk

Prediction supply chains can manufacture risk as well as insights.

Tech policy has struggled to develop appropriate responses to the potential harms of predictive data science. Without traceability guidelines, the only way to determine component parts is to examine the final product. Attempting to assess highly processed algorithmic products after the fact has its limitations. Technologists have tried to reverse engineer algorithms with modest success (Diakopoulos 2014). Audits and post hoc evaluations are like performing a forensic analysis of poisonous hot dogs instead of enacting food regulations to prevent harm in the first place. It may not be necessary to experience bad effects if sufficient guidelines are in place. Regulators currently seek to set reasonable limits such as the General Data Protection Regulation in the European Union and the AI Bill of Rights in the United States.

A supply chain perspective can identify a wider range of improvements that are actionable in law and policy. Different choices at each critical point could produce alternative viable results. This systematic approach moves data science away from being a deterministic technology that produces the "right" magic box answer and toward the complex product that it is. An inference may be resolved by pursuing a sociological question rather than a mathematical one. To paraphrase the actor Lily Tomlin who asked "If love is the answer, can you please rephrase the question," we have to think carefully about the questions we ask if prediction is the answer..

Debates over whether data science belongs in the social sciences or in computing skips over the fact that prediction is primarily an economic activity. Accumulating massive data repositories is like owning productive land in previous eras. The land not only represented affluence but also generated wealth. The land leased to farmers or miners would yield new goods that could be sold. Organizations that control massive resources have little incentive to support individuals, the public interest, or long-term incentives. Data streams are traded just as minerals and rare spices were once exchanged by dominant actors before fair trade agreements.

Given the economic orientation of prediction, ethics in data science is necessary not only because we need to think about appropriate behavior but because the benefit of a few who control these technologies must be balanced against the interests of the many who live with the consequences. The groups who control these technologies are under no moral obligation to provide a public service beyond their own incentives. The next era of data science must consider how to democratize control of predictions.

The following illustration introduces the stages in the prediction supply chain and their staggering risk accumulated by a welfare payment program in Australia.

1.5 OCI Robodebt

The Online Compliance Intervention system (OCI) was launched in 2016 to detect overpayment of welfare benefits in Australia. Ironically, the federal system cost the Australian government billions of dollars and in the process ruined lives and destroyed political careers. Referencing the movie *RoboCop* (Verhoeven 1987), the press dubbed OCI "Robodebt," for how the predictive system automatically accused people of fraud.

Australia intended for OCI to modernize its Centrelink welfare system. A cost-benefit analysis that justified the new system claimed that in previous years nearly one million welfare recipients had been overpaid (Parliament of

Australia 2017). Recovering funds from fraudulent claims became a primary incentive for automating welfare payments. Over three years, seven hundred thousand Australian residents were wrongly accused of fraud (Parliament of Australia 2021). Indigent welfare recipients had to repay the government thousands of dollars at a time. Repayment with interest. The predictions made misguided assumptions about itinerant work that resulted in overpayments (Henriques-Gomes 2020; Karp and Knaus 2018). The government accused people of fraud instead of recognizing their own algorithm's overpayment problem.

Like other predictive data systems, the Australian system was designed to save money and increase the government budget. In a related attempt, the welfare office reduced staff—just as the number of exceptions that staff had to handle increased. By the time multiple investigations stopped OCI, the government owed more money in damages than they recovered from alleged fraud (Henriques-Gomes L 2019). Australia spent $1.8 billion AUD to compensate for wrongful accusations in one class action case. Although the 2019 case represented only ten thousand people (Henriques-Gomes L 2023), Australia continues to face additional civil litigation from others seeking redress through individual lawsuits over OCI Robodebt (Parliament of Australia 2021). Some applicants under the pressures of repayment took their own lives (Henriques-Gomes 2021).The political party and politicians who championed the system were not voted back into office amid the scandal (Royal Commission 2023).

Risk of failure is often underestimated in predictive data technology. To treat a predictive algorithm as an immutable magic box is to introduce a Trojan horse into the organization. Predictive algorithms not only can result in substantial harms to individuals but can severely disrupt administrative operations. Insufficient testing beyond the typical cases may result in heavy burdens on non-algorithmic systems (Rhue and Washington 2020). Increasingly, people who are wronged by algorithms demand compensation and do so publicly. When Apple issued high credit limits only to husbands and not wives, several high-profile couples complained on social media. In the least, the public begins to question the legitimacy of organizations that release faulty predictive systems.

The following sections sketch the logic of the book's organization with a case study of the OCI Robodebt predictive welfare fraud system. The prediction supply chain makes a distinction between each incremental stage, explaining an aspect of OCI Robodebt that went wrong and how it could be improved. After indicating the fault lines across five decision points, the case illustrates the compounding effects of sourcing, modeling, comparing, optimizing, and learning. The Robodebt nickname of the Australian welfare system represents the robotic unemotional thinking that can sometimes prevent data science from achieving its full potential.

1.6 Robo Source

The first concern of any supply chain is to locate raw materials. In the prediction supply chain, data are the supplies that will be processed and transformed. Digital material needs to be identified, evaluated for quality, and selected for appropriateness. The credibility of future prediction depends on finding the right materials.

Sources were essential to the Robodebt's problems. To receive benefits, applicants declared how much money they might earn. The application form asked for income or income estimates. OCI Robodebt had another source for discovering income. Government agencies in Australia can exchange data about citizens. As soon as the tax agency received income reports, it would send the information to the welfare agency. The sources for Robodebt primarily came from applications and other government agencies as many applicants left blank the response to the income question. Income was not a required field. However, it would prove to be an essential field.

The government distributed welfare benefits based on current income levels. The goal of the policy was to supplement individual income, not to provide a uniform payment. The welfare payments for someone earning $500 AUD a week would be half of someone earning $1,000 AUD a week. Understanding a trend in earnings was critical to distributing payments. Applicants who did not complete that field on the form inadvertently relied on an algorithm to estimate income. The algorithm made assumptions that led to incorrect estimates. OCI Robodebt calculated income based on the last available tax data. Applicants who had higher past income compared to current levels were overpaid. OCI Robodebt did not consider the naturally occurring difference between anticipated income and reported income.

Because fraud was defined as a discrepancy between the application and the tax agency, people whose estimated future earnings did not match actual taxed earnings were flagged. Applicants were accused of fraud because a leading indicator did not have the predictive power of a lagging indicator. However, overpayments were deemed to be a moral failure of the applicant. The applicants had no control over the outcome and did not explicitly consent to having the algorithm estimate their wages.

The "Source" chapter explores the first step in the prediction supply chain and invites data scientists to think like a painter who intentionally assembles available material to build a composition. The selected materials provide solid evidence for the intended picture the prediction will paint. OCI Robodebt seemed to not understand how its data sources interacted with each other. The system did not take into consideration how availability related to quality and timing.

Simple mistakes—or in this case, an omission—with such large consequences deserve some level of informed consent. Why couldn't someone let applicants know that the wrong income value could land them in jail? Informing applicants of the importance of income estimates was the least that the Australian government could have done. Better understanding of the original sources could have led to more accurate payments and would have resulted in fewer accusations of fraud.

1.7 Robo Model

The second stage of the prediction supply chain is to clarify what will be produced. Personal data is transformed into different products just as raw materials turn into mass-produced consumer goods. A manufacturer would need to know if a supply of cotton is destined to become a shirt or a rope. Each product requires quality of material and processing to achieve the desired results. The "Model" chapter considers symbols, the predictive goal, and all its associated assumptions. Striving for validity, models represent an ideal or the prediction's default assumed characteristics.

OCI Robodebt created a model to estimate the income of welfare applicants. The algorithm paid benefits based on a two-week average of income. If the applicant left the income estimate blank, the algorithm used information of last reported income from the tax office. The calculation for income in OCI Robodebt assumed that residents receiving payments had stable work.

The validity of a two-week income average is strongly questionable for the given population. People who have one employer and a steady annual income have predictable biweekly income. The injustice of this model choice is that the jobs available to people receiving welfare benefits are not this consistent. An average of earnings was never going to be ideal for people who require occasional welfare benefits.

The decision to average wages did not match the profile of people working in informal economies. A waiter cannot approximate tips. A taxi driver cannot estimate fares. Someone out of work after a busy holiday season could easily be accused of fraud. OCI Robodebt made payments based on holiday wages, and when actual earnings did not meet these high estimates, the government demanded repayment. Of course, the algorithm could have used data sources that tracked annualized income. The poor choice of sources put more pressure on the algorithmic models to perform well.

Just like in the discipline of history, sources can contradict each other, especially when compared over time. Thinking like a historian invites data scientists to recognize the circumstances influencing the sources they select. Historians establish credible narratives with often fragmentary contradictory evidence by weighing relative values. OCI Robodebt did not consider both the quality and the timing of the income data. Instead, it gave all information equal weight, despite when it was received.

A more realistic model of applicants' lifestyles would have led to better accuracy in the initial benefit payments and fewer accusations of fraud. The model could have been adjusted for seasonal earning trends. Another model could have made lower, less generous, estimates to avoid any probability of repayment. The algorithm did not reflect the life patterns of the people whose lives were being predicted. Without that basic face validity, the resulting predictions were often off target.

1.8 Robo Compare

Comparison is the essential expertise necessary to create predictions. Data scientists aggregate and transform original digital materials into meaningful groups through comparisons. The "Compare" chapter considers how to detect differences and define similarities through pattern matching.

The Australian government made a selective choice to not find patterns about the people accused of fraud. Although fraud was detected at a regular clip, the government interpreted this as a mass effort to defraud the government by unique actors. Knowing that the algorithm consistently made the same mistake would have been valuable feedback and a plausible alternative explanation for the overpayments. The autonomy of applicants accused of fraud was quickly diminished. The cost of being accused of fraud included repaying the money received back to the government with interest. But there were other costs, including a criminal record, difficulty finding employment, exclusion from other government benefits, and foreclosure. Putting people into categories has consequences, and OCI Robodebt never acknowledged the full social impact of how applicants were categorized.

OCI Robodebt compared actual income to anticipated income to categorize applicants into two sets. One set contained people whose income estimates were correct. The other set contained people who relied on the faulty algorithm's income estimate. The people whose income estimates were wrong initially received an overpayment and subsequently a letter demanding repayment. The welfare system labeled the second set as fraud and leveled legal obligations on them. The credibility of people in the fraud group was constantly questioned as they tried to resolve the issue. Algorithms that make stark social comparisons quickly disempower. Building sets for comparison is not alone a problem. The problems begin when the distribution of resources is radically different between groups. Categories often have material consequences because they can imply a social hierarchy. Divisions can stoke animosity between groups of people. Placing people in undesirable categories without a basis for appeal is antithetical to societies that encourage opportunity.

Categories assigned by the algorithm seemed inevitable and immutable since the sources and models were not openly available. Applicants were not aware of why they were put in this category. Without an awareness of what information led to the accusation, applicants could not change their status in the eyes of the algorithm. Only during multiple legislative inquiries was it revealed that the income calculation was critical to making comparisons. In the least, the government could have made it possible to challenge being placed in a category that had catastrophic disadvantages.

Categories are not natural. They reflect community values. For centuries, the library profession has considered how to determine similarity for multiple intellectual communities simultaneously. Library catalogers, specifically, build knowledge infrastructures and establish rules that incorporate outliers, exceptions, and potential unknown items. Data scientists who think like a librarian intentionally create an intellectual order that recognizes both consistency and flexibility of meaning. Librarians balance the power of classification with the dignity of intellectual freedom.

Comparison is the core activity in data science, yet social classifications are rarely static. Some comparisons can level collective punishment, severely limiting individual autonomy.

1.9 Robo Optimize

The fourth stage of the prediction supply chain examines necessary trade-offs to achieve efficiency. Just as a factory is designed to waste few resources, algorithms are streamlined so some activities take precedence. Optimization forces decisions about importance and priorities. Choosing priorities inherently enacts moral frameworks that justify why one choice eclipses another.

The letters OCI Robodebt sent to those accused of fraud explained how much money they owed, when they had to repay, and the penalty for failing to respond. OCI did not justify the accusations in these letters. Applicants did not know when the overpayment occurred nor how overpayment was calculated. The letters aggregated and summarized details. This obscured details that might be in the interests of applicants.

OCI Robodebt retained all advantages for the government while placing all burdens on the applicants. Anyone accused of fraud was immediately banned from all government assistance programs. This alleviated budgetary pressures across multiple agencies and saved the government money. Furthermore, the government seemed to not even think about the stress or material impact on someone accused of defrauding the government. The government's financial and budgetary interests were the overriding priorities for OCI Robodebt.

Applicants' responses were severely limited through institutional control. Compliance in the form of repayment was the only given action. Applicants accused of fraud were given no alternatives. Because the letters were cryptic, calls into the welfare office increased. People waited multiple hours to talk to someone to get any advice. As a further cost-cutting measure, the government, anticipating less work with the new automated system, laid off welfare office staff. There was no procedure to challenge the accusation or change the applicant's fraud classification. An implicit social contract was broken when no reason was given for the accusation. Administrative due process is the expectation that procedures will be followed as stated in policy and followed under all circumstances (Calo and Citron 2021). Procedural fairness in OCI Robodebt was not prioritized.

Thinking like a philosopher invites data scientists to justify an algorithm's priorities or at least to acknowledge the trade-offs. Philosophical positions furnish compelling portraits of the competing forces that shape the prediction supply chain. Drawing on the work of great philosophers contextualizes data science priorities. The "Optimize" chapter introduces seven common philosophical positions to explain differing approaches to data science: utilitarianism, deontology, virtue ethics, social contract theory, feminist ethics, theology, and rational choice economics.

The OCI Robodebt algorithm could have been designed to balance the relative importance of budgetary, civic, organizational, and ethical priorities. The letters could have explained who determined fraud and how it was calculated. The government could have prioritized the interests of applicants as taxpayers and members of the polis. Instead, cost recovery dominated the priorities of the Australian government and its third-party contractor. OCI Robodebt prioritized the organizational interests of the government over the interests of both solitary applicants and accused applicants collectively.

Data science optimizations often fail to justify their actions or accept responsibility for secondary effects of optimized outcomes. Algorithmic optimization enacts priorities and moral values.

1.10 Robo Learn

After optimizing, the final stage in the prediction supply chain is to learn from the inferences. Data patterns reveal insights that the world has never known. This stage determines how new knowledge is distributed and who benefits by learning from the information.

OCI Robodebt learned that people with occasional work can easily over- or underestimate income. The system did not employ this trove of knowledge to reflect on itself, the system, or any patterns of fraud. Instead, OCI Robodebt hoarded, for its own benefit, all new knowledge generated by the algorithm. The applicants and the tax agency did not learn any insights based on the data they shared with the welfare agency. Members of the public, who essentially paid for the system with their tax dollars, did not know how the system worked. The welfare agency did not reveal how it generated payments and fraud accusations. The system did not consider sharing information as important. Applicants could not learn what they did wrong nor refute the claim. Without an awareness of what information led to the accusation, applicants could not correct data or provide additional information.

All data scientists have a vested interest in optimizing their own benefits, which, in the case of Robodebt, meant a steady stream of fraud accusations. A third-party contractor built the automated system for OCI. The contractor received a percentage of the funds recovered through accusations of fraud. The government received money back from welfare recipients. Together, OCI and the contractor benefited from the new knowledge generated from this system. The algorithm ignored the needs of applicants in favor of their own desire for cost recovery. The Australian government exercised a large and consequential information asymmetry over individuals and used it to extract money.

Beneficence, a core motivation in research ethics, is not just good intentions. It is an obligation to enhance the possibility of an advantage for people who share data. Thinking like an architect asks data scientists to not just design a beautiful building but solidly construct something that will not collapse and kill people. The "Learn" chapter introduces the *logic of aggregation* framework that helps researchers connect who provides the source to who benefits from what is learned from the data.

OCI Robodebt could have been designed with the needs of individuals in mind without consideration of financial profits. The contractor could have prioritized improving the initial calculations for disbursement. More accurate welfare payments not only would have eliminated many fraud accusations but also would have given reduced revenue opportunities. The government could have waited to lay off office staff until after the system was successfully implemented. While the OCI Robodebt saved money, the expenses for implementing an insufficient system were costly to the individuals and, ultimately, to the organization. Ethical studies keep their own benefits in check especially in light of any harm caused to participants.

1.11 Lessons from Robodebt

Algorithms rely on symbolic interpretation as much as math. Individuals challenging an automated system have the additional cognitive work of interpreting the situation through the eyes of the organization and its algorithm. Organizational success comes at the expense of individual administrative burden. Unlike an economic penalty focusing on the exchange of goods and services with a price mechanism, automated decision systems fail by exacting a time cost, which I call *procedural attention*.

OCI Robodebt obscured where the work was being done. The administrative work shifted from the government to applicants. Those who wanted to fight the fraud accusations had to devote time and attention to understanding how the algorithm interpreted existing public policy. Efficiency should be justified not only in making decisions but in the procedural burdens in correcting decisions.

Because mistakes happen at scale, there needs to be a systematic way to handle errors at scale.

In the "Predict" chapter, I present a policy proposal that can help organizations calculate the efficiency of disputing a claim, so they have a more nuanced perspective of the success of a predictive system. This mitigates errors within the production process by changing both public policy and internal data policy to receive better feedback.

Australia's OCI Robodebt system could have limited accusations of fraud by finding more accurate sources and optimization. Because the system did not share what it learned with others, the implementation was particularly obscure. The deployment of OCI Robodebt exacerbated and compounded problems from the earlier stages. Having solid plans would have limited the harms inflicted in the active system. Together, the sources, models, comparisons, optimizations, and implementation created an unsustainable predictive algorithm.

The multiple layers of effort within the prediction supply chain provide a foundation to unpack what went wrong. The prediction supply chain is a tool to distinguish between levels and layers of accountability.

1.12 Thinking Like a Chef

The culinary arts may seem a far cry from traditional humanities, much less data science. Yet the combination of flair and discipline to make a good meal is like making a good prediction. Data science and the culinary arts have two things in common. First, they share a highly technical production process. Second, they also share the need to obscure details and complications to create an object extremely legible to average people.

Along with taste and looks, the culinary arts have to grapple with the real constraints of food science, otherwise the soufflé will sink or the soup will burn. Human physiology, biochemistry, and even physics come into play when cooking. Chefs also have an eye on the meal's nutritional value, so it provides sufficient proteins, nutrients, and vitamins. Nourishment and chemistry, however, merely prepare the setting for the expression of human culture.

Chefs follow the laws of natural science to produce nourishing food that appeals to the eye and the palate. What emerges from the kitchen looks appetizing and enticing. To a diner, exceptional aesthetics of taste and sight conceal all the mechanics. The bottom line for food is whether the flavor and texture meet expectations. Culinary education would be incomplete if it ended with agricultural science, yet data science programs sometimes stop short at methods courses.

Data science often seems tasteless or stale.

Random data between slices of algorithms are like lunchmeat sandwiches that provide a quick meal with low nutritional value. Processed foods blend salt, sugar, fat, and preservatives to meet taste standards at the lowest possible cost in a way that profoundly mirrors the development of lazy predictive data analytics. Data science will not get better without accountability when the advertised steak sandwich actually contains bologna. Only someone with discriminating taste buds can even begin to unravel the composition of a bouillabaisse. Understanding a prediction requires a similar level of mastery but few paths to acquire these skills. Data scientists who think like a chef forgo cheap canned meats and even cookbooks.

Legendary data scientists are like professional cooks who ignore recipes to build flavorful textures from only an awareness of salt, fat, acid, and heat (Nosrat 2017). Just as senior data scientists rely on more than technical skills to perfect their craft, any chef knows that rare spices and new equipment are seldom sufficient to produce an excellent meal. People skilled in the culinary arts can reshape a meal entirely with only minor expert interventions. The key to virtuosity is curiosity, which means asking how and why questions while transforming digital materials.

Thinking like a chef means bringing technical skills to bear on artifacts designed for human consumption. Predictive data science could be alert to social textures and sour tastes like the abuse of power. Chefs have a cultural awareness and a heightened awareness of context. Data scientists, like chefs, need to recognize that they are not creating one isolated thing but are contributing to a broader cultural production.

It is generally assumed that restaurants do not serve food that kills people. There is a baseline level of care. No matter how many people handle the food, nor how many ways it is prepared, what is delivered on the plate will not be toxic. This simple principle could be useful in data science.

References

Beamon, Benita M. 1998. "Supply Chain Design and Analysis: Models and Methods." *International Journal of Production Economics* 55 (3): 281–94. https://doi.org/10.1016/S0925-5273(98)00079-6.

Borgman, Christine L., Peter T. Darch, Irene V. Pasquetto, and Morgan F. Wofford. 2020. "Our Knowledge of Knowledge Infrastructures: Lessons Learned and Future Directions." Working Paper. University of California escholarship. https://escholars hip.org/uc/item/9rm6b7d4.

Bowersox, Donald J. 2013. *Supply Chain Logistics Management.* 4th ed. New York: McGraw-Hill. http://www.mhhe.com/bowersox4e.

Calo, Ryan, and Danielle Citron. 2021. "The Automated Administrative State: A Crisis of Legitimacy." *Emory Law Journal* 70 (4): 797–845.

Cespedes, Frank V., and H. Jeff Smith. 1993. "Database Marketing: New Rules for Policy and Practice." *Sloan Management Review* 34: 7–22.

Dhar, Vasant. 2013. "Data Science and Prediction." *Communications of the ACM* 56 (12): 64–73. https://doi.org/10.1145/2500499.

Diakopoulos, Nicholas. 2014. "Algorithmic Accountability." *Digital Journalism* 3 (3): 398–415. https://doi.org/10.1080/21670811.2014.976411.

"Former Director for Tuskegee Syphilis Study Believes Work Was 'Completely Ethical.'" 1972. *All Things Considered.* Washington DC: National Public Radio. https://www.npr.org/2020/03/03/808621619/former-director-for-tuskegee-syphilis-study-believes-work-was-completely-ethical.

Ginsberg, Jeremy, et al. 2009. "Detecting Influenza Epidemics Using Search Engine Query Data." *Nature* 457: 1012–14.

Halevy, Alon, Peter Norvig, and Fernando Pereira. 2009. "The Unreasonable Effectiveness of Data." *IEEE Intelligent Systems* 24 (2): 8–12. https://doi.org/10.1109/MIS.2009.36.

Heller, Jean. 1972. "Syphilis Victims in U.S. Study Went Untreated for 40 Years." *The New York Times*, July 26, 1972, sec. Archives. https://www.nytimes.com/1972/07/26/archives/syphilis-victims-in-us-study-went-untreated-for-40-years-syphilis.html.

Henriques-Gomes, Luke. 2019. "Robodebt Scheme Costs Government Almost as Much as It Recovers." *The Guardian*, February 21, 2019, sec. Australia news. https://www.theguardian.com/australia-news/2019/feb/22/robodebt-scheme-costs-government-almost-as-much-as-it-recovers.

Henriques-Gomes, Luke. 2020. "All Centrelink Debts Raised Using Income Averaging Unlawful, Christian Porter Concedes." *The Guardian*, May 31, 2020, sec. Australia news. https://www.theguardian.com/australia-news/2020/may/31/all-centrelink-debts-raised-using-income-averaging-unlawful-christian-porter-concedes.

Henriques-Gomes, Luke. 2021. "Judge Criticises Government for Allegedly Refusing to Tell Grieving Mother about Son's Robodebt." *The Guardian*, May 6, 2021, sec. Australia news. https://www.theguardian.com/australia-news/2021/may/06/judge-criticises-government-for-allegedly-refusing-to-tell-grieving-mother-about-sons-robodebt.

Henriques-Gomes, Luke. 2023. "Robodebt: Five Years of Lies, Mistakes and Failures That Caused a $1.8bn Scandal." *The Guardian*, March 10, 2023, sec. Australia news. https://www.theguardian.com/australia-news/2023/mar/11/robodebt-five-years-of-lies-mistakes-and-failures-that-caused-a-18bn-scandal.

Karp, Paul, and Christopher Knaus. 2018. "Centrelink Robo-Debt Program Accused of Enforcing 'illegal' Debts." *The Guardian*, April 4, 2018, sec. Australia news. https://www.theguardian.com/australia-news/2018/apr/04/centrelink-robo-debt-program-accused-of-enforcing-illegal-debts.

Lazer, David, et al. 2009. "Computational Social Science." *Science* 323 (5915): 721–23. http://dx.doi.org/10.1126/science.1167742.

Maloni, Michael J., and Michael E. Brown. 2006. "Corporate Social Responsibility in the Supply Chain: An Application in the Food Industry." *Journal of Business Ethics* 68 (1): 35–52. https://doi.org/10.1007/s10551-006-9038-0.

Nosrat, Samin. 2017. *Salt, Fat, Acid, Heat: Mastering the Elements of Good Cooking.* Simon & Schuster Nonfiction Original Hardcover. New York: Simon & Schuster.

OECD. 2013. "The Organisation for Economic Co-Operation and Development Due Diligence Guidance for Responsible Supply Chains of Minerals from Conflict-Affected and High-Risk Areas." 2nd ed. http://www.oecd.org/corporate/mne/mining.htm.

O'Rourke, Dara. 2014. "The Science of Sustainable Supply Chains." *Science* 344 (6188): 1124–27. https://doi.org/10.1126/science.1248526.

Parliament of Australia. 2017. "Better Management of the Social Welfare System Initiative Report of the Community Affairs References Committee." Parliament Report. Canberra, Australia. Australia. https://www.aph.gov.au/Parliamentary_Business/Com mittees/Senate/Community_Affairs/SocialWelfareSystem/Report.

Parliament of Australia, Canberra. 2021. "Centrelink's Compliance Program." Australia. https://www.aph.gov.au/Parliamentary_Business/Committees/Senate/Commun ity_Affairs/Centrelinkcompliance.

Provost, Foster, and Tom Fawcett. 2013. *Data Science for Business: What You Need to Know about Data Mining and Data-Analytic Thinking.* Sebastopol, CA: O'Reilly.

Royal Commission. 2023. "Royal Commission into the Robodebt Scheme." https://robod ebt.royalcommission.gov.au/publications/report.

Rhue, Lauren, and Anne L. Washington. 2020. "AI's Wide Open: Premature Artificial Intelligence and Public Policy." *Boston University Journal of Science and Technology Law* 26 (2): 353–78. https://ssrn.com/abstract=3720944.

Scism, Leslie, and Mark Maremont. 2010. "Insurers Test Data Profiles to Identify Risky Clients." *Wall Street Journal*, November 19, 2010, sec. Tech. http://www.wsj.com/artic les/SB10001424052748704648604575620750998072986.

U.S. Department of Health, Education, and Welfare, and National Commission for the Protection of Human Subjects of Biomedical and Behavioral Research. 1979. "The Belmont Report. Ethical Principles and Guidelines for the Protection of Human Subjects of Research."

U.S. Department of Homeland Security, et al. 2012. "The Menlo Report: Ethical Principles Guiding Information and Communication Technology Research." Cyber Security Division, U.S. Department of Homeland Security Science and Technology Directorate. https://www.dhs.gov/sites/default/files/publications/CSD-MenloPrinciplesCORE-20120803_1.pdf.

Vidal, C.J., and M. Goetschalckx. 1997. "Strategic Production-Distribution Models: A Critical Review with Emphasis on Global Supply Chain Models." *European Journal of Operational Research* 98 (1): 1–18. https://doi.org/10.1016/S0377-2217(97)80080-X.

Wible, Brad, Jeffrey Mervis, and Nicholas S. Wigginton. 2014. "Rethinking the Global Supply Chain." *Science* 344 (6188): 1100–03. https://doi.org/10.1126/scie nce.344.6188.1100.

Wright, Christine M., Michael E. Smith, and Brian G. Wright. 2007. "Hidden Costs Associated with Stakeholders in Supply Management." *Academy of Management Perspectives* 21 (3): 64–82. https://doi.org/10.5465/AMP.2007.26421239.

1

Source

Data Are People Too

1. DATA ARE PEOPLE TOO

The first stage of the prediction supply chain is to gather data. Data scientists source digital material that aligns with what they want to learn. Sources are aggregated to generate credible predictive knowledge. Gathering data begins the path toward delineating the core forecasting decisions the data science will support. Often dismissed as data cleaning, preparing data for analysis is vital intellectual work that creates the foundation for the legitimacy of the resulting decision. Ethical data scientists are less interested in availability and instead are intentional about selecting appropriate data. The pursuit of knowledge does not need to necessarily violate norms of consent. This includes an awareness that digital material sometimes can misrepresent as well as it reflects reality. Predictive models often label groups of people as bad or use other pejorative attributes. In the movie *Who Framed Roger Rabbit* (Zemeckis 1988), the cartoon character Jessica Rabbit objects to assumptions that she is unfaithful to her husband because of the way she looks. Jessica complains that she is not bad, but just drawn that way. Data draws pictures of us that may not reflect how we see ourselves. Appropriately aligning sources to make a prediction begins by recognizing that data are people too. Data sources ideally find harmony between the content, the people represented, and predictive goals. Humanity can be equally knowable and elusive in digital representations.

Ethical Data Science. Anne L. Washington, Oxford University Press. © Oxford University Press 2023.
DOI: 10.1093/oso/9780197693025.003.0003

1.1 Data Doubles

What did you do last Thursday at 10:35 am? If you have a predictable answer, you just met your data double. Your data double brings together many digital patterns. A sensor captures your license plate on a toll road. The public transit card tracks your movements as you deliver your child to school. The grocery store shares your purchases with your credit card. The telecommunications company pings your phone's location through cellular towers.

Taken together, the digital traces that occur every Thursday morning make your behavior predictable. The sociologist Evelyn Ruppert originally defined data doubles in the context of a census or other population statistics (Ruppert 2011). A data double is a constellation of biographic, biometric, transactional, sensor, and identity classifications that cluster people into groups for analysis.

Our data doubles serve as the primary source for most predictive data science. Yet a data double is only a fragment of your experience. The license plate reader cannot detect that you plan to donate the car to charity. No indicators track that someone gave up his seat for you on the bus. The credit card will never know that you flirted with the store cashier. The telecom company is ignorant that you left your phone in a taxi.

Data sets are a snapshot of time and space. The frame of the photo cannot include both the entire Eiffel Tower and your nose. Data represent the angle, lighting, and composition—in short, the perspective of the data collector. Governments that can compel information and corporations that can collect data are always snapping the shot. Our data doubles are a picture postcard of our lives, and an organization is always behind the camera.

What if digital traces helped us to individually see ourselves as part of a whole? My employment data double could calculate the difference my Library Science degree made in my earnings history. My civic data double would break down legislative voting patterns for the candidates I supported in the last election. My consumer data double informs me which café serves a high percentage of decaf coffee to increase the chances I get a fresh pot.

Sadly, none of these data doubles exist. Why? This information does not serve the needs of any organization that has the power to collect it. While some researchers may generate a specialized data set to pursue a research question, it still falls under the purview of their institution's interests. Our data doubles often do not reflect civic or social roles and rarely support an individual's personal economy. Understanding a data source requires recognizing that it was collected for a reason. There may be incentives to collect some information and perhaps not collect other information.

Where do data scientists get their sources? The first concern of any supply chain is to locate something to process. Predictive systems need digital material, but where should it come from? This chapter considers how data scientists can avoid common problems in securing appropriate resources and reflects on scholarship on decision-making. In the following case, a data scientist prioritized personal curiosity, data availability, and expediency over their predictive goals and privacy interests of the people they represent.

1.2 Found Data, OK?

OkCupid users were looking for love, not publicity, yet their intimate profiles were posted to the internet as a data set in 2016. A graduate student at the University of Aarhus noticed that the tests on the free online dating site were similar to psychology evaluations he was studying. He decided to learn if cognitive ability was statistically correlated with items like tattoos, piercings, religion, political affiliation, gender, race, and preference for ethnocentric dating. The student did not find any pertinent correlations with tattoos, but he did run afoul of many ethicists when he posted the data set with actual names and locations of over 68,000 people. The data set contained all dating profiles he could get to. Thousands paid a price for his desire to confirm that zodiac signs were not statistically significant.

Someone signing up for a free dating profile may want to disclose tattoos to a potential partner, but probably never considered that this information would be placed in a data set for any random person to read. Software developers call this "database creep," where a data set created for one purpose always winds up being used for additional reasons. The primary context was a dating site where you want to exchange truthful details confidentially with a potential partner. In the secondary context, the dating profile was part of a public research forum.

Many data scientists consider any structured information available for their own analysis if there are no payment barriers or scraping challenges. They might argue that anonymization is unnecessary because all digital profiles are public, even if on a platform. However, any user of a platform is not entitled to the contents of the entire platform. Data sets often are licensed, meaning specific conditions guide the terms for reuse. While access to OkCupid was free from costs, the dating profiles were not free for analysis. Even open data sets may have licensing restrictions or some limits on reuse.

In the end, OkCupid legally forced the student to stop sharing the data set because as a platform user he violated OkCupid's terms of service. OkCupid filed a digital copyright infringement against the site where the data was posted, and the student they had to take it down. The data set is no longer publicly available, but the situation highlights problems with found data. Found data is a general term for data sets like this. Anyone with enough technical talent will download and repurpose whatever they can get. Availability to the data scientist is the most salient aspect of found data. These data sets are often crowdsourced or may not be curated at all, but they are always available without cost to the researcher.

The OkCupid release exemplifies not only ethical concerns but also credibility problems of data science. Are we to believe that the OkCupid research is the final word on cognitive abilities and tattoos? Is this an ideal data set to test questions about ethnocentric dating, a topic of interest to the researcher? Is there any skepticism about the reliability of the tests taken under non-experimental conditions? Would the results be similar on a paid dating site? Are dating profiles accurate data doubles (Oyer 2014)?

Using the OkCupid example, we can consider several questions about the relationship between the population, the content, and predictive goals. First is whether the population within the data set makes sense for the purpose. The researcher might have justified using single people seeking relationships as an appropriate population for assessing cognitive ability. Otherwise, the researcher might describe how this population differs from those in the original survey on cognitive ability. Another line of inquiry would consider the content in the source itself. The researcher would be able to state inherent obstacles to using dating profiles as accurate evidence of sensitive personal information. A discussion of profiles as evidence would explain the difference between dating profiles and profiles for other purposes. Finally, the study could have situated what the researcher wanted to learn in relation to the source. The entire premise of the study is that the OkCupid surveys were the same as common psychometric tests. The researcher could have explained how those tests were previously deployed and whether the OkCupid context was comparable. It would be enlightening to know whether anyone has previously published studies comparing tattoos to cognitive ability. If there was no evidence in his study, perhaps other scholars had found positive correlations between zodiac signs and physical attributes. Overall, the researcher did little to line up a data source appropriate to the predictive goals.

Unethical data science entirely overlooks the salience of the data set sacrificing alignment for convenience. The easiest actions dominate all decisions, including learning about the topic. It is not clear that this was the ideal data set for developing new knowledge about cognitive ability. The researcher's ease overshadowed the need to satisfy the prediction objectives. The controversy about the ethics of the data set distracted from the quality of the underlying data science. Although such lawsuits are rare, data scientists may have to consider whether testing their skill or satisfying their curiosity may result in legal action.

As the first step in the prediction supply chain, sourcing lays the intellectual foundations for prediction. Data are sourced, selected, and aggregated to meet predictive goals. Data scientists constantly evaluate the compatibility of the data set's content with what they want to learn about people. It may not all line up perfectly, but an awareness of the gaps adds to the credibility of the data science. In addition to evaluating the suitability of external sources, data scientists must also reflect on their own choices and reasons for gathering material. Ethical data science intentionally assembles the strongest available evidence with an awareness of who controls those sources.

1.3 Whose Control?

Digital representations of human behavior can come from many sources such as government mandated disclosure, voluntary personal information, sensor tracking, or business transactions.

Who controls the data? The availability of material for analysis is greatly dependent on the people or groups that administers the data. Infrastructure, standards, measurements, and policies shape what we know as data. Not all material is recorded. Not all material is kept.

A data set represents a specific dynamic between the people described and the organization with the authority to collect their representations. Patricia Hill Collins asserts that power is maintained on multiple dimensions including the institutional, the symbolic, and the individual (Collins 1993). Power over data representations and their distribution represents similar dimensions of control. When you see a data set, you also must see the advocates, associations, government agencies, unions, businesses, and other groups that argued for its existence and shaped its contents. Political scientist Deborah Stone warns that data sets represent what counts, not necessarily what we want to count (Stone 2020). Data science is beholden to decisions made much earlier when someone chose what was important enough to put in a database. What is available will reflect priorities from somewhere else or another time. Understanding the origins of the data shape the picture of why it was created and how it was intended to generate knowledge.

As the first step in the prediction supply chain, sourcing lays the intellectual foundations for the predictive goals. Data are sourced, selected, and aggregated to meet predictive goals. Data scientists constantly evaluate the compatibility of the data set's content with what they want to learn about people. In addition to evaluating the suitability of external sources, data scientists must reflect on their own choices and reasons for gathering material. It may not all line up perfectly, but an awareness of the gaps adds to the data science credibility. Simply, data scientists cannot always rely on ideal data sets. Ethical data science intentionally assembles the strongest available evidence with an awareness of who controls their sources.

The rest of this chapter considers how data scientists can avoid common problems in securing appropriate resources for their predictive goal, such as how to align populations, interpret content, and watch for data silences.

1.4 Align Populations

No one will think you are a dog on the internet, even if you start liking posts about squirrels, buying chewy meaty treats, and scrolling through images of fire hydrants. The underlying assumption is that humans with a bank account use the internet. But everything may not be as it may seem online.

Large data sets necessarily represent a majority position. Majority populations may not have the incentives to be kind to groups with less power. Worse, a sizable portion of the majority may intentionally make associations that overwhelm the dignity and autonomy of others represented in fewer numbers (Bender et al. 2021). Co-creation inevitably has this emblematic tension between the majority and peripheral parts of a network (Young, Wigdor, and Kane 2020). Reddit, for instance, for many years contained deeply partisan groups that used slurs toward subpopulation groups. Wikipedia routinely removes articles about women as insignificant. Both Reddit and Wikipedia are the basis for large language collections. Sometimes web-based data sets merely end up being the loudest guy in the bar instead of a thoughtful collection of a wide range of humanity. Language about marginalized or minority groups may necessarily be derogatory or incomplete if size is the only dimension of importance.

Digital sources may comprise unanticipated populations through mischievousness, political strength, or deceit. Some digital misdirection is playful. Activists targeted a politician who opposed gay marriage in 2012 by digitally associating his name with aspects of those unions he would not want to know about. Congressman Rick Santorum had to run for president to drown out the prank with information about his political career. This was not the first successful attempt to take over search results. The term "Google bomb" was applied as early as 2002 when a search for "miserable failure" would return an image of the US president.

User-generated content reflects the interests of those who have the time to learn the systems and recruit others. In 2011, the US presidential administration wanted to hear directly from the people and set up a petition. The top request was to legalize marijuana, which was not a widely held opinion at the time. Another was to repeal legislation that outlawed same-sex marriage. During a contested US presidential campaign, a loosely organized group of worldwide fans famously snapped up all the tickets for a political rally without any intention of attending. The campaign anticipated a packed house only to find a trickle of people in a near-empty stadium while fans of the K-pop band BTS celebrated. Fandoms are generally seen as benign groups of people very excited to bond over pop culture. The BTS Army consistently employed the power of its thousand-strong fandom in serious matters from ruining a candidate's rally, to promoting environmental causes, or donating over a million dollars to Black Lives Matter causes. Data sources may contain evidence of pressure from a small group of people who choose to exert a big influence.

The economist Nicolas Taleb calls this minority rule as he explains why most lemonade in the United States is kosher and why most lamb in the United Kingdom is halal despite these populations being very small (Taleb 2019). The majority can be accommodating and does not mind if they are eating kosher or halal, while the smaller groups have less flexibility for matters important to them. It is a reminder that complex systems have emergent properties that may not be easily predictable.

The line between getting your friends to participate in civic discourse and sowing partisan division is not always clear. Early internet pranks set the stage for the spread of false medical and misleading political information through networks similar to Cold War disinformation networks. Media scholars such as Joan Donavon and Siva Vaidhyanathan provide multiple examples of how user-generated content on platforms can be manipulated. Crowdsourced protests have morphed into serious attempts to compromise access to good information. Institutions and individuals have figured out how to force algorithmic rankings to promote fringe perspectives. Adversarial actors perfected these techniques to infiltrate platforms with active measures to seed division and chaos especially in the face of scarcity. After the Christchurch, New Zealand, mosque massacre, groups flooded search engines with inaccurate details, which were picked up by journalists and published as facts in legitimate news publications. Any data scientist using user-generated content to represent "everyone" must be aware of the limitations of this line of thought in the contemporary digital environment.

Large digital sources can easily drown out views from smaller populations. On the other hand, digital sources could be absolutely dominated by small, determined groups. Ethical data scientists have an awareness of these dynamics and ask if the people in the data set are expected to be there.

1.5 Align Content Interpretations

Ever try to explain to your family the context of a joke that seemed really funny to everyone at work? Ever try to share a picture from a private party with work colleagues who were not amused?

Digital information is available to multiple audiences, but it may not translate from one to another. In 2010, a teacher in training posted on Myspace an image of herself drinking. The university saw her drunken image and denied her degree. This story was repeated in 2011, when a parent saw a party photo of a teacher, who was subsequently fired. Maybe it is still happening, but the news media does not report this anymore. Stories like these point toward the importance of interpretation.

A posting on social media is particularly challenging for outside groups to interpret.

Attempting to steer children away from joining gangs as teenagers, city governments began to monitor social media accounts of preteens. In New York City, the Juvenile Robbery Intervention Program monitored Facebook and Twitter accounts of teenagers living within targeted geographic areas to prevent them from committing robberies outside of their neighborhoods. The police created lists of potential gang members in part by measuring culpability with Twitter retweets and Facebook likes. Both portals have very limited affordances for showing approval. Teenagers seeking attention and approval from peers may present themselves differently than how they are in real life. Retweeting a photo associated with a gang is not the same as being a member of the gang (Stevens et al. 2019). Tapping the Facebook like button is not an unwavering endorsement. While the number of retweets and likes is a quantitative measure that lends itself to comparison, it is a stretch to deem it equal to criminal culpability. Teenagers seeking attention and approval from peers may present themselves differently than how they are in real life. Just like the teachers who were fired, someone may attempt to be accepted by one audience and instead generate disgust and repulsion from another audience.

Worse, some of that social media information was gotten through impersonation. According to a 2013 *New York Times* report, two adult male police officers gained access to private Facebook conversations by actively representing themselves as attractive teenage girls (Ruderman 2013) to lure male gang members. This may have exacerbated the performative aspects of the teenager's online behavior. Whereas the OkCupid case involved someone gaining access to the platform only to extract data from other users for research, the users here represent an organization, in fact one that is supposed to work in the public interest. While many law enforcement organizations currently have memoranda of understanding about using data (Wexler 2021), those agreements were not widely known at the time. As early as 2011, New York City criminal investigations used social media information as admissible evidence despite generating culpability through deception and then misinterpreting the affordances of the platform.

Grabbing data is never enough. Pause to consider the existence of the data for the subpopulation included in the study. Ethical data scientists ask if they can understand the context of data collection sufficiently to interpret meaning.

1.6 Align Goals Around Silences in the Digital Record

Why is it possible to know how many weekend movie tickets sold but not the number of high-stakes incidents where police officers used lethal force? This is the question that the director of the Federal Bureau of Investigation (FBI), James B. Comey, asked in 2015 at the Summit on Violent Crime Reduction. In the private meeting, Comey lamented the state of available federal statistics on police shootings. Police unions claimed that the 2014 police killing of Michael Brown, an unarmed teenager, was an isolated incident. The community of Ferguson, Missouri, claimed it was a pattern of police brutality. There were no local data sources to resolve the issue, and no federal oversight bodies that could suggest trends elsewhere.

A data scientist who grabbed the easiest to find FBI data set may have gotten an incomplete perspective on the situation. The Law Enforcement Officers Killed and Assaulted data set has meticulously tracked lost officers since its creation in 1996. This may lead someone to believe that the FBI crime database, active since 1930, is equally diligent. Yet the FBI crime database contains only a few incidents of police killing civilians. Someone would have to know that despite being an authoritative source, the FBI relies on voluntary reporting from police departments.

Crime statistics are some of the oldest widely available data. Despite this abundance, many things are not counted. The legal scholar Rashida Richardson argues that criminal justice algorithmic tools are based on information that is flawed, one-sided, and sometimes tied to unlawful policing practices (Richardson 2022). The paucity of information after the police killed Michael Brown in Ferguson led the *Washington Post* and *The Guardian* newspapers to begin a project called The Counted. By October 2015, the US Department of Justice announced it would begin to collect federal statistics on police killings.

Similar to the silence in the archives, digital silences represent a lack of evidence. What documents were not kept? Whose voices were not worthy to record? What vocabularies describe less-powerful people? Which records were never created? The internet has a multitude of written opinions, but it does not track people with oral traditions, those who cannot write freely, or those who lack access to technology. Silences are a result of power and influence at the point of acquisition (Sutherland 2019). An archival silence is a gap in the historical record that can lead to a distortion of what we can know in the future.

Mimi Onuoha, a conceptual digital artist, created a file cabinet of empty folders to represent data sets that do not exist. The artwork "Library of Missing Datasets" includes the "Global web user measurements that include virtual private networks" and "Undocumented immigrants currently incarcerated and/

or underpaid" and "Sales and prices in the art world" (Onuoha 2016). Unlike missing data that statisticians manage through mathematical estimates and imputation, missing data sets are voids in our quantified understanding of the world. This art asks us to reflect on what evidence is missing of other people, places, and events.

Data scientists need to see if a data set exists that meets their predictive goals, with an awareness that there might not be data for what interests them. Ethical data scientists describe the limitations of the sources in meeting their predictive goals. For instance, the FBI crime database would be a good measure of police reporting of civilian killings but not a measure of all civilian deaths at the hands of police. Predictive goals should be tailored to describe what can be measured in the available sources.

1.7 Source Ethical Data Science

The first action in an ethical prediction supply chain is to do no harm by considering if the source is representative of the population and then making careful selection within the source. Data almost always offers things that we do not track. Perhaps some rows of a spreadsheet will be removed because they are not appropriate. Perhaps only a few columns are relevant to the question in mind. A key aspect of evaluating data sources is discernment about what to leave in and what to leave out.

Data are rarely used for one purpose. At the point of sourcing data, it is important to consider how those digital representations were made, by whom, and for what purpose. Consider whether any populations will be negatively exposed to harm if the data from your project has any additional use.

Predictions can function like public policy proposals. Some people will be greatly helped, while others may receive little assistance. In public policy analysis, populations are divided into those who are targeted by the policy and those who merely will be impacted if it is implemented. David A. Rochefort and Roger W. Cobb argue that an agenda for policy change is driven in part by how the populations impacted are defined, and they offer the following groups (Rochefort and Cobb 1994). The target population is seen as deserving, worthy of service, and receiving the intended policy advantage. The dependent population has little political control over the policy decision and may be further divided into those who are deserving or undeserving of the advantage. The deviant population is negatively constructed, has no political power, and may be blocked from enjoying the policy advantage. The intended target of the policy has the most power over the politicians and the policy design.

Sourcing with an ethical lens asks us to consider which populations are impacted by the project. Is there an implicit deviant population whose feedback on the system will be ignored? Are some populations seen as more deserving of good data science? Are you aware of powerful and political savvy groups that want the predictive systems designed around their needs?

Machine learning benchmarks and data sets are rarely meticulously curated. Few receive any institutional supervision or curation. Until there are more legitimate ways to evaluate the provenance of data sets, researchers must remain highly alert before incorporating a new data set into their predictive model.

Where should you not look for a data source? The lines keep shifting. In the 1990s, looking through a person's email would have been taboo, but the Gmail service now shuffles through every word in corporate and personal inboxes on a central server to avoid spam. In the 2000s, when health-care policy emphasized privacy, health data would have been clearly off limits—yet today people use multiple devices daily to measure personal information like physical movement and heart rate. The idea of having a microphone and camera in the home would have been an unimaginable infringement on consent, but the era of smart beds and voice-activated lighting has changed all of that.

Relaxing standards for data collection places a greater burden on data scientists to implement concepts of consent while aligning population, content, and predictive goals with care.

1.8 Prediction as Decision-Making

Predictions help people make decisions. Choosing a restaurant. Making a meal. Finding something to wear. All can have wildly different markers of success depending on the situation. Automated decision systems like any of these everyday decisions needs a direction.

To build early artificial intelligence systems, cognitive scientist Harold A. Simon studied how people make decisions and found that a central part of decision-making is an internal representation of the goal. Would the advice you'd give for choosing a wedding gift be the same advice for choosing a birthday present? While guests give presents to hosts at both events, something else must explain why socks may be appropriate for one occasion but not the other. One reason for the differences is that a wedding implies more than one recipient, while a birthday suggests one person. Also, a wedding, in most cultures, is a unique celebration that demands an extraordinary gift instead of a birthday, which is an annual occurrence. An abstraction of gift selection needs social context in addition to knowing the actors, objects, and actions.

Decisions rely on layers of abstract symbols. Symbols are internal representations that designate relationships and actions between objects in the external world (Simon 1996). Simon reminds us that abstract symbols are always goal-seeking, and the external world sets the conditions for attaining these goals. The anthropologist Lucy Suchman shifts our thinking to include reflexivity, which invites us to situate all symbolic systems as conceptual devices and rhetoric leading to realization (Suchman 2007). Suchman's classic example is about navigating a raft on the open sea. One approach is to reach the destination on a planned route that charts out a course from detailed study. Another approach is to know the destination and meet the realities of the water and weather with a set of skillful practices. Internal representations intersect with larger symbolic systems that serve the interests of the economic, social, and technical ecosystems. Predictive sources are no different.

Knowing the initial state the prediction begins in will help to identify where your decisions start and another system ends.

Predictions take on the shape of their environments. Each decision sits within another system. Choosing between the red pill and the blue pill is possible because two colors were manufactured. A decision to fly or drive to Michigan can only be made because there is ample infrastructure to do both. A classic early coding mistake is to forget to reset default values. If someone asks you to describe how to tie a shoelace, would you remember the first step is putting the shoe on someone's foot? The initial state for an action acknowledges there are other interlocking systems.

Public policy is full of examples that show how there can be significant disagreement on how to build an abstraction of a problem. Entry into a country without appropriate paperwork sparks strong partisan feelings. The US immigration legislation in response to a 2014 increase in migrants at the border reflected stark differences in abstractions. Those who saw it as a human rights emergency wanted to frame it through the lens of housing, health, and other aspects of social welfare. Others saw the attempted crossings as illegal and sought to strengthen criminal law related to immigration. A stronger conceptualization of immigration would select from available information to match the predictive expectations of these very different abstractions.

Data scientists select parts of data sources and concepts crucial to the abstraction. Someone with a different perspective or access to other information can build a parallel set of objectives to meet similar predictive goals. Spinning through large data sets is fun, but a general direction will get to more reliable results faster. Predictive goals are a way to automate decision-making by giving the computer system information about what we want it to do for us. A coordinated plan orients activity but must always face practices and conditions that control its ultimate realization.

1.9 Research Ethics: Informed Consent

Informed consent is the beginning of ethical research involving human subjects, yet it is elusive in reference to large-scale data sets. Privacy and consent of individuals are often completely overlooked in favor of using all material from everyone at scale.

Informed consent is an active authorization free from coercion. The process of informed consent reasserts volition for participants in situations where researchers control their emotions, ask them to recall a difficult memory, reveal family secrets, or use DNA cells for experimentation. Voluntary participation is a crucial aspect of research ethics. Participants in research studies have the right to say no. At any moment they can volunteer to end the study. The path toward getting volunteers starts with informed consent.

To truly volunteer, the person must be given sufficient information that is comprehensible and clear about the risks and benefits. Participants also have the right to know what the research context is and how data about them is transferred between researchers and institutions. A voluntary research participant is an independent person able to comprehend the decision and disclosures. Some populations are considered vulnerable because they have limited or no power in relationship to large institutional forces controlling their lives. Because consent and willingness are core values, current research ethics regulation in the United States severely limits access to incarcerated, pregnant, or underage people.

Computer scientists using digital representations of humans on the internet generally do not fall under human subjects research. For instance, there were no approval mechanisms for the student who grabbed the dating profiles from OkCupid. Yet our digital records contain aspects of our daily activity that, in many ways, are more revealing than a single interview or even a series of observations done in typical research settings.

Legal notice and consent on digital forms is different than informed consent. The US Federal Trade Commission complaint against Sears Holdings Management Corporation in 2009 established that notice within detailed legal agreements was insufficient for the type of data collection that monitored all user activity (Hoofnagle 2016). Digital consent is still deeply contested (Citron 2022).

Digital consent can be blurred, buried, or diluted to make it difficult to know what we are consenting to and for how long. Regulators in the European Union demanded consistent and uniform consent so people can sufficiently understand how to participate. Data scientists will rarely have clear guidelines on whether one person out of a million opposes being included in the data set. In general, informed consent means you have carefully considered the needs of people and populations in the data.

1.10 Thinking Like a Painter to Source

Data science could be more intentional about the portraits it is capable of painting through data. A painting is a visual expression of what the artist sees. Painters articulate their observations of the world through deliberate choices of color, texture, juxtaposition, and lighting. Watercolors capture bright daylight on a summer day. An oil painting conveys a dark interior lit by a single candle.

The study of painting invites an awareness of how outcomes are shaped by the selection of materials. A vision of the final composition drives a purposeful medley of tools and media. Artists learn the merits of each medium and then apply the medium in their work for maximum results.

Data scientists starting a project could learn from a painter's considered selection of techniques and material in assembling a composition. Techniques do not detract from the final goal but instead add to the work's fullest expression. Slow-drying paints give the artist an opportunity to build layers and make changes over time. Size, shape, and bristle define a painter's primary utensil: a brush. A painter chooses a round-tip brush with a long handle to add detail to a canvas set vertically on an easel. A short-handled ink brush, however, is ideal for leaning over to do calligraphy. Each material creates an overall experience for the artist and lends a unique quality to the final composition. Data scientists could better calibrate expectations if they were able to articulate how their technical selections contribute to the overall predictive picture.

Painters recognize that materials are dependent on each other. A canvas primed for watercolors limits the ways the image could be rendered in acrylic. Sable-hair brushes are very absorbent, making them ideal for watercolor paints but not very good for acrylics. A painter who selects a wide brush for filling in the background may find it inconvenient when trying to convey nuanced detail. Which canvas and brushes are just two of the choices painters make to express their vision just as predictions require many technical decisions.

Data scientists could approach data sources the way painters approach their choices. A painter's canvas is like societal circumstances that set the backdrop for prediction and data collection. Consider a study that made predictions based on health-care spending. This study reified racial disparities by predicting that people with more money needed more health-care, which privileged mostly White patients. (Benjamin 2019; Obermeyer et al. 2019). Data scientists have to be aware of the context of creation. For instance, some DNA databases are compiled solely from coercive situations, like arrests or indigent populations at public hospitals. Predictions using this data set will oversample on people from lower social economic backgrounds.

Predictive services that try to ascertain behavior from photos are like trying to paint a tiny Vermeer with a wide brush. The machine learning classifier trained to determine criminals actually picked up on differences in clothing (Wu and Zhang 2017) because people in mugshots were less likely to be wearing a suit and tie. A study of dating profiles that attempted to determine sexual orientation really distinguished between grooming habits (Arcas, Todorov, and Mitchell 2018). Many of the studies that claim to predict emotion, criminality, or deviance from facial characteristics actually pick up visual manifestations of social preferences.

The skills painter have can help data scientists choose materials to best convey observations of the world. The Gender Shades project (Buolamwini and Gebru 2018) evaluated facial recognition tools at the intersection of skin tone and gender-identity by evaluating World Parliament official portraits so the sources truly mirrored world populations. The source brought greater depth and validity to the results of the Gender Shades study. Thinking like a painter means selecting and processing sources with intention and with an eye on the ultimate predictive goal.

1.11 Chapter 1 Summary

Data come from somewhere. In the act of analysis, data science converts material from one context into another. Transformation and moving between environments holds power that data science is beginning to reckon with. Ideally, data sources fit predictive goals, but often the best choice is approximate. Statistics can be done on a subset of data and still create valid results. Digital representations of people require particular care so that the specificity of the predictive goal matches the specificity in the data. Staying focused on the overall decision needs of the prediction supply chain is one way to not become preoccupied by the power of the math or overcome by curiosity. Remember that the digital traces you analyze could make people vulnerable.

Sourcing data is important not only for what it predicts but for implications downstream. The sourcing of data involves the complex tangle of populations represented, interpreting content, predictive goals, and informed consent. Data scientists must be alert to changing social expectations around data collection and sourcing. Sourcing a prediction supply chain sets the intellectual foundations for valid and logical results.

The next chapter considers how to model predictions.

1.12   APPENDIX EXERCISES—Chapter 1 Source

Points to consider:

- Know your predictive goal.
- Find sources that reflect consent from participants.
- Ask about data-licensing restrictions and terms of service.
- Make the credibility of the evidence stronger.
- Avoid sources that only represent dominant social groups.
- Watch for data moving between contexts that require additional interpretation.

References

Arcas, Blaise Aguera, Alexander Todorov, and Margaret Mitchell. 2018. "Do Algorithms Reveal Sexual Orientation or Just Expose Our Stereotypes?" *Medium Microsoft Research* (blog). January 18, 2018. https://medium.com/@blaisea/do-algorithms-reveal-sexual-orientation-or-just-expose-our-stereotypes-d998fafdf477.

Bender, Emily M., et al. 2021. "On the Dangers of Stochastic Parrots: Can Language Models Be Too Big?" In *Proceedings of the 2021 ACM Conference on Fairness, Accountability, and Transparency*. Virtual Event Canada: ACM, 610–23. https://doi.org/10.1145/3442188.3445922.

Benjamin, Ruha. 2019. "Assessing Risk, Automating Racism." *Science* 366 (6464): 421–22. https://doi.org/10.1126/science.aaz3873.

Buolamwini, Joy, and Timnit Gebru. 2018. "Gender Shades: Intersectional Accuracy Disparities in Commercial Gender Classification." *Proceedings of Machine Learning Research* 81 (February): 77–91.

Citron, Danielle Keats. 2022. *The Fight for Privacy: Protecting Dignity, Identity, and Love in the Digital Age*. 1st ed. New York: W.W. Norton & Company, Inc.

Collins, Patricia Hill. 1993. "Toward a New Vision: Race, Class, and Gender as Categories of Analysis and Connection." *Race, Sex & Class* 1 (1): 25–45.

Donovan, Joan, Emily Dreyfuss, and Brian Friedberg. 2022. *Meme Wars: The Untold Story of the Online Battles Upending Democracy in America*. New York: Bloomsbury Publishing.

Hoofnagle, Chris Jay. 2016. *Federal Trade Commission Privacy Law and Policy*. Cambridge; New York: Cambridge University Press.

Obermeyer, Ziad, et al. 2019. "Dissecting Racial Bias in an Algorithm Used to Manage the Health of Populations." *Science* 366 (6464): 447–53. https://doi.org/10.1126/science.aax2342nt/sci/366/6464/447.full.pdf.

Onuoha, Mimi. 2016. *The Library of Missing Datasets*. https://github.com/MimiOnuoha/missing-datasets.

Oyer, Paul E. 2014. *Everything I Ever Needed to Know about Economics I Learned from Online Dating*. Boston, MA: Harvard Business Review Press.

Richardson, Rashida. 2022. "Racial Segregation and the Data-Driven Society: How Our Failure to Reckon with Root Causes Perpetuates Separate and Unequal Realities." *Berkeley Technology Law Journal* 36 (3): 1051–90. https:// doi.org/10.15779/ Z38PN8XG3V.

Rochefort, David A., and Roger W. Cobb. 1993. "Problem Definition, Agenda Access, and Policy Choice." *Policy Studies Journal* 21 (1): 56–71. doi: 10.1111/1541-0072. ep11784506.

Ruderman, Wendy. 2013. "For Troubled Teenagers in New York City, a New Tack: Forced Outreach." *The New York Times*, March 3, 2013. https://www.nytimes.com/2013/03/04/ nyregion/to-stem-juvenile-robberies-police-trail-youths-before-the-crime.html?pag ewanted=all.

Ruppert, Evelyn. 2011. "Population Objects: Interpassive Subjects." *Sociology* 45 (2): 218– 33. https://doi.org/10.1177/0038038510394027.

Simon, Herbert Alexander. 1996. *The Sciences of the Artificial.* Vol. 3. Cambridge, MA: MIT Press.

Stevens, Robin, et al. 2019. "Sex, Drugs, and Alcohol in the Digital Neighborhood: A Multi-Method Analysis of Online Discourse amongst Black and Hispanic Youth." https://doi. org/10.24251/HICSS.2019.261.

Stone, Deborah. 2020. *Counting: How We Use Numbers to Decide What Matters.* 1st ed. New York: Liveright Publishing Corporation, a division of W.W. Norton & Company Inc.

Suchman, Lucille Alice. 2007. *Human-Machine Reconfigurations: Plans and Situated Actions.* Vol. 2. Cambridge; New York: Cambridge University Press.

Sutherland, Tonia. 2019. "The Carceral Archive: Documentary Records, Narrative Construction, and Predictive Risk Assessment." *Journal of Cultural Analytics.* 4 (1): 1– 21 https://doi.org/10.22148/16.039.

Taleb, Nassim Nicholas. 2019. *Skin in the Game: Hidden Asymmetries in Daily Life.* London: Penguin Books.

Vaidhyanathan, Siva. 2011. *The Googlization of Everything: And Why We Should Worry.* Berkeley, CA: University of California Press.

Wexler, Rebecca. 2021. "Privacy Asymmetries: Access to Data in Criminal Defense Investigations." *U.C.L.A. Law Review* 68 (1): 212–87. https://www.uclalawreview.org/ privacy-asymmetries-access-to-data-in-criminal-defense-investigations/.

Wu, Xiaolin, and Xi Zhang. 2017. "Automated Inference on Criminality Using Face Images." Preprint article. arXiv. https://doi.org/10.48550/arXiv.1611.04135.

Young, Amber G., Ariel D. Wigdor, and Gerald C. Kane. 2020. "The Gender Bias Tug-of-War in a Co-Creation Community: Core-Periphery Tension on Wikipedia." *Journal of Management Information Systems* 37 (4): 1047–72. https://doi.org/10.1080/07421 222.2020.1831773.

Zemeckis, Robert, dir. 1988. *Who Framed Roger Rabbit.* https://www.imdb.com/title/ tt0096438/.

2

Model

Dear Validity, Advice for Wayward Algorithms

1. DEAR VALIDITY, ADVICE FOR WAYWARD ALGORITHMS

The second stage in the prediction supply chain is building an authentic representation. Prediction depends on models to structure relationships between objects and concepts. Models convey the interdependence between events, ideas, and other forms of evidence. Chances are the available data found in the first stage may not perfectly reflect the predictive goal nor meet standards of mathematical beauty. Data scientists must decide what data to leave in and what to omit so the project makes sense. Access to data is meaningless without considering how to use the available data judiciously. Ethical data science limits predictions to plausible insights and does not simply blame anyone the powerful expect to blame. Like the police captain in the movie *Casablanca* (Curtiz 1942) who ignores the shooting he just witnessed, some data science projects overlook the evidence and merely round up the usual suspects. Authenticating research outcomes as logical and defensible is a check on whether models correspond with actual observations. Models are a way to advise intractable algorithms and coax them toward well-behaved predictive outcomes. The best predictions are specific and can articulate how less-than-ideal cases will be handled. Building a predictive model reflects reality as much as it attempts to change reality. This

Ethical Data Science. Anne L. Washington, Oxford University Press. © Oxford University Press 2023.
DOI: 10.1093/oso/9780197693025.003.0004

chapter encourages questioning ideal models, thinking about outliers in training data, checking for validity, and forming credible narratives based on principles of justice.

1.1 Giving Advice

What advice do you give people visiting you?

You probably want your visitors to enjoy themselves, but how each person defines that is an open question. You may have a different dining suggestion for an old college friend than for a retired couple attending their nephew's wedding. The wealthy retired couple may think a three-star restaurant is an excellent dining experience. A college friend who still has student loans may not want to pay for a Michelin-starred meal. Embedded within all advice is a definition, or at least a vague idea, of success. Let's consider a few ways to model advice for an enjoyable visit to New York City based on past success, popularity, or a definition.

History may determine success. If the last visitor enjoyed something, future visitors may too. You recommend your favorite restaurant because you assume your experiences will be repeated. Advice, like many algorithms, still function even in suboptimal situations. The visitors may be disappointed in your favorite spots but unlikely to declare the trip a total failure because one restaurant did not have gluten-free pasta.

Popularity can also be a motivating factor for defining a good visit: if a large number of people like the restaurant, your visitors will too. You recommend a restaurant that is popular at work without thinking what traits you share with your colleagues. At a minimum, anyone designing success factors based on personal experience must be able to name what they have in common with other people. This awareness may help to imagine a recipient of this advice who may be very different. Of course, not everyone enjoys the most popular places.

A narrow definition of success has only one indicator, such as every vacation in New York City must include a visit to the Statue of Liberty. This advice has the hidden assumption that everyone wants to sail to a remote island in a busy harbor and can effortlessly climb 350 stairs to the top. It also ignores obstacles such as recent knee surgery or an aversion to heights. Success dependent on only one criterion creates very stark boundaries and can severely limit participation. Sometimes a single generalized model, like the trip to Lady Liberty, overlooks so many other situations that it utterly fails to support all but a narrow set of people while claiming universality.

The perfect itinerary to New York City probably depends on many factors, such as how long the visitors stay, how many are visiting, and the nature of their visit. You may break down success into specific elements like where to eat, what to see, and how to get around. Your advice might mix your favorites with things that suit the context along with your visitor's preferences.

Advice is similar to a predictive model. Predictive data science also relies on history, demand, and strict tests.

Both models and advice express a preferred optimal state. They create a general ideal example and then apply it to specific instances. Central to giving good advice and building models is an ability to understand abstractions. Let's begin by considering how to turn advice for visitors into advice for a predictive algorithm.

1.2 We Hire Us

A major tech company wanted advice on screening job candidates and asked its data science staff to come up with a predictive system. The hiring algorithm was intended to predict the best applicants by determining what made past job candidates successful. The data science team had access to high-quality data, over ten years of applications from successful and unsuccessful job candidates. The team ripped into the texts to identify fifty thousand words common on applications of new hires. They built hundreds of recruiting models for each career so an accountant would be evaluated differently than a marketing candidate. All of this was technically correct and well-planned, however the recruiting predictions were never used. Why? Amazon abandoned the hiring algorithm in 2016 because it only selected male candidates (Ajunwa 2016). This did not meet its standard for implementation.

While the designers had unrivaled ideal-quality data sources, there were several ways the scope of the predictive model failed to appreciate context. An awareness of the past, dominant culture, and realistic goals can lead to building in appropriate assumptions into the abstractions that create models.

First, historically technology start-ups are heavily skewed toward people who identify as men. To expand the employment base beyond this population, it would need to recognize this lopsidedness and try to correct it. The simple predictive goal was the algorithmic equivalent of "more of us, please." Discrimination against protected classes of people is illegal in many jurisdictions. Using this tool to only hire men or to eliminate everyone else would be against the law and unnecessarily restrict talent.

Second, the text analysis did not consider the impact of the dominant culture on the breadth of language. The ideal candidate had the collective traits of previous new hires based on language patterns in applications and resumés over ten years. Reflecting the majority of past hires, the hiring algorithm learned to penalize words not associated with men such as "women's soccer" or "transgender studies." Historically, women's colleges were downgraded, so applicants who attended Wellesley or Spelman were at a disadvantage. A recruiting algorithm that relies on popularity will identify good candidates but may consistently miss others.

Finally, the predictive goal was narrowly defined. The team probably wanted to find the best job candidates or hire another Jeff Bezos. Instead, they modeled the task to identify people with applications similar to current employees. At best, the model duplicated existing skills found in the current workforce which would not contribute to the planned expansion. This type of modeling is not isolated to Amazon's recruitment algorithm. Modern recruiting algorithms from commercial firms promise similar magic solutions yet without the transparency of data and outcomes that the internal algorithm could rely upon.

Most predictive models will advise people making high-level decisions. Predictive models can give bad advice that looks like good advice. Careful consideration of the type of advice necessary would help to design models that can be useful in decision-making. Not every data science project has astute managers like the ones at Amazon who noted the consistent omission in the algorithm's predictions and declined its advice.

How do data scientists build models? Understanding how models reflect predictive goals and how to determine if you are predicting a theory of the solution or a theory of the problem are some of the tools for creating ethical data science.

1.3 Which Ideals?

Predictive goals illustrate an ideal. Models connect concepts and data representations together into an ideal package. An ideal is a judgment about what is the best. People can reasonably differ on what is the ultimate aesthetic representation. The key here is considering which ideals shape the norms of prediction. The items that break the logical coherence of the ideal model reveal unspoken boundaries that divide predictions into normal and deviant cases. Knowing the assumption behind the rules helps to prepare for handling exceptions. Models tend to articulate a theory of the problem or a theory of the solution (Majchrzak and Markus 2013). Some models represent the originating conditions, positing a theory of the problem. Other models may ignore why something is occurring and focus on viability of interventions, positing a theory of the solution. Understanding what is being idealized can better explain the underlying goals of the prediction.

A data science model is designed to create inferences or predictions to address a particular issue. Predictive models want to guess what might happen in the future. Some models express causality, what causes something else. Other models suggest correlations, what frequently occurs with something else. All models hypothesize by using conceptual relationships, contingencies, and connections.

A model explains through abstraction. Models represent some phenomenon that exists in the social, environmental, or built world. However, models can never contain absolutely everything and make choices about what to include or exclude. A model builds associations between labels, objects, actions, and time to explain how things work. A model makes assumptions about the problem and about possible solutions, which will determine if it will apply to new situations. Models are optimized, or tailored, for an ideal set of conditions or populations. Thinking about exemplars and training data will build valid models that can better function within predictive decision-making.

Each classic pitfall of modeling is explored in detail in the following sections. Ideals from twentieth-century photography raise awareness of the role of history and its impact on visual machine learning models. Average estimates point toward becoming alert to the interaction between dominant cultures and outliers. An example from public health underlines the benefits of juggling specific definitions for the best fit.

1.4 Speaking of Models, Meet Shirley

The young person on the card was called Shirley. The image of a real fashion model distributed on cardboard by film manufacturers was also an exemplar model. A Shirley card is an analog equivalent of training data. The legacy of Shirley cards represents typical challenges in selecting exemplars and ideals that data scientists could encounter today.

Kodak Corporation created one of the first Shirley cards to test appropriate contrasts for light-sensitive emulsions on film. The Shirley card was popular in the mid-twentieth century soon after color film appeared in commercial markets. The ideals represented on these cards helped photographers to calibrate for reflections and color balance. Together, Shirley cards established the norm for human flesh tones in visual images.

All film manufacturers began to widely distribute similar images as a way to give advice on photographing people with their film under different light conditions. A 1993 Polaroid Shirley card has blocks of primary colors and shades of neutral ones surrounding an image of a blonde in a dress with bright colors (Roth 2009). On a 1978 Kodak card, a young woman with long wavy brown hair smiles over a white drape that showcases luminous pearls at her neck. Her light skin stands out in contrast to the dark highlights in her hair. The British Broadcasting Channel relied on an image of a blue-eyed dark-haired pale woman as the basis for calibrating television cameras across thirty countries that contain primarily people with brown skin. Japanese manufacturer Fuji films found this range unsatisfactory and developed a range of images for calibrating people with black hair and different skin tones. Photographers calibrated light meters for pale-skinned people with shiny thin hair that reflected light no matter who was posing for the photo.

While these corporations have the right to create film stock for its preferred or even a majority targeted group, the twentieth-century Shirley card model failed in depicting the real world accurately. The Shirley card standard made it impossible to clearly see two people with different skin tones in the same photo. Calibration techniques that made lighter skin more prominent would in turn make facial features on darker skin unreadable. Parents complained about blob yearbook photos when cameras were set up once and never changed. To compensate for the limits of this model, dark-skinned journalists were asked to wear skin-lightening makeup (Roth 2009). This problem did not stay in the analog world. Digital image processing software continued the tradition of featuring images of women with light skin as examples for Photoshop (Roth 2009).

The Shirley card symbolized how to represent human skin in analog photography, but its impact may still linger in digital images today. Visual machine learning systems learn from repositories of existing photographs as training data. Modeling the future on the past is efficient but can bake in historic assumptions that may no longer be ideal. Visual machine learning recreates the Shirley card ideal instead of recognizing the need for optimal lighting for all human skin and hair.

While Shirley cards were finally inclusive of all skin tones, the legacy is repeating in other digital systems. In 2020, Twitter discovered that its photo preview algorithm always cropped out the person with darker skin tones. Another artificial intelligence (AI) system modeled a definition of beauty, from the data, as only a light-skinned person with European features. In July 2020, the AI software Depixelizer removed any distinctive facial characteristics from any low-fidelity image of a person with Asian, African, or Latino heritage. It had the striking result of turning the first Black president of the United States into a White guy. The logic of the Shirley cards thus continues in the digital world, where an ideal exemplar of skin tone and hair texture is used to improve the efficiency of sorting through visual imagery. Shirley cards and contemporary AI models of beauty illustrate how efficient models can also lead to exclusion.

In the following example, we can see the impact on people's lives when they break implicit models of the system's ideals.

1.5 Training Data on Reference Man

While the Shirley cards represent ideals, training data represents popularity. Training data defines the ability to generalize predictions widely and sets the scope for all underlying models. It plays a critical role in the range of possible outcomes and actions. In critical conditions, it must be possible to make exceptions and modifications for a spectrum of human experiences and proportions.

Models are perfected, and in some cases developed, using training data. In supervised machine learning, labeled data sets help calibrate predictions. In unsupervised machine learning, large amounts of information identify statistical patterns of recurrence and frequency (Halevy, Norvig, and Pereira 2009). A language model is an example of unsupervised machine learning. For instance, GPT-3 is trained, in part, on all the words in Wikipedia and on Reddit to understand the probability that the word "thank" is followed by the word "you" (Brown et al. 2020).

Training data, however, can overrepresent some material than others that naturally occur. Large free data sets are rarely expertly curated (Washington et al. 2022). A visual translator for alternative text images is populated with labeled objects to automatically generate image captions (Birhane, Prabhu, and Kahembwe 2021). However, the machine learning algorithm learned from a data set containing nonconsensual explicit images and tags for adult content. This introduced inappropriate descriptions to professional photos. The risks involved in training systems built on faulty assumptions are equally pronounced in tangible examples. Many of us experience the flaws of ignoring outlying cases in standards for the built environment.

Our world is built for Reference Man.

Look out! Reference Man boldly endures an annual average temperature of twelve degrees Celsius. Holy smokes! Our hero crunches the competition with a body mass of twenty-four. Ka-pow!! This unassuming twenty- to thirty-year-old male appears everywhere. Reference Man is not from the imagination of comic book great Stan Lee but is a standard created by the International Commission on Radiological Protection (ICRP).

Reference Man is not a standard model. Reference Man is THE standard model. In anticipation of possible nuclear harm, this model helps calculate long-term shelter, and metabolic and nutrition requirements for society. There are a few variations, recognizing that not everyone is 5'7" and 150 pounds. The 1995 revised ICRP standard includes a model for 120-pound females who are 5'8" tall. The Asian Center for Reference Man Studies also developed an alternative model. However, the Reference Man standard today has influence over most of the world and physical infrastructure. Reference Man determines the dimensions of an airplane, the size of a door, or the shape of the car seat. Reference Man is similar to the Shirley card—but represents an ideal average.

Averages are a good place to start when building a model. But what is average and who determines it? Averages expect that about half the population is above and half the population is below these values. Unlike a median, that represents a real observation in the center of all values in a set, the average is a calculation. The average is the arithmetic mean calculated by dividing the total number of observations by the sum of all observations.

Getting the range of possibility wrong is not always merely inconvenient, it can be the difference between life and death.

Airbags prevent accidental death by inflating a cushion around the car dashboard on impact. Initially, when airbags became standard, the automobile fatality rates increased for female drivers of below average height. Why? Airbags inflated at Reference Man's chest, which is exactly into the face of a shorter person. The airbags designed on average for tall people were deadly to anyone smaller (Criado-Perez 2019). Strong models can move easily from where they were empirically tested and confirmed. When the abstractions are stable enough to apply in other settings, academics consider the model to have generalizability.

Data scientists must consider how to anticipate the spectrum of use and design systems that allow regular use or protect people no matter how tall, how small, or what shape they are.

1.6 Theory of the Problem or the Solution?

As conceptual representations, models arrange ideas into logical order. Some models want to understand how things got this way. Other models may want to fix things. Most form tentative explanations through a range of implicit choices such as training data, performance indicators, or ideals.

The decade of big data from 2008 to 2018 proclaimed the end of theory in favor of inductive learning. While true that careful academic models now have serious competition, throwing data at a question does not always give the best answer. Amazon had a sound plan for a predictive hiring algorithm but had not thought it all the way through. Theorizing still has a place in data-centric research. Without explicit recognition of at least the reasons for completing the study, it is easy to make assumptions that send you in the wrong direction.

Think of each predictive model as an explanation, or theory. Theories may bring insight into repeated occurrence without necessarily resolving the issue. Management scholars Ann Majchrzak and M. Lynne Markus built a taxonomy of types of explanations, including theories that explain the problems surrounding the phenomenon or ones that explain possible solutions. While there are additional explanations in their taxonomy (Majchrzak and Markus 2013), the theories of problems and theories of solutions are most relevant here.

A theory of the problem explains patterns of empirical evidence by answering how and why questions about the phenomenon (Markus 2014). These are plausible explanations of how the phenomenon works or why it exists. On the other hand, some theories attempt to bring closure. A theory of the solution explains the viability of interventions (Markus 2014). Building on a clear perspective of the problem and its causes, a theory of the solution attempts to determine ideal ways to address the phenomenon. Both theories of the problem and theories of the solution rely on observed patterns.

If you want to understand dependencies, you may be formulating a theory of a problem. If you are asking how things change, a theory of solution might be what you are planning. Either one can help to uncover additional assumptions about the underlying phenomenon of interest. A map that transformed public health shows how these theoretical positions can filter into models.

1.7 Scratch a Model to Find a Theory

The British physician John Snow lived in London during the particularly lethal 1854 cholera outbreak. Having formed the Epidemiological Society of London four years earlier, Snow was intensely interested in understanding the spread of the disease that was killing fifty people a day (Tulchinsky 2017). Cholera was rampant in newly overpopulated areas of London that did not yet have sanitation systems for removing waste and supplying water. The consensus at the time was that cholera spread through the bad-smelling vapors of raw sewage. A model of cholera fatalities by neighborhood supported this "miasmas" theory that this was an airborne disease.

The slums of Soho had a high number of cholera cases. Snow noticed that proximity to neighborhood open cesspits did not alone explain patterns of cholera outbreak among his Soho patients. He formulated a different theory of the problem based on sanitation, not sewers (Snow 1856). The epidemiology model that Snow built included detailed variables about drinking water to understand what he saw in his clinic. He mapped cholera deaths using two spatial locations: residence and communal water pumps. A cluster of deaths close to the Broad Street water pump convinced city officials to close it, and the epidemic subsided soon after.

Cholera is now accepted as not an airborne disease but one that spreads by drinking contaminated water. Snow's models added a new concept in the form of water sanitation and changed the level of analysis from neighborhoods to residences to explain the phenomenon. Importantly, it was not possible to biochemically confirm that cholera came from the water and not the air until medical biology progressed decades later (Tulchinsky 2017).

In essence, Snow's model of water sources was a theory of the problem. It was in competition with a model that only contained data about locations of smelly sewers. Early-stage observations often explain problems based on strong patterns in existing phenomenon. By formulating a sound theory of the problem, Snow was able to save thousands of lives until a solution was identified. A theory of the problem finds causality within recurring empirical evidence. It may not be able to explain the efficacy of solutions, but it explains what contributes to why something is happening.

Building models requires understanding assumptions in exemplar models, averages in historical training data, and hidden assumptions about the problem or the solution.

1.8 Model Ethical Data Science

Data scientists model predictive goals around a specific perspective of how things work. No need to design a light meter that calibrates for multiple skin tones if there is no expectation that people with different skin tones would be in a photograph together. Only stock extra-large suits if there is no expectation that smaller people will become astronauts. Design automobile airbags to save the lives of tall men because there is little expectation that shorter people will drive.

A data science model is an abstract representation of reality. Models create inferences or predictions often with a specific population, location, or issue in mind. They are optimized for an ideal set of conditions or populations. Being able to name these settings is an important step in ethical data science. To meet the predictive goals, it is necessary at this point to determine which sources to combine, which observations to ignore, or which concepts are missing.

The data scientist at this stage remembers their role as advisor to wayward algorithms and begins to slowly understand context. When is a standard deviation known or unknown? What is the appropriate goodness-of-fit statistical tool? . How does the platform work? Are the responses in 140- or 280-character sections? Be clear about the status quo and measurements. Define concepts through data selection. Determine conceptual relationships to prepare for predictive goals.

Political scientist Deborah Stone reminds us that what counts depends on who counts. Numbers are produced for people and organizations with power (Stone 2020). What can be found in data sets represents the interests of whoever commissioned them. The massive data sets are only available because organizations that can compel or collect this information pay to store it. Someone else without those interests may generate different data sets.

Predictive models are also built to serve organizations, often in an attempt to save money or time. Using handwriting samples to approve loans makes little logical sense except that it would streamline operations at many banks. Data scientists must reflect on how to maintain the validity of their research within these nested systems and goals.

Ethical data science makes predictions that are specific and credible by recognizing what it can and cannot do with the available sources. In creating models, data scientists must balance what the data users designed it to do, what the algorithm patrons want to learn, and how the world actually works.

1.9 Validity

Predictions successful in one setting are frequently deployed elsewhere. Data scientists need to determine whether and how the switch from one setting to another is appropriate for their predictions. The formal term for this is validity.

Underlying this process is a question about how people, places, actions, and ideas become quantified measures. Models represent one of many possible interpretations. Validity asks us to assess how well reality is quantified for analysis. Assessments of validity are traditional in statistical reasoning and apply to other models.

Statisticians use validity to ascertain the quality of a model. Validity tests were designed to help fit problems to available data. Questions of interest frequently did not match available data. The data may not answer a question directly or it may offer choices that do not track to the model. While blessed with large data sets, data scientists still must understand what to leave in or remove so things make sense.

Before the era of large digital data sets and "big data," statisticians had to routinely rely on a sample of data. The Guinness Brewery hired the statistician William Sealy Gosset in 1900 to develop a method to assess the quality of the malt beer without having to test every barrel, which he called a t-test. The t-test is still used to make estimations from small samples today. Statistical validity recognizes that not all available data describe the phenomenon exactly and that we must develop mathematical models to build valid claims from samples.

Naturalistic field studies do not rely on math to evaluate validity. Instead, inductive, qualitative, or abductive researchers assess quality using concepts of reliability and objectivity (Lincoln and Guba 1985). The following are some ways to evaluate both internal validity and external validity of data science projects.

Internal validity asks if the research design is logically coherent. Models must first have their own logic, and internal validity establishes a form of credibility. Comparing a temperature in Fahrenheit to a temperature in Celsius is a simple example of logical incoherence but it happened on a joint USA-EU space mission. Internal validity asks about the consistency, structure, and clarity (Rubin and Rubin 2005). Threats to internal validity can be handled with an awareness of measurements and design protocols. The more likely challenge for data science models is external validity.

External validity checks whether the model correspond to the actual phenomenon. Counting people in a bar is a suboptimal abstraction for understanding alcoholism. Model abstractions are valid when they bear a resemblance to the question being asked. As discussed in chapter 1, data quantification is not random and follows political or economic interests. Data scientists building strong predictive models have an intuitive understanding of the source's quantification strategy. Threats to external validity in data science include conflating population groups, ignoring base rates, relying on historically biased data sources, or failing to address traditional validity checks. Research should also be dependable, showing a consistent chain of evidence and demonstrating a lack of systematic bias in sources and interpretations. Confirmability is the deepest challenge for data science because of the uneven access to data and computing resources to replicate or reproduce studies.

Validity is the first invitation to think about boundaries. Chapter 4 examines the importance of thresholds for making comparisons. In this chapter, we focus on the overall project to identify where it starts and stops to make a valid and successful prediction. No matter how large the data set, these boundaries can have a substantive impact on the validity of the results.

Imagine that a social scientist combined massive sources on New York City's children between 1865 and 2020, drawing from immigrant diaries and social media, and successfully identified predictive trends about Irish twelve-year-olds. A social scientist would be asked many questions about the validity of the model and the applicability of the predictions. Do they apply to all Irish children? All immigrant twelve-year-olds? All children who lived in the former British empire? Does the model apply to children who immigrate from areas with political turmoil? How did the model take into account that before 1922, everyone was labeled as British because the Irish state did not exist? Are the findings related to New York City's unique stature as a gateway for immigration? Would the findings be valid in other cities? Social scientists conceptualize and generate data for a specific question within a given context, often following the national standards for research conduct.

Predictions often shift to other people, locations, or time periods. Discussing these shifts is a necessary step in social science, and data science could benefit from the same practice. Especially for predictions that can have strong impacts on human lives, understanding the nuance of different normative patterns is critical.

Research regulators hold social science and biomedical researchers to a high standard to create rigorously valid research. In that process, they are required to justify their research design decisions and show the steps they take to generate authoritative findings. Studies involving digital material do not have to meet the same standard. But an understanding of this process can be helpful in producing more ethical data science.

1.10 Research Ethics: Justice

Justice is a core principle for ethical research involving human subjects. The Belmont Report, which regulates research ethics in the United States, seeks to avoid exploitative research by emphasizing equal distribution of burdens and advantages (U.S. Department of Health, Education, and Welfare and National Commission for the Protection of Human Subjects of Biomedical and Behavioral Research 1979). Research should not deny a benefit someone is entitled to have. Moreover, investigators must express a good reason if someone is treated differently. This immediately raises crucial but deceptively simple questions: Who is equal, and how do we define inequality?

Predictive data systems appear to treat everyone equally. Data justice can be defined in many ways (Bui and Noble 2020). Some ignore specific characteristics in a search for fairness. Others label characteristics to identify injustice. In either case, exact calculations to withhold or distribute benefits may appear stricter than what might make sense in other settings.

Amazon Prime members living in majority-Black zip codes in 2016 were excluded from same-day service in the cities of Atlanta, Washington, DC, Oakland, New York City, and Chicago. While it is true that demography may not have been considered in the company's analysis, the exclusionary results are still the same. The model had a disparate impact on the community. Amazon never really explained why Roxbury had two-day Prime service even though its trucks repeatedly crossed through the Black community to provide faster service to every single surrounding neighborhood. After a Bloomberg report and a request by the Boston mayor, Amazon agreed to expand same-day delivery to all Boston neighborhoods (Ingold and Soper 2016). Only those aware of the underlying demographic data would have been able to identify the disparity and bring justice to the people without the service. In the case of Amazon, a benefit was systematically withheld, but in the augmented reality game, areas were excluded.

Pokémon GO seemed to only concentrate its popular augmented reality game outside of Black neighborhoods. The location-based phone app intended to build new community ties and increase physical activity. The Urban Institute compared the Washington, DC, game locations with census track data and discovered that fifty-five portals appeared in majority White neighborhoods compared to nineteen portals in majority Black neighborhoods (Kooragayala and Srini 2016).

Conversely, other locations, such as cemeteries and war memorials, had game portals that they did not want. Pokémon GO modeled its portals on locations found on a crowdsourced platform. Crowdsourced information is limited to the people who participate. A justice perspective might have considered using more than one crowd to source from. Another solution might have been to simply have a corporate ethic that would refuse locations in places honoring the dead. The company also might have reached out to specific physical locations to invite them to participate in the crowdsourcing to generate better data sets for themselves and future location-based games.

Making a distinction between labels and structural categories will be essential to interpreting and implementing data justice. Orange cars, for example, have a higher resale. They are rare in comparison to most cars on the market, but it is not the color alone that explains their value. Instead, it is the qualities of someone who might originally ask for a factory-painted car of that color that drives its value. Orange cars represent a type of driver who is very specific about what type of car they drive. On the other hand, the colors of M&M's function as a label because each color represents a distinction that does not make a difference. Red and yellow M&M's are interchangeable except, unless perhaps, you are under a certain age. In both cases, the color is not important, but one is a label and the other is an assemblage of several meanings.

Data sets, like in the Amazon or Pokémon cases, may not even contain characteristics representing protected legal classes such as age, income, ethnicity, race, ability, or gender. However the history of social use of these labels means that they will be legible in the data, often undetected except by those with personal experience. Protected classes are not mere labels but structural categories that represent a series of social policy choices made by powerful actors against others (Richardson 2022). The movement of fairness, accountability, and transparency in machine learning attempts to tackle these issues by correcting for some of these social conditions with mathematical adjustments (Mehrabi et al. 2021; Hutchinson et al. 2021).

Another approach to justice is to recognize how digital systems may continue earlier forms of exploitation (Mohamed, Png, and Isaac 2020). These efforts recognize that predictive data systems can have the authority and force of colonial forces, and they look to history for deconstructing power differentials. The cognitive scientist Abeba Birhane calls for rethinking the entire endeavor by centering the experiences of vulnerable groups (Birhane and Cummins 2019) and advancing a form of data justice that seeks human flourishing for all (Birhane et al. 2022).

Justice in research ethics appeals to a question of fairness. Data scientists could strive to meet the same principle by endeavoring to treat people consistently, and if not, explain why.

1.11 Thinking Like a Historian to Model

Predictions create narratives and implied relationships. Data scientists who think like historians arrange available evidence into credible narratives of the previous patterns. Skill deftly evaluating fragmented sources and contradictory evidence is core to historic thinking in data science models.

Historians study change over time. Not merely a chronicle, a history reveals motivations and explanations. The past informs the present and may suggest repetition in the future. Like historians, data scientists should recognize the circumstances that influence the patterns they find.

History, according to Peter N. Stearns, is a laboratory where earlier events substantiate the causes and conditions of today (Stearns 1998). Forging conceptual relationships between people, events, and conditions, history, in short, builds a model. Historians tend to specialize in a period, an idea, places, or people so they can understand the context of their sources. Data scientists could emulate this practice by collaborating with subject matter experts who have deep knowledge.

The study of history recognizes that the past is always fragmentary. The historical record is inconsistent, incomplete, hard to find, or could be entirely missing some aspects. The past is pieced together through the material readily available, although it may not be the best source. Historians select a range of relevant sources representing multiple views to build a more complete narrative of actual events. The digital human record is unlimited in comparison to paper records, yet it is equally fragmentary in terms of access. Large data sets are licensed, under copyright, private, or otherwise have limited access. Sources may contain both confirmatory proof and conflicting evidence that require pause and interpretation.

Historical skills can help data scientists appraise the worth and contribution of informational fragments to the larger narrative. There is always something we do not know, have not recorded, or cannot access.

Fragmented sources lead to contradictions. One source may say one thing, while another source may refute it. Which source is reliable? Scholars are trained to interpret and evaluate contradictory historical evidence, in addition to noting which perspectives are missing from the historic record. As evidenced in the problems with Mechanical Turk image labels, machine learning and data science elevate conformity (Irani and Silberman 2013). Critical benchmark research evaluates the credibility of web sources to show how assumptions of uniformity do not hold across all populations.

Thinking like a historian means assembling fragmentary, contradictory sources of questionable quality into a coherent, credible narrative of cause, effect, and correlation. Instead of ignoring differences, see if contradictory evidence can refine predictive goals. Data scientists who think like historians would carefully weigh the relative value of all sources to piece together a credible narrative of the past.

Ethical data scientists comb through their sources to determine which evidence will drive the prediction.

1.12 Chapter 2 Summary

Models set the shape of predictions. A predictive model is a representation of reality that is designed to optimize specific inferences. Together, data sources and concepts best represent the ultimate predictive goal. Like any plan, model abstractions eventually are tested in real situations. Modeling determines a prediction's ability to meet its intended goal in authentic conditions.

Assessment is the essence of the second stage of the prediction supply chain. The quality of each data column, each source, and even the overall predictive goal are all up for consideration. Validity assesses how dependable, consistent, and credible predictive models are. Training data, exemplar models, and representative averages all play a part in this final planning stage. Importantly, models are opportunities to question assumptions and begin to make room for eventual outlying data points or circumstances. A strong model enhances the likelihood that the predictions smoothly ease into operation without compromising validity.

This chapter encourages thinking about credible narratives and the plausibility of predictive insights. While the gods are motivated by hubris and all-knowing power, most of us working with data sets recognize shortcomings. Being realistic about the validity of predictive capabilities brings credibility to data science. The next chapter discusses making comparisons in predictive models.

1.13 APPENDIX EXERCISES—Chapter 2 Model

Points to consider:

- Ask about interpretations of the predictive goal.
- Clarify operating assumptions in order to generalize results.
- Know how to measure key performance indicators.
- Avoid training data that does not match the predictive goals.
- Watch for opportunity costs and consider whether it is NOT doing something that is relevant to the predictive goal.
- Make models as accurate as possible for the default population while considering how to handle rare occurrences and outliers.

- Watch for organizational efficiency that may have a "round up the usual suspects" approach.
- Eliminate parts of sources that do not reflect full consent from participants.

References

Ajunwa, Ifeoma. 2016. "The Paradox of Automation as Anti-Bias Intervention." *Cardozo Law Review* 41 (March). http://dx.doi.org/10.2139/ssrn.2746078.

Birhane, Abeba, and Fred Cummins. 2019. "Algorithmic Injustices: Towards a Relational Ethics." http://arxiv.org/abs/1912.07376.

Birhane, Abeba, et al. 2022. "Power to the People? Opportunities and Challenges for Participatory AI." In *EAAMO '22: Equity and Access in Algorithms, Mechanisms, and Optimization.* . Arlington, VA: ACM, 1–8. https://doi.org/10.1145/3551624.3555290.

Birhane, Abeba, Vinay Uday Prabhu, and Emmanuel Kahembwe. 2021. "Multimodal Datasets: Misogyny, Pornography, and Malignant Stereotypes." http://arxiv.org/abs/2110.01963.

Brown, Tom B., et al. 2020. "Language Models Are Few-Shot Learners." Preprint article *arXiv:2005.14165 [Cs]*,. http://arxiv.org/abs/2005.14165.

Bui, Matthew Le, and Safiya Umoja Noble. 2020. "We're Missing a Moral Framework of Justice in Artificial Intelligence: On the Limits, Failings, and Ethics of Fairness." In *The Oxford Handbook of Ethics of AI*, edited by Markus D. Dubber, Frank Pasquale, and Sunit Das, 161–79. Oxford; New York: Oxford University Press. https://doi.org/10.1093/oxfordhb/9780190067397.013.9.

Criado-Perez, Caroline. 2019. "The Deadly Truth about a World Built for Men—From Stab Vests to Car Crashes." *The Guardian*, February 23, 2019, sec. US news. http://www.theguardian.com/lifeandstyle/2019/feb/23/truth-world-built-for-men-car-crashes.

Curtiz, Michael, dir. 1942. *Casablanca*. https://www.imdb.com/title/tt0034583/.

Halevy, Alon, Peter Norvig, and Fernando Pereira. 2009. "The Unreasonable Effectiveness of Data." *IEEE Intelligent Systems* 24 (2): 8–12. https://doi.org/10.1109/MIS.2009.36.

Hutchinson, Ben, et al. 2021. "Towards Accountability for Machine Learning Datasets: Practices from Software Engineering and Infrastructure." Preprint article. *arXiv:2010.13561 [Cs]*. http://arxiv.org/abs/2010.13561.

Ingold, David, and Spencer Soper. 2016. "Amazon Doesn't Consider the Race of Its Customers. Should It?" 2016. http://www.bloomberg.com/graphics/2016-amazon-same-day/.

Irani, Lilly C., and M. Six Silberman. 2013. "Turkopticon: Interrupting Worker Invisibility in Amazon Mechanical Turk." In *Proceedings of the SIGCHI Conference on Human Factors in Computing Systems*, 611–20. CHI '13. New York, NY, USA: ACM, 611–20. https://doi.org/10.1145/2470654.2470742.

Kooragayala, Shiva, and Tanaya Srini. 2016. "Pokémon GO Is Changing How Cities Use Public Space, but Could It Be More Inclusive?" *Urban Wire: The Blog of the Urban Institute*. August 1, 2016. https://www.urban.org/urban-wire/pokemon-go-changing-how-cities-use-public-space-could-it-be-more-inclusive.

Lincoln, Yvonna S., and Egon G. Guba. 1985. *Naturalistic Inquiry*. Beverly Hills, CA: Sage Publications. http://www.loc.gov/catdir/enhancements/fy0658/84026295-d.html.

Majchrzak, Ann, and M. Lynne Markus. 2013. *Methods for Policy Research: Taking Socially Responsible Action.* 2nd ed.

Markus, M. Lynne. 2014. "Maybe Not the King, but an Invaluable Subordinate: A Commentary on Avison and Malaurent's Advocacy of 'Theory Light' IS Research." *Journal of Information Technology* 29 (4): 341–45. https://doi.org/10.1057/jit.2014.19.

Mehrabi, Ninareh, et al. 2021. "A Survey on Bias and Fairness in Machine Learning." *ACM Computing Surveys (CSUR)* 54 (6): 1–35. https://doi.org/10.1145/3457607.

Mohamed, Shakir, Marie-Therese Png, and William Isaac. 2020. "Decolonial AI: Decolonial Theory as Sociotechnical Foresight in Artificial Intelligence." *Philosophy & Technology*, 33 (July): 659–84. https://doi.org/10.1007/s13347-020-00405-8.

Richardson, Rashida. 2022. "Racial Segregation and the Data-Driven Society: How Our Failure to Reckon with Root Causes Perpetuates Separate and Unequal Realities." *Berkeley Technology Law Journal* 36 (3): 1051–90. https://doi.org/10.15779/Z38 PN8XG3V.

Roth, Lorna. 2009. "Looking at Shirley, the Ultimate Norm: Colour Balance, Image Technologies, and Cognitive Equity." *Canadian Journal of Communication* 34 (1): 111–36. https://doi.org/10.22230/cjc.2009v34n1a2196.

Rubin, Herbert J., and Irene Rubin. 2005. *Qualitative Interviewing: The Art of Hearing Data.* Vol. 2. Thousand Oaks, CA: Sage Publications.

Snow, John. 1856. "On the Mode of Communication of Cholera." *Edinburgh Medical Journal* 1 (7): 668–70. https://www.ncbi.nlm.nih.gov/pmc/articles/PMC5307547/.

Stearns, Peter N. 1998. "Why Study History?" 1998. https://www.historians.org/about-aha-and-membership/aha-history-and-archives/historical-archives/why-study-hist ory-(1998).

Stone, Deborah. 2020. *Counting: How We Use Numbers to Decide What Matters.* 1st ed. New York: Liveright Publishing Corporation a division of W.W. Norton & Company Inc.

Tulchinsky, Theodore. 2017. "John Snow, Cholera, the Broad Street Pump; Waterborne Diseases Then and Now." In *Case Studies in Public Health*, 1st ed. Boston, MA: Elsevier.

U.S. Department of Health, Education, and Welfare. 1979. "The Belmont Report. Ethical Principles and Guidelines for the Protection of Human Subjects of Research." National Commission for the Protection of Human Subjects of Biomedical and Behavioral Research.   https://www.hhs.gov/ohrp/regulations-and-policy/belmont-report/ index.html.

Washington, Anne, et al. 2022. "Uncoupling Inequality: Reflections on the Ethics of Benchmarks for Digital Media." In Proceedings of Hawaii International Conference on System Sciences. https://doi.org/10.24251/HICSS.2022.352.

3

Compare

No Comparison Without Representation

1. NO COMPARISON WITHOUT REPRESENTATION

The third stage of the prediction supply chain is to find patterns. Data scientists compare digital material against models or other ideals. This is the core activity of data science—making decisions about what is similar. Whether they are called bins, features, characteristics, clusters, attributes, codes, or categories, these sets define similarity or difference. Pattern-matching criteria for difference are rarely documented much less discussed intellectual activity that serves as an extension of social orders. Being pigeonholed in a category can be uncomfortable, even at an interpersonal level. In the movie *Guardians of the Galaxy*, before a dangerous combat mission, the character Quinn asks his new colleague, Gamora to enjoy music (Gunn 2014). Gamora refuses because she views herself as a warrior and as an assassin who does not dance. Similar incompatibility between lived experience and labels occurs in data analytics, which is why research ethics asks investigators to have respect for persons. History shows that rigid population divisions can stoke political oppression, often stimulated by fruitless and racist endeavors of proving one group of humans as superior. Ethical data science is aware that comparisons can imply hierarchical social relationships that may generate stigma. Ignoring salient features may compromise the legitimacy of the prediction, which is why comparison requires representation. Data scientists

Ethical Data Science. Anne L. Washington, Oxford University Press. © Oxford University Press 2023.
DOI: 10.1093/oso/9780197693025.003.0005

could find matching items while respecting multidimensional identities of the people represented in the data and models. This chapter examines the role of standards, binary limitations, the material force of categories, and digital dignity.

1.1 Tomato; To-MAH-To

Is a tomato a vegetable or a fruit? Maybe you ate tomatoes for dinner in salsa, pasta, or a salad. If vegetables are savory foods, then tomatoes are certainly a vegetable because they are not sweet. Any peek inside a cookbook finds that tomatoes are not listed under desserts or fruits. Tomato recipes are listed under vegetables. While everyone you know may agree this is true, is there a formal definition that goes beyond a popular heuristic?

If we are building a system that will have a major impact on society, we should rely on something other than our own informal understanding of the world around us. Let's consider how scientists classify a tomato. In botanical science, a fruit is a ripened flower containing seeds. According to botanical classification, a tomato is grouped with other fruits such as cucumbers, olives, and avocados. That all these items are classified as fruit may seem strange. But botanists do not have a definition of a vegetable. The scientific classification of a tomato, Solanum lycopersicum, has been in use since Carl Linnaeus's 1753 *Species Plantarum*. Do not despair if this centuries-old definition is news. Classifications change over time.

A vegetable is a culinary term we might all commonly use within our regional cuisines, but it is not a scientific classification. It is a label that is totally culturally determined and therefore mutable across locations. A contemporary scientist sees a tomato as a fruit, but so did customs officers for most of the nineteenth century.

Back in 1893, the United States came down on the veggie side when the US Supreme Court decided that tomatoes, for regulatory purposes, would be considered a vegetable. The case foiled tomato importers trying to avoid tariff hikes. In *Nix v. Hedden*, 149 US 304, the Court ruled that tomatoes imported under the vegetable designation would be subject to US Customs regulations based on the Tariff Act of 1883.

Classification choices often spark political debate such as the uproar over the 1981 declaration that ketchup and relish would be counted as vegetables in US federally funded school lunches. The 2011 revision of the US Department of Agriculture nutritional goals for meals in public schools established two tablespoons of "tomato paste and puree" as a vegetable on pizza. These definitions had a material impact on the health and nutrition of millions of children. State planning and coordination of large populations can greatly impact the physical landscape and social experience (Scott 1998). While some may consider governing the sole important task of the public sector, regulation plays an expansive role in establishing categories.

A round, red, juicy tomato can be grouped in many ways depending on who is looking. A chef sees a vegetable, which can be verified with a commercial category scheme. A botanist sees a fruit based on its scientific name. Categories are not static. Making comparisons based on well-defined or representative sets is not as simple as separating apples and oranges, fruits and vegetables, or tomatoes and broccoli.

If this was so complicated for a food that many of us have eaten our whole life, imagine the level of difficulty in putting people in groups. One object, one person, one lifetime can juggle and maintain multiple simultaneous identities. Sociologist and cultural theorist Stuart Hall reminds us that encoding and decoding meaning is a complex culturally specific process of interpretation (Hall et al. 2003).

Despite these vagaries of meaning, comparison is at the heart of most scientific endeavors. Empirical science relies on discovering variance and explaining why distinction and discrepancy occur. Data scientists build on this lineage to ask if this is the same as that and then generate insights from those evaluations. It is a very elaborate pattern-matching exercise.

Predictive data science forms groups and labels them for analysis. This chapter expands the conversation to consider how categories are an extension of social orders and how to not use categories to fracture society. Let's begin by seeing the impact of classifying people.

1.2 Exceptions to the Rule

Not everyone fits neatly into a category.

Data science sometimes designed for wide dissemination must remember that there will always be exceptions to the rule. In the built environment, quick fixes can bridge poor design. Left-handed people know where to buy different types of scissors. Motion-activated soap dispensers that only detect movement from people with relatively light skin can be fixed by surrounding them with bright light.

Digital predictive system can sometimes stop working altogether when they encounter an exception. In the worst situation, anyone who does not fit the idealized model is essentially refused access to service. Data science is built for efficiency, and efficiency requires known and defined boundaries. The downside of efficiency is that when a model encounters something different, it can behave unexpectedly.

Dating apps which match couples struggle with how to describe people accurately in order to facilitate searching. A racial binary often dissolves into a proxy for skin color. Race and ethnicity categories often force people with parents from different heritages to make a tough decision. While these explicit definitions can be challenging, one online dating app used implicit category definitions that unleashed attacks on some clients.

Tinder is a visual dating app where potential couples respond to photos of each other. Unlike other dating sites that support "traditional marriage," Tinder advertised itself as a place for all couples. Just swipe to make a match. The model had built-in assumptions to serve men seeking men, women seeking women, and heterosexual couples. But where would a match with a gender nonconforming person fit? Exacerbating the problem was that Tinder users had the ability to report fraud or accuse other users of deception. People who expected heteronormative pairing reported transgendered profiles as deceptive. Users were banned essentially because their photos did not depict normative ideas of gendered facial features Sato (2021). The majority population used the apps community reporting tools to ostracize a subpopulation and exert punitive power. Tinder took steps to resolve the issue but not before competitors' community support groups such as the #alltypesallswipes movement tried to help people avoid getting harassed and banned on matching services. There may have been no intention to make some clients uncomfortable, but the app chose to develop its algorithmic model on only one segment of the population.

The disconnect was not only in the types of comparisons available but also in specifying the predictive goals. Proclaiming that the dating app served all couples did not align with ignoring the interests of a defined subpopulation group that was crucial to their business model. An app that matches couples needs to attend to population categories relevant to dating such as hormonal, sexual, and gender identities. In contrast, those categories may be irrelevant for a cooking app that would want to know dietary preferences or allergies. An awareness of salient categories within the specific predictive setting must be articulated in tandem with the goal for the comparison to function as expected.

The dating app case brings up a subtle problem. Without representative data, the dating app could not learn appropriately. Not only did the app fail specific users, its model failed because of flawed interpretations of what was similar and what was different. The only way to assess the risk in advance would be to consider who is included and excluded from the original data sets. This is a responsibility that data scientists are rarely trained to do. Interpretive researchers call this "negative evidence" (Mason 2002) to draw attention to voices absent from the empirical record.

How do data scientists make comparisons? Comparisons in the third stage enact ideals established during the second stage in the prediction supply chain when models are set. Understanding how to define difference, use standards, and avoid binaries are tools for ethical data science comparisons. Contrasting and comparing items starts with thinking about whose value judgments determine the sort.

1.3 Who Is Sorting?

Who is sorting, and what determines similarity or difference?

Data science combines sources and models to determine reasonable associations between items to support inferences. Comparisons dominate data science but often without a mechanism to draw attention to the logic and assumptions behind what determines similarity. Research based only on observations will be skewed because most sets do not contain rare exceptions (Taleb 2007). The more rare the event, the more important theory becomes because there is so little observational evidence. One simple approach to solve this is to choose which authority will determine the composition of the group.

Data scientists without domain expertise have to decide which authority to rely on when explaining comparisons, and there are many options. Communities may create their own definitions to determine how they want to be named and differentiated. A concerned passionate authority may serve as an ally who elevates community definitions as standards. Some may want the legitimacy of a dispassionate neutral authority, such as a committee. Some may want to rely on historic and generational patterns. Others may want to only determine difference through measurable qualities. Public policy and regulatory statutes provide another alternative to establish categories and boundaries for items related to commerce. Ethical data scientists are able to articulate how they determined similarity or difference.

Comparison is the process of determining whether items have something in common. Everyone makes comparisons. Will tomorrow be similar to today? Is this sweater the kind he likes? Is she one of them? Making comparisons also creates sets. In mathematics, elements in a set share some definition. A set can be described by what makes items similar. A set could also be characterized by why items are excluded.

There are many words for making sets for scientific analysis. Machine learning describes groups formed from unsupervised learning as "features." Computer scientists may refer to similarities as "clusters." Data mining likes the term "buckets." Data scientists have a process called "binning," where data are distributed by intervals equally into bins for comparing distributions. Statisticians may consider this a form of classification. Record linkage supports longitudinal research where entity resolution is not obvious. Qualitative researchers meticulously evaluate non-numerical data to assign codes. I refer to all of them here to imply that there is in-depth scholarship on grouping observations for analysis.

Understanding the values that drive pattern matching can lead to more accurate intellectual order in data science.

The classic struggles for comparison are explored in the following sections on standards, binary settings, determining differences, and similarities.

1.4 Standards

Data science relies on standards to differentiate items. Characteristics, locations, behaviors, events, transactions, and sensor data are quantified in regular ways for more accurate definitions of similarity. The power of standards is rooted in their widespread interoperability and steadfastness.

Standards facilitate comparisons by maintaining stability for commensuration. Standards are guidelines that promote uniformity in measurement or design. To cut curtains of the same length, use the same yardstick. Something must remain fixed so that differences can be detected. Standards systemize a problem and solve it through universal repetition.

Standards can also be localized, which is why acting like your shoe size in Europe means acting like a forty-year-old, but in Minneapolis it is acting like a nine-year-old. A standard often becomes a commercial or regulatory specification, such as an agreement to make notebooks 8.5×11 inches in the United States.

When conditions change, standards change. Scholars of record linkage in historical census data build new statistical solutions for handling these types of issues (Ruggles, Fitch, and Roberts 2018). Consider trying to follow stock ticker symbols through mergers and acquisitions. Sears and Roebuck Company on the New York Stock Exchange had the ticker symbol S for decades. When Sears and Kmart merged into the Sears Holding Company, the single-letter ticker symbol available for the first time since 1906 was snapped up by Sprint. Sprint Corporation subsequently became a subsidiary of T-Mobile. Standard transitions can be viewed from the path of the ticker symbol S from Sears to Sprint, or from the perspective of an entity: Sears was S, then KMRT after another merger, and then SHLD before filing for bankruptcy. Standard identifiers are not static.

The politics of standards is rooted in how and when they update. Sometimes visible only to experts, standards encourage coordinated action often in response to accidents, disasters, or misadventure to be avoided. The sinking of the *Titanic* sparked decades of improvements in wireless technology, such as the universal SOS distress signal. City dwellers who enjoy water sanitation standards can thank a particularly lethal cholera outbreak in London (Snow 1856). Even ethical research requirements are standards that emerged from problematic studies (Heller 1972; "Former Director for Tuskegee Syphilis Study Believes Work Was 'Completely Ethical'" 1972).

Standards can be seen as responses to problems, often political ones, faced by people governing large populations. Standards are negotiated artifacts. They represent compromises, agreements, fights, and placations. Data science draws on the power of standards to make inferences.

1.5 Beyond the Binary

Can't we have more than two?

Binary options give you two choices. On/off. Push/pull. All binary choices result in a Boolean computer code that chooses between a zero or a one. Computing is full of binary choices. Consider a default setting that forces everyone to make an adjustment if it doesn't suit them. Computers are able to count above one but often insist on historic binary choices that do more to enforce norms and limit diversity.

Early US census forms presented only a racial binary of either Black or White, ignoring all other categories or origins of people. The constantly changing US census demographic categories highlight the need for adjustment. Colleges are responding to students who want to share their full identities by adjusting registration systems to accommodate additional information.

The classic case is the gender binary that forces people to choose either male or female on forms. Ironically, the binary continues to be enforced by pronoun selection on many systems. For example, Facebook announced its new gender identity categories with fanfare in February 2014 when it released fifty-six options in its English-language social networking site. Everyone on the site also chose whether to use the pronouns he/she/they/ze. Despite this radical change in demographic categorization, there was little outcry from the business community, which relies on Facebook advertising because the algorithm automatically labeled anyone not explicitly female (she) as male. Despite holding rich and wide-ranging information, Facebook simply reasserted the binary that the system itself attempted to rebel against. Facebook corrected this pattern after many years of tossing out self-identified categories in favor of a binary convenient for advertisers.

A binary assessment of human traits often can lead to flat conclusions that say more about the investigator's limited thinking than anything about human social groups.

The 2017 Xiaolin Wu and Xi Zhang's paper, "Automated Inference on Criminality Using Face Images," claimed to determine who was a criminal with machine learning (Wu and Zhang 2017). A classifier was built on a binary of criminal and noncriminal people. The predictive system did sort people easily into two groups, but the signal was not criminality but clothing. The group who wore button-collared shirts were labeled the noncriminals, while anyone who wore a T-shirt was labeled a criminal. Algorithms solve for the easiest possible distinction. The signal picked out commonalities that had nothing to do with the predictive goals of the people in the study.

Binaries can so limit expressions of humanity to the point that they can become meaningless. The world-class runner Caster Semenya wrote on Twitter on March 26, 2022, that according to World Athletics, she was male in the 400m and 800m and female in the 100m and 200m (Semenya 2022). The same athletic standards body gave one person differing gender categorizations. A multiracial family in apartheid South Africa could never be appropriately recognized by the state (Bowker and Star 1999). Attempts to define strict boundaries between population groups in bureaucratic systems often exclude people who do not pass purity tests anticipated by models.

A binary choice severely limits human autonomy because it reduces options to a simple if-then choice. Normative values can sometimes associate ordinary conditions of humanity with forms of deviance. Attempts to go beyond the binary immediately move from a debate over a simple default settings into broad reflection on who is or is not normal in society.

1.6 The Material Force of Categories

One photo shows a man wearing a black suit and a blue tie. Another photo shows a man in a hoodie, while another shows a man in a tank top. Are these images of the same person? The artist Bayeté Ross Smith created sequences of photographic images in *Our Kind of People* (2015) to invite viewers to reflect on how clothes shape how people are judged. Just as clothes can change what people think of us, categories change our place in society.

Comparisons can result in real-world violence. People who do not conform to anticipated expectations can be pushed out or punished. Population statistics collected by governments have been misused for extermination and ethnic cleansing (Seltzer and Anderson 2001). For instance, US citizens classified as Japanese in the 1940 census lost their property and businesses when they were put in internment camps during wartime. Geoff C. Bowker and Susan Leigh Starr described this as the material force of categories. Stand in the wrong line at passport control or go to a bathroom where you are not welcome and suddenly a mere label becomes what Durkheim called a social fact (Bowker and Star 1999).

Categories create and reify social conditions. Strong thresholds between people based on behavior and physical characteristics can function as tools of social control. A data science team claimed that they were able to predict sexual orientation from dating profiles. Another group repeated the study and discovered that the model simply picked up on strong signals of beards, glasses, and eye makeup (Arcas, Todorov, and Mitchell 2018) and claimed the study was phrenology. Phrenology tries to predict mental conditions based on physical characteristics and is very popular with some data science teams. Typically, these tools accompany attempts to exploit social power. Some countries consider homosexuality a crime, and predictive systems like this could result in real violence. Appreciation of difference is not the same around the world.

Throughout history, population groupings have stoked division and oppression using differences to denote who is considered human and nonhuman. This is why this book asks data scientists to think of data as people too. Data science has a responsibility to understand how organizing knowledge can impact populations. Prediction can shift people into different social contexts that can materially shape their daily experiences. The pattern matching that is essential to data science can compromise human autonomy when it sorts people into rigid social categories that imply hierarchal power relationships.

Systems that expressly invite everyone must function for populations that are the minority in number. Meeting the needs of 80 percent of the public may be good enough for a research project. Operational systems deployed to serve the broader public must be able to serve everyone, including the outliers and rare occurrences. Public interest technology must be built for the freaks and the geeks, as well as the normative majority.

1.7 Searching for Similarity

Search for images of babies on your favorite internet search engine. In 2021, on a popular search engine, few had brown eyes and only one had dark skin. Most were adorned with colors that denote blue for boy and pink for girl. Arguably, a baby represents the continuation of all forms of humanity, yet on search systems, babies are pale blondes with rosy lips and blue eyes. There are no images representing babies born in Nairobi, Rangoon, or Taipei.

Data science benchmarks, artificial intelligence training data, internet search systems, and other expansive large-scale sets have the capacity to represent humanity in all of its complexity. But they rarely do.

General labels, such as "baby," are limited to only a few human body types. The opposite is also true. Non-pale, non-male people do not get general purpose labels, such as professor, other than their difference to this enforced norm.

Searchers must look for Filipino scientist or Black doctor and hope to avoid explicit images. The scholar Safiya Noble revealed how search systems related women with specific heritage characteristics to adult content (Noble 2018). Yet we know there are women who are firefighters and men who are nurses.

Some labels are derogatory. The software engineer Jacky Alciné sent a 2015 tweet showing that Google's auto-tagging service had labeled people without pale skin as gorillas in his photos (Vincent 2020). Google apologized and promised that it would no longer use that term in images. A follow-up study three years later found that Google Photos simply made it impossible to search for terms like gorilla, chimp, monkey, or other specific primates whose names are used as pejorative slurs (Simonite 2018). The problem was not solved, although the embarrassment was eliminated by restricting the range of things available for search. Generally, people in an iPhone photo are not in the same environment as an animal in the wild. It seems like the system took all labels at face value.

The derogatory labels become material that feeds into other automated systems. The UN campaign for gender equality ran ads in 2012 showing the Google autocomplete from the prompt "Women should not." Large language models frequently make associations that perpetuate stereotypes that dehumanize (Bender et al. 2021). Data science benchmarks that strive for generality often are overwhelmed with poor construct validity, creating very uneven quality results (Paullada et al. 2021). Some differences are more than skin deep. Pearl Bailey and Carol Channing both had an African-American grandmother, but most systems would classify them by their skin color. There is ample photo evidence of biracial twins who look completely different. Our current systems that determine sameness are not designed to handle these natural variations in human populations.

In 1950, the "Family of Man" exhibit toured widely, showcasing lifestyles and human life forms around the planet. It depicted people in dwellings passed down through millennia, such as hand-built homes and palaces built by servants. Photos of children, teenagers, workers, and the elderly included communities with an average height of 4'5" and those where everyone stood over 6 feet tall. The Trappist monk, Thomas Merton, described his amazement at flipping through the exhibit book he found at a used bookstore. Merton wrote that the variety of images confirmed to him that humanity is one and that everyone has the same face.

The breadth of humanity summarized in three thousand images published more than seventy years ago has more breadth than the five billion images available on machine learning benchmarks today. Books are limited by page numbers and printing conventions. The internet does not have the same physical limitations but still constrains possibilities. There is no mathematical or resource limitation that points to why digital systems choose depth, or quantity over breadth, or variety. Why can't we design technical systems that better reflect the infinite categories of humanity rather than assert the limitations of paper systems?

Despite the capacity for any digital ecosystem to represent more than one characteristic, we repeatedly focus on a negative model or deficits that reinforce sameness.

1.8 Compare Ethical Data Science

The third action in the ethical prediction supply chain is to compare responsibly. No comparison without representation. Data and actions traceable through this process should help to support decisions at this point. Traceability will give further assurance in how to compare and contrast data. However, no data sets are complete or do not show the frayed edges of multiple classifications over time. It is not possible to know everything about data sets, but it is possible to learn enough to make informed assumptions.

The central question to consider here is whether data science diminishes the capacity for humans to make independent choices.

Comparisons that support human autonomy bring up theological concepts of free will. Do we choose our own fate, or are our life paths predetermined? Great thinkers in Yoruba philosophy, Buddhist teachings, Sanskrit Vedas, and quantum mechanics have contemplated the extent that the universe is deterministic. Statisticians continue the tradition with debates over causal inference, asking when it is appropriate to conclude that conditions and actions control outcomes.

The Matrix movies present a popular interpretation of autonomy which reduces everything to a binary. Centuries of philosophy are condensed on-screen to a choice between a red pill and a blue pill. Red gives knowledge and the burden of making independent choices. Blue maintains a deterministic system and a form of ignorant bliss. The Matrix, like many technical systems, poses an artificial limit expressed as a binary. Why only two choices, with no yellow, mauve, and chartreuse pills? The natural world offers a multitude of choices where there is not just one purple flower but millions. Morpheus at least offered a choice so Neo had some type of informed consent. Research ethicists will note that Neo had no ability to refuse the invitation all together and opt out of participation.

Unethical data science comparisons take blunt binaries seriously. There is no awareness of strengths of signals in the data, such as noticing that no one in the mugshot wore a tie. There is no curiosity about unexpected patterns or unexpected connections. No sharp eye checks on underrepresented groups such as rural communities, unemployed people, non-Western locations, binary races, or lower castes. Some predictive algorithms echo the legacy of phrenology and eugenics to scientifically determine who is an undesirable human. Quantification and advanced math in the past justify domination or subordination for economic exploitation.

Data science can provide powerful insight into society and comparisons go well beyond creating sets. Data science adds to the existing knowledge and the comparisons, and sets are merely a tool to get to facilitate gathering empirical evidence. Balancing freedom and fate were tough questions millennia ago. Today these questions have a deeper salience as automated systems nudge us toward a new form of determinism. The logic of organizational efficiency that dominates prediction has little tolerance for individual whimsy and self-determination.

1.9 Research Ethics: Autonomy

Autonomy in research ethics is equated with freedom from outside control. Research participants must act willingly and from their own volition, without coercion from researchers or others. According to the standards developed over the twentieth century, research can only be conducted on volunteers through the process of informed consent. Only someone who is acting independently can issue consent to participate in a study (Faden, King, and Beauchamp 1986). Each research participant must be an autonomous person who can take autonomous action.

An autonomous person authorizes their own time, attention, and actions. Importantly, an autonomous person has the ability to refuse to participate. Autonomous people are knowledgeable of and take responsibility for the risks, benefits, and constraints in which they operate. It is only through an awareness of the full balance of possibilities that informed consent can be given.

Central to research ethics is voluntary participation and the ability to say no at any time. What is important to data science is that these standards emerged from a long tradition of addressing the impact of research on social worlds. Concepts of informed consent and vulnerable populations give us language to understand the potential impact of data technologies.

Predictive systems are often called autonomous, which confuses the research sense of autonomy.

The Greek origin of the word "autonomy" is a combination of the words meaning self (autos; αυτός) and law (nomos; νομός). Autonomy literally means independent self-governance. Autonomous technology makes self-standing determinations to take calculated action—but there are questions whether this is true autonomy in the philosophical sense. Autonomous vehicles. Autonomous weapons. They act independently based on inferences from digital sources and have the freedom to do so. Ideally, they can determine how to handle variations without intervention. Autonomous weapons shoot targets without anyone pulling the trigger. Autonomous robots complete routines without explicit directions. Autonomous vehicles navigate streets without a driver. No need for a human to issue a command. The "autonomous" label in front of twentieth-century innovations brings the technology into the twenty-first-century realm of data.

Despite its use in computing, autonomy has a singular human meaning. Human autonomy is an ability to exercise choice. Autonomy is highly relevant for technology that categorizes people to intentionally circumscribe their range of action. It is still appropriate to ask if individuals have control over their own fate in automated systems built by organizations for operational efficiency.

The concept of autonomy as it applies to research ethics can give a new perspective to data science practice. Research ethics protocols heighten an awareness of the constraints that systems of classification and comparisons can put on individual autonomy.

1.10 Digital Dignity

Dignity protects an intrinsic sense of self-worth. Dignity assumes that people have individual freedoms to exist as humans. Respect for all human bodies and respect for property are two common ways to communicate self-worth. Can predictive data science not disturb or interrupt our lives as it makes comparisons between us and other people?

The state, organizations, and other people do not have control over the liberty of one individual. Digital autonomy is having control over digital representations of you. In his essay on utilitarianism, John Stuart Mill defined dignity as "pride or love of liberty or personal independence" (Mill 1863). Giovanni Buttarelli, a primary figure in the European Union's General Data Protection Regulation (GDPR), frequently said that the driving force behind the policy was digital dignity.

Human rights law is a specific form of legislation that enshrines concepts of dignity by recognizing the independence of all human beings. It promises that everyone can be free from fear or want. Article 1 of the UN Declaration of Human Rights stated that "all human beings are born free and equal in dignity and rights." In the United States, the Bill of Rights establishes dignity through property rights such as the Fourth Amendment, which declares that the government cannot search or seize property without cause.

Yet dignity and autonomy are often dismissed for some populations. Technology often splits people into those who are experimented on to protect others. Surveillance tools and blanket data collection in the past have been tested on vulnerable populations who have minimal rights. Afghan refugees were exposed to early biometric technology by the United Nations to control the flow of people (Jacobsen 2010). Iris retina screening technology is a unique form of identification. The UN High Commission for Refugees forced the screening on anyone who wanted to be repatriated home across the Afghan/Pakistan border between 2002 and 2007. Children as young as six were involved in the mandatory scheme on this unproven technology. Virginia Eubanks (2018) contrasted the lack of dignity in prosperous societies, where poor and working-class people are marginalized in a "digital poorhouse." The German government in 2017 considered proposals to allow officials to seize smart phones of asylum seekers and duplicate all data on them (Latonero 2016). Examples from science and technology studies continually show that people with low rights or no political power become data subjects in technology experiences, despite belonging to clear vulnerable populations.

Researchers and data scientists can impact a social world in positive or negative ways. Anyone studying a vulnerable population, even with the intention to help, has more power over this group and may increase the level of inequality experienced in those populations. Ethical data science has a duty to protect the individual dignity even as it builds insights from aggregated their information. Digital dignity starts with a right to privacy (Citron 2022). Computer scientist Latanya Sweeney in a 2013 study noted that 87 percent of Americans can be identified from their zip code, birthday, and gender (Sweeney 2013).

Ethical comparisons involve avoiding vulnerable populations and digital material that might be perceived as impacting someone's sense of dignity. It also recognizes long-term impacts of these available data.

1.11 Thinking Like a Librarian to Compare

Libraries organize knowledge. Librarians, specifically catalogers, build intellectual infrastructure to compare and contrast information. Librarians operate within worldwide knowledge systems by acting globally and finding locally. Data scientists could learn how to ascertain similarities consistently from the library and information sciences professions.

No one would trust a library that put novels on the nonfiction shelf or slipped a gardening book in with quantum mechanics. Libraries make it easy to find similar books. Items that resemble others are put on the same shelf or have links to similar items in a digital catalog.

Knowledge is global. Information is produced in every language in every location across the world. The shape and membership of catalogs change by circumstance and populations, yet catalogs are interoperable with other systems.

Catalogs can explicitly serve different localities and intellectual communities simultaneously. Catalogs even recognize that there are multiple ways to even record authors, from last names first or to matrilineal surnames. Cataloging standards are coordinated by several large international professional associations and consortiums.

Knowledge becomes standardized in catalogs. Catalogers describe information resources, which becomes metadata in digital systems. In some cases, the words are not as important as any consistent label. For what many of us would call the Second World War, the Library of Congress Subject Heading is "Great War 1939–1945." And the September 11, 2001, events are classified as "Attack on America." While these labels seem dated now, they still have some lasting value. Additional labels or cross-references can augment a label that has been applied consistently. Coherent catalogs can articulate why items are similar and how they differ by establishing rules.

Knowledge production is constant. Catalogs aggregate information incrementally. Instead of just one system for everyone forever, catalogers anticipate different ways of expressing knowledge. Therefore, librarians routinely develop crosswalks so that a chemist can still find material in biology. This means it is easier to adjust to multiple knowledge dimensions within one object. In a library catalog, a tomato can be listed as both a fruit and a vegetable to accommodate all forms of knowledge. Library catalogs make room for ambiguity, the unknown, and future interpretations.

Knowledge infrastructures must be responsive to change. Large collections of information demand consistent arrangement. Librarians are often on the forefront of social movements because of their unique perspective on changing culture. Sanford Berman, from his position as cataloger at Hennepin County Libraries in Minnesota, began to throw flames at the Library of Congress because of the outdated classifications of people. Subject headings are always behind societal changes, which is why most cataloging rules routinely provide a mechanism to review descriptions. Cataloging rules are frequently updated to accommodate new formats and methods.

Classification theory engages with the theory of knowledge, or epistemology. Epistemology is a branch of philosophy that considers how new knowledge emerges, why we believe it, and how it is justified. Classification theory recognize that knowledge accumulates and broadens over time.

Theories of classification developed by librarians over centuries offer us insight into some challenges in data science comparison.

Data science enacts comparisons with far-reaching effects, little documentation, and significantly less oversight (Paullada et al. 2021). Machine learning benchmarks have been explicitly denounced for failing to establish an intellectual order that allows for valid comparisons (Bender et al. 2021). While achieving equity is the ideal goal, a good first step is to clarify the motivating principles about declaring difference.

Data science could imitate a cataloger's ability to maintain consistency while being flexible to local differences. Thinking like a librarian means creating intellectual order so items can be aggregated across multiple dimensions with confidence.

1.12 Chapter 3 Summary

This chapter recognizes the power of comparisons. Standards play a critical role in making appropriate comparisons, but standards can also change. Classifications are not static, and one object can maintain multiple simultaneous identities. Rigid categories based on human traits can limit individual autonomy and dignity. The third stage of the prediction supply chain creates intellectual order by determining difference.

1.13 APPENDIX EXERCISES—Chapter 3 Compare

Points to consider:

- Make classifications less rigid.
- Avoid singular taxonomies.
- Watch for unstated social norms that may be regional, local, or in other ways not universal.
- Watch for classifications that penalize.
- Strive for outlier equity.
- How do you record choices about comparisons?
- What metrics or constraints would document differences?

References

Arcas, Blaise Aguera, Alexander Todorov, and Margaret Mitchell. 2018. "Do Algorithms Reveal Sexual Orientation or Just Expose Our Stereotypes?" *Medium Microsoft Research* (blog). January 18, 2018. https://medium.com/@blaisea/do-algorithms-reveal-sexual-orientation-or-just-expose-our-stereotypes-d998fafdf477.

Bender, Emily M., et al. 2021. "On the Dangers of Stochastic Parrots: Can Language Models Be Too Big?" In *Proceedings of the 2021 ACM Conference on Fairness, Accountability, and Transparency*. Virtual Event Canada: ACM, 610–23. https://doi.org/10.1145/3442188.3445922.

Bowker, Geoffrey C., and Susan Leigh Star. 1999. *Sorting Things Out: Classification and Its Consequences*. Cambridge, MA: MIT Press. https://mitpress.mit.edu/books/sorting-things-out.

Citron, Danielle Keats. 2022. *The Fight for Privacy: Protecting Dignity, Identity, and Love in the Digital Age*. 1st ed. New York: W.W. Norton & Company, Inc.

Eubanks, Virginia. 2018. "A Child Abuse Prediction Model Fails Poor Families." *Wired*, January 15, 2018. https://www.wired.com/story/excerpt-from-automating-ine quality/.

Faden, Ruth R., Nancy M.P. King, and Tom L. Beauchamp. 1986. *A History and Theory of Informed Consent*. New York: Oxford University Press.

"Former Director for Tuskegee Syphilis Study Believes Work Was 'Completely Ethical.'" 1972. *All Things Considered*. Washington DC: National Public Radio. https://www.npr.org/2020/03/03/808621619/former-director-for-tuskegee-syphilis-study-believes-work-was-completely-ethical.

Gunn, James, dir. 2014. *Guardians of the Galaxy*. https://www.imdb.com/title/tt2015381/.

Hall, Stuart, 1980. "Cultural Studies and the Centre: Some Problematics and Problems." Edited by Stuart Hall, Dorothy Hobson, Andrew Lowe, and Paul Willis., eds. 1980. In *Culture, Media, Language: Working Papers in Cultural Studies, 1972–79*. 1st ed. 1–33. London: Routledge https://doi.org/10.4324/9780203381182.

Heller, Jean. 1972. "Syphilis Victims in U.S. Study Went Untreated for 40 Years." *The New York Times*, July 26, 1972, sec. Archives. https://www.nytimes.com/1972/07/26/archives/syphilis-victims-in-us-study-went-untreated-for-40-years-syphilis.html.

Jacobsen, Katja Lindskov. 2010. "Making Design Safe for Citizens: A Hidden History of Humanitarian Experimentation." *Citizenship Studies* 14 (1): 89–103. https://doi.org/10.1080/13621020903466399.

Latonero, Mark. 2016. "An App to Save Syria's Lost Generation?" *Foreign Affairs*, May 23, 2016. https://www.foreignaffairs.com/articles/syria/2016-05-23/app-save-syrias-lost-generation.

Mason, Jennifer. 2002. "Making Convincing Arguments with Qualitative Data." In *Qualitative Researching*, 2nd ed., 173–204. London ; Thousand Oaks, Calif.: Sage Publications.

Mill, John Stuart. 1863. *Utilitarianism*. https://archive.org/details/a592840000milluoft.

Noble, Safiya Umoja. 2018. *Algorithms of Oppression: How Search Engines Reinforce Racism*. New York: New York University Press.

Paullada, Amandalynne, et al. 2021. "Data and Its (Dis)Contents: A Survey of Dataset Development and Use in Machine Learning Research." *Patterns* 2 (11): 100336. https://doi.org/10.1016/j.patter.2021.100336.

Ruggles, Steven, Catherine A. Fitch, and Evan Roberts. 2018. "Historical Census Record Linkage." *Annual Review of Sociology* 44 (1): 19–37. https://doi.org/10.1146/annurev-soc-073117-041447.

Sato, Mia. 2021. "The Pandemic Is Testing the Limits of Face Recognition." *MIT Technology Review*, September 28, 2021. https://www.technologyreview.com/2021/09/28/1036279/pandemic-unemployment-government-face-recognition/.

Scott, James C. 1998. *Seeing Like a State: How Certain Schemes to Improve the Human Condition Have Failed*. New Haven, CT; London: Yale University Press.

Seltzer, William, and Margo Anderson. 2001. "The Dark Side of Numbers: The Role of Population Data Systems in Human Rights Abuses." *Social Research* 68 (2): 481–513.

Semenya, Caster. 2022. "@caster800m March 26." *Twitter.* https://twitter.com/caster8 00m/status/1507666418065629189.

Simonite, Tom. 2018. "When It Comes to Gorillas, Google Photos Remains Blind." *Wired*, January 11, 2018. https://www.wired.com/story/when-it-comes-to-gorillas-google-photos-remains-blind/.

Smith, Bayeté Ross. 2010. *Our Kind of People*. Photographs. http://www.bayeterosssmith.com/our-kind-of-people.

Snow, John. 1856. "On the Mode of Communication of Cholera." *Edinburgh Medical Journal* 1 (7): 668–70. https://www.ncbi.nlm.nih.gov/pmc/articles/PMC5307547/.

Sweeney, Latanya. 2013. "Discrimination in Online Ad Delivery." *Communications of the ACM* 56 (5): 44–54. https://doi.org/10.1145/2447976.2447990.

Taleb, Nassim Nicholas. 2007. *The Black Swan: The Impact of the Highly Improbable*. 1st ed. New York: Random House.

Vincent, James. 2020. "What a Machine Learning Tool That Turns Obama White Can (and Can't) Tell Us about AI Bias." *The Verge*, June 23, 2020. https://www.theverge.com/21298762/face-depixelizer-ai-machine-learning-tool-pulse-stylegan-obama-bias.

Wu, Xiaolin, and Xi Zhang. 2017. "Automated Inference on Criminality Using Face Images." Preprint article. arXxiv. https://doi.org/10.48550/arXiv.1611.04135.

4

Optimize

Data Science Reasoning

1. DATA SCIENCE REASONING

The fourth step of the prediction supply chain is to enact priorities through algorithms and calculations. Algorithms make choices, efficiently directing resources to meet predictive goals. Each comparison is optimized based on explicit or implicit ideas of precedence for the predictive goal. Optimization calibrates an algorithm by making decisions about what is important. An algorithm can overoptimize, meaning it focuses so much on one goal that it ignores other equally important goals not specifically articulated. The novelist Octavia E. Butler reminds us that change can bear seeds of benefit or seeds of harm in the beginning of her Earthseed trilogy *Parable of the Sower* (1993). Research ethics emphasizes the inherent trade-offs and limitations in all research studies. Ethical data science recognizes and can reason about alternative priorities. The best optimizations are clear about motivations and can explain why one priority has more weight than another. This chapter encourages data science reasoning.

Ethical Data Science. Anne L. Washington, Oxford University Press. © Oxford University Press 2023.
DOI: 10.1093/oso/9780197693025.003.0006

1.1 The Efficient Commuter

What's the usual way you get to work? A generic answer might simply calculate the shortest distance in a minimal amount of time. But the quickest path may not be the only thing to consider in establishing a routine. A work commute happens regularly, at least twice a day, so you might want to think carefully about how to manage your time, money, energy, health, or other resources. But everyone has a different definition of wasted resources.

Even if you and your colleagues lived in the same neighborhood, each of you would have a different commute based on your priorities. A driver might be motivated by the beautiful view of the river in the morning and not want to take the fast roadway. A bicyclist might want exercise and seek out longer routes with steep hills. Someone may take public transportation to save money. The environment might be an important value to the cyclist and the public transit commuter, but in the end, their routines are set by different priorities. Not choosing is still a choice. The commuter who prioritizes only time and distance simultaneously downplays social, interpersonal, or financial aspects of the commute.

Technically, an efficient commute with the shortest distance is the right answer, but the final decision balances many other trade-offs. And there are several unstated assumptions to even consider that this is the right answer. It assumes that compensated work takes place outside the home and the commute involves travel to one specific location. It ignores everyone who does not have a regular office or who commutes between more than one job.

Optimizing a predictive algorithm is like trying to decide the best way to get somewhere. Even with an agreed-upon destination, everyone may have their own idea of the optimal route. There can be many reasons that quantitative measurements are not as important as the journey.

Mathematically elegant solutions are always implemented within existing value systems. While there will always be a standard calculated answer, other factors will come into play to meet goals. An awareness of what value systems may form critical secondary perspectives will help juggle priorities so predictive goals can be met within realistic circumstances.

Let's consider how priorities compete when predictive algorithms are released to the public. Hopeful students had their dreams thwarted when an algorithm denied them entrance to prominent universities.

1.2 Failing Students

The World Health Organization declared the COVID-19 pandemic just as students in the United Kingdom were scheduled to spend hours with strangers to take a career-critical test. UK students seeking undergraduate admissions must sit an exam which will determine which university they attend. The government body responsible for administering the exams needed a quick solution. The UK Office of Qualifications (Ofqual) turned to data science in June 2020 to determine which student would be admitted where. The Ofqual admissions algorithm was replaced by teacher scores within only a few weeks under wide public condemnation.

What went wrong? Like Robodebt ignoring the perspective of applicants, students had little agency in the Ofqual calculation. Ignoring individual student success made it easier for schools, universities, and government agencies to manage the 2020 admissions. While it was logical from an efficiency perspective, it came at the detriment of some students.

The calculation for estimating 2020 general exams scores was based on institutional data. The historical grade distribution of final grades at each school from 2017 to 2019 determined the level of grade inflation for all students attending that school. All of these data were based on previous students' data. These historical trends could eclipse individual student performance. Finally, the calculation included the number of students in each class. If the class was too small (under fifteen people), students received their teachers' recommended grades. Ofqual calculated the likelihood of a grade distribution for each school and then used the rank list of students to determine a grade. How students performed on earlier standardized tests was only reflected in the distribution of grades within the school.

In short, the predictive grades were not based on actual student performance. Entrance to university was based on trends about the school or the teacher but precious little about individual achievement. MP Christian Wakeford reported in a hearing that straight-A students in his constituency received a D on the predictive exam score (Hern 2020). Initially, only schools had the right to appeal grade estimates. Ofqual assumed that the institution would find the problem before the families did and file for each student. Some schools felt that students had to have a performance direction, which meant they would not support an appeal for a higher grade if it was not part of a statistical trend. In other words, students who did well unexpectedly were penalized. Students could only appeal if they felt they were individually targeted for discrimination.

Ofqual did not publish their statistical model in advance to avoid having anyone calculate their results in advance of everyone receiving grades. Further exacerbating this situation, many adult learners study for college admissions outside of any institution. There were no interim data such as mock exams or institutional grades to rely on, so adult learners could do nothing but wait until the exams happened in person again.

The most impacted group could easily be identified as high-attaining children at low-performing schools. The size of this population was small in terms of overall numbers, with one estimate at 2 percent of young people—but there were six million exams. At one point, Ofqual considered reaching out to students performing differently in schools without inflated grades to ask them to appeal. On legal advice, Ofqual decided not to run additional models or rules over these populations because it might amount to making arbitrary judgments out of scope with their statutory authority. Instead of a programmatic solution, Ofqual shifted the burden to those its model impacted, deciding the best way was an appeal process for outliers to claim the standardized process had an adverse impact on their outcome.

Ofqual intended to create more fairness between schools so there would be less variation in grades. However, given that Ofqual calculated a greater weight for class sizes with fewer than fifteen students, the result was that elite schools received higher scores as they predominantly had smaller class sizes. The difference between the algorithmic grades and teacher assessment were 10.42 percent for low-income groups and 8.34 percent for high-income groups (Katwala 2020). Ofqual considered these disparities within normal range of actual exam outcomes. The level of accuracy available through this mechanism was never going to meet expectations. Toward the end of a daylong testimony, Roger Taylor, chair of Ofqual, summed it up when he said that by replicating the most likely results, his office replicated differences in educational opportunity.

In an August 14, 2020, letter to Ofqual, the Royal of Statistical Society noted two important points about this method (Murray 2020). First, the choice to arrange students by rank would have a large impact on middle-ranked students where there was less certainty about distinctions. While the predictions for best and worst students were fairly obvious, predictions would not be significantly precise for students in the wide middle, especially in large schools. Second, they questioned the assumption of statistical stability of analyzing data at the level of the school. This left student success at the mercy of which school they attended and its class sizes. Ofqual did not make the statistical advice they received public until the middle of the scandal.

The Ofqual predictive algorithm established priorities that severely hurt easy-to-identify subpopulations and literally failed them on the exam. The predictive goal of getting a limited number of students to university under pandemic social-distancing rules was adequately met. However, Ofqual severely undervalued priorities deemed important to the public, such as fairness, individual achievement, and class mobility. The data science solution for college admissions optimized convenience for all organizations involved but completely failed individual students.

How do data scientists optimize algorithms? This stage focuses on explaining and justifying the reasoning behind data science choices. Understanding the reasoning that justifies priorities can lead to finding solutions for cases that are not optimized. This part of the prediction supply chain begins to be more public-facing, considering how the prediction will be presented to others. It is also a way to check that data science priorities line up with other things that are important.

1.3 Whose Priorities?

Each if-then juncture of an algorithm is an opportunity to enact priorities. People designing algorithms determine what is and is not important at each step with an awareness that priorities for efficiency compete. It is not possible to save money on gas while also saving time going the longer route. One goal, one population, one outcome is preferred over another.

Whose priorities justify the distribution of risks and rewards?

Algorithms are mathematical solutions that need some human direction about how to solve problems. The step-by-step instructions within an algorithm constantly choose one thing over the other to meet its predictive goals efficiently.

The problems algorithms solve are first translated into quantitative measures. Order, thresholds, weights, even inclusion are some of the priorities to consider. For instance, the algorithm may need to know whether a higher value is better or maybe to not give equal weight to another value. The order of calculations can make a difference or even which values are deemed important enough to include in the calculation. As seen in the Ofqual example, a different set of priorities may lead to new data science insights. When predictive systems are released at scale, forgotten, or overlooked, priorities can quickly overwhelm the original intentions. Data scientists must always be aware of trade-offs because algorithms are always optimized.

Moral philosophy may seem far removed from emerging technology, but the ideas debated for millennia still have resonance. Philosophy furnishes compelling portraits of the competing ethical forces that shape the prediction supply chain. Philosophers create coherent structures for organizing human knowledge and motives. Ethics clarifies the reasoning that governs decisions. Applied ethics specifically considers how principles inform practice.

Optimization is the efficient use of resources. Efficiency asks what is the minimal effort necessary to achieve maximum results. Computational optimization, in its strictest definition, seeks to make algorithms faster. Data science optimization seeks to meet predictive goals with an optimal use of resources. By definition, anything that happens outside those original optimal conditions will give wrong answers, be slower, or simply fail.

Data science optimization builds on earlier chapters. Data sources establish the scope of predictive goals. Models define an ideal state for prediction. Comparisons establish how pattern matching will identify similarity and difference. Optimization puts models, data, and comparisons into action to calculate predictions while balancing priorities. Predictive algorithms calculate possible outcomes using models to compare digital sources.

Optimization is used in data science to balance priorities. Algorithmic optimization enacts priorities through calculations. Predictive algorithms are optimized toward goals that represent specific motives, preferences, or principles. Ethics represents the governing ideals underneath motivating factors. Ethical data science is able to establish frames of reasoning and to express trade-offs. This chapter asks data scientists to question efficiency, justify priorities, and express underlying principles.

1.4 RoboCop Principles of Efficiency

Efficiency is ruthless in making systems really, really good at one thing. Just one. An efficient system is geared toward completing a singular outcome exceedingly well within a given environment. Efficiency is driven by both specific conditions and a set of principles. Principles can contradict each other, and efficiency in one area can drive inefficiency elsewhere.

The science fiction movie *RoboCop* features a humanoid robot who kills ruthlessly to control crime in a future Detroit, Michigan. The Australian cost-saving scheme was nicknamed Robodebt after the 1987 movie *RoboCop*. The fictional and actual cases illustrate how priorities influence actions.

RoboCop is efficient at delivering punishment. The robot police officer moves from observations directly into action. Robodebt was efficient at accusations of fraud. Robodebt's predictive data system sent indigent people into further poverty by accusing them of fraud and demanding repayment. Robodebt and Ofqual moved so quickly into action that there was no room for reflection. Generally, a quick response is desired when predictive systems are created. Quick decisions with irreversible outcomes are less desirable.

RoboCop's killing of potential threats on sight left little room for negotiation or reconsideration. To soften its singular goal, RoboCop is given three public directives to only kill in order serve the public trust, protect the innocent, and uphold the law. Principles are general statements of what is important and what takes precedence. Most professions have some form of ethical code. Doctors, for instance, take an oath to do no harm to patients. Although there have been many attempts to develop ethical codes for data science (Washington and Kuo 2020), nothing has been finalized. While many of these codes state large humanitarian ideals, they overlook the economic reasons that drive most predictive systems.

The principle that dominates predictive data science is financial efficiency. The initial Australian government analysis to justify Robodebt solely focused on the overpayments of people who received benefits. The cost of lawsuits was not included in any calculations of efficiency. The social turmoil the predictive system caused was incalculable. Australia, the US state of Michigan, and the Netherlands all built welfare systems that prioritized organizational efficiency and lost money in the end. Governments that automate systems to save money can ignore the perils of overoptimization.

Principles can contradict each other. This is where trade-offs in efficiency come in. At some point it will be necessary to determine what priority prevails. Robodebt decided that fairness and transparency were secondary values. Without any way to question, dispute, or redress the findings of the algorithm, applicants had limited choices. Welfare recipients were not trusted when they said the system was not working, while the technology, no matter how opaque or inaccurate, was trusted. The Robodebt program might have been an honest mistake in implementing a new system, but the politicians continued to assert that they wanted to stigmatize anyone using the social safety net. The automated system intentionally enabled the subordination of entire subpopulations at scale. The efficiency politicians wanted was contradicted by the inefficiency of employees taxed with more work when the algorithm made mistakes.

RoboCop is controlled by another general principle, which is to not act against any executive of the company that created it. These directives are not enough, however, when RoboCop faces a dilemma between competing principles. Breaking the law is usually enough for RoboCop to kill someone. When an executive at the company breaks the law, it is impossible for RoboCop to both uphold the law and never harm an executive. RoboCop cannot function without additional clarification between principles.

Efficiency rarely distributes risks and rewards equally. Because efficiency makes some things faster under specific conditions, other things may slow down or break. Questioning efficiency is a way to uncover assumptions about the distribution of risks and rewards in suboptimal conditions. Principles for efficiency can be obvious to the organization or the industry funding the algorithm, but people with different guiding values may challenge these priorities.

1.5 No Justification, No Peace

Algorithms are great at making decisions, but without justifying those decisions in a way that regular people can understand, they may never be successfully deployed. Unknown priorities and unwelcome optimizations can both lead to social disturbances that can upend predictive systems.

The inherent information asymmetry between study participants and data science researchers is one area for potential harm. While this is an accepted aspect to many insiders, it can breed mistrust to those without a data science perspective. Accumulating information that could be used in negative ways is a form of power that many recognize as potentially dangerous.

Parental concerns highlighted this in the case of a K–12 data science effort in New York City. It started with a 2012 agreement between government officials and a large foundation to develop a shared learning infrastructure that could help schools, regulators, teachers, parents, and students have access to the same assessment and instructional material. It was a valiant attempt to modernize digital recordkeeping for the country's largest school district. While a central repository makes lots of technical sense to a data scientist, it requires an abundance of trust.

InBloom, an education technology company, went down in public relation flames when parents saw what information was being stored without sufficient explanation about how it might be used for or against their kids. This statewide system kept highly specific details on relationships such as a student's adoptive sister, natural sister, half-sister, parent significant other, or probation officer. Given that some of these categories could change over time, it was not clear how frequently this information would change or if everyone would be permanently associated with each other in these records. In the misfortune of a discipline incident, students were also classified by the type of weapon they had and who was the victim, perpetrator, witness, or reporter. Given the existing data-sharing relationship between the education system and other state authorities—in what some call the school-to-prison pipeline—privacy advocates were alarmed that a scuffle on a playground could become part of a criminal record.

On the other hand, an algorithm that addresses a universally agreed-upon public need may still miss the mark. For some people, the sole justification for any policy change is what they want, the way they want it. A perfectly fair and equitable prediction may agitate people who do not want an algorithm to make decisions for them. Even worse is ceding power to an algorithm that turns around and equally shares something perceived as their privilege. Understanding how priorities are set and who feels entitled to special treatment is important to anticipate this second type of disruption.

The Boston school system was looking to save money and optimize the school bus route in 2018 (Goodman 2019). Two MIT doctoral students won a competition to design an ideal system that equally distributed early wake-up times and got the buses to the right places for the start of the school day. No one anticipated that efficient distribution would meet fierce opposition. A fair system meant that someone might lose something they currently had. The 15 percent of Boston parents who had the most political power followed politicians from meeting to meeting across the city to complain because the system no longer specifically gave them an advantage. Parents who opposed the time change for their children did not want the system implemented for anyone. In public policy, the people receiving a benefit are considered the target population (Rochefort and Cobb 1994). All Boston parents were the school bus policy's target population, but a small group of parents insisted that they alone were the target and that their preferences had to be accommodated. Equity meant improvements for all, but it can also mean that some people with privilege experience a loss.

People experiencing predictive systems want to know how they work. Optimizations will always leave someone out. Public policy also often gives some groups priority over others. Optimizations once released to the public are very much like new legislation that lays out a new policy agenda. Data scientists may need to be prepared to carefully engage with target populations, dependent populations, and even those populations deemed undeserving (Rochefort and Cobb 1994) to implement a successful predictive system.

No data science justifications can sometimes mean no peace in society.

We explore trade-offs and differentiate seven philosophical positions that might motivate data science optimization. Drawing on the work of great philosophers helps to contextualize choices and the reasons behind priority rankings.

1.6 The Philosophy Cafe

This section reviews some core philosophies that can help uncover the reasoning behind data science practices. But first, let's consider these lofty ideas for a mundane decision. What will you eat at the philosophy cafe? A prominent moral philosopher is seated at each table in the philosophy cafe. Customers must choose a table and explain their menu choice using the reasoning each school of philosophy offers.

The choice is not obvious.

Imagine that you have a limited diet. The philosophy cafe only serves meat, gluten, and dairy foods. They do not even serve decaffeinated coffee! You are with a group of people who can eat anything on the menu, but you do not eat any of those foods. You have traveled all day to get there and are hungry. It is an isolated place, and there are no alternative options. The choice of tables and philosophical positions include: utilitarianism, deontology, virtue ethics, social contract theory, feminist ethics, theology, and rational choice. Following are descriptions of each table, its core idea, the philosophers, how they might influence what to eat, and how each might drive the rationale behind data science projects.

1.7 Red Table—Utilitarianism

The first table you see when you walk in the door has a red tablecloth. The utilitarianism thinkers wanted to be near the door. Mostly because the consequentialists, who are a branch of this thinking, like it. Utilitarians believe that there are unitary common goals that can be achieved. People would justify their reasoning by the number of people supported. The greatest good is done for the greatest number. Two philosophers associated with this belief are Jeremy Bentham and John Stuart Mills. In today's world, these are people who use spreadsheets to calculate the right answer. An elaborate pro/con list determines the best choice. The best part of utilitarianism is that it is strongly focused on a goal and its realization. The other perspective is that they may undervalue all the costs in their quest to satisfy the goal.

How do you justify your menu choice to the utilitarians? They would expect to hear an unequivocal goal first. For example, eating is the goal, therefore you would weigh the costs and benefits of eating this specific food. Alternatively, if the restricted diet is the goal, you must weigh the costs and benefits of going hungry. Large companies often practice a form of utilitarianism where the goal is to satisfy popular tastes, often to satisfy goals of efficiency and economy.

1.8 Orange Table—Deontology

This table is always exactly two chair lengths away from any other table. The deontologists like rules that can be applied universally. Deontologists believe that there is a moral code that can be applied consistently. They support their choices by stating which moral code they follow and how it applies in the situation. The orange table is always behind the red table. While the utilitarians may believe that the ends justify the means, the deontologists would say the means justify the end. Deontologists focus not on where to go but how to get there. Also known as duty ethics, deontology assumes that human action has an adherence to duty. Famous deontology philosophers include Emmanuel Kant and Thomas Hobbes, although many dispute if these philosophers agreed on much. A modern deontologist would love checklists. Rules are clear. It is just a matter of following them.

Anyone sitting at the orange table would justify their decision by stating which moral code or which rule they are following. Perhaps you will eat meat because the rules of hospitality drive your thinking and you do not want to be rude to the locals. Perhaps you will not eat meat because you strongly believe consuming animal products violates your personal moral code. Privacy legislation underscored a duty ethics approach, where compliance to regulatory rules dominates. The end-user license agreements or any checklist approach is favored here. On the positive side, duty ethics approaches to data science create an audit trial that can form the basis for law and regulation.

1.9 Blue Table—Virtue Ethics

This table is near the window. The virtue ethicists like to look at the sky as they strive for high moral achievement. They believe in the strength of human character. Aristotle is at the head of this table with his fifth century BC writings about eudaimonia. Virtue ethics wants people to be happy, content, and moral. These people may write in-depth personal reflections to make decisions.

Aristotle may want to hear a justification for your meal decision that maintains your moral stature. If you strongly believe that environmental principles mean that no food should be wasted, there will be no question that you will eat at the cafe. If eating today would in any way compromise your sense of morals and would stain your soul as a permanent vice, it would be best avoided. Modern digital technology often does not find room for morals. However, some apps, such as meditation timers, strive to promote moral achievement within a market economy.

1.10 Green Table—Social Contract Theory

The next table is in the middle of the space surrounded by everyone else. The people who follow social contract theory as a form of ethics believe in community. They advocate for collective responsibility over individual rights. Early social contract philosophers were John Locke, Thomas Hobbes, and Jean-Jacques Rousseau. Important contemporary theorists include John Rawls, who posited a theory of justice, and Tommie Shelby, who applied these concepts to state constructions of race. The social contract is an exchange of some freedom for the safety and comfort of living in community. These people are more likely to make decisions in a town hall format.

Your choice on the menu would be one that is socially responsible. Perhaps you will not eat because you believe that the meat industry does not use land responsibly. In terms of data science, a social contract theorist believes that the organizations with whom you share data owe you a safe environment. It balances the loss of freedom within monopolistic platforms with a responsibility to create a space where harm does not occur.

1.11 Yellow Table—Ethics of Care

This table moves around, based on a consensus each time someone joins the table. The ethics of care philosophers believe in interpersonal harmony.

They believe that people make decisions to maintain significant personal relationships. They strive to cultivate an inner circle within their family, neighborhood, friendship, religion, hobby, or affinity group. A core theorist, Carol A. Gilligan, labels this as feminist ethics. Critics of White feminist thought, such as the Combahee River Collective, were still motivated by the importance of care (Combahee River Collective 1979; Taylor 2017). The theorist bell hooks argues that a commitment to mutual respect is essential to combat oppressive systems that attempt to divide humanity (hooks 2015). These philosophers respond to and care about how people are feeling within social situations and societal conditions. These people are likely to talk, share, or discuss with others their choices.

If you were sitting at this table, you would jointly decide the best way for everyone to get fed and still respect boundaries. Some people may have what they want, and others may not. In prediction, the data scientist would act as a fiduciary, someone whose sole interest is protecting your data and making it safe for you. This concept of information fiduciary (Balkin 2017) has become a popular way to describe a missing aspect of most technology policy efforts.

1.12 Purple Table—Theology

The theologians sit near the staircase in the cafe. Theology aspires to a higher power through traditional texts handed down through centuries. It encompasses multiple religions, from popular Abrahamic religions, such as Islam and Judaism, to other traditions like the Baha'i. Each religion relies on contemporary interpretations of important texts. For instance, Christianity interprets the Bible, while Hinduism reads Vedic texts. These documents guide how to live in order to improve one's relationship with the divine. Everyone at this cafe table has some religious affiliation that guides their behavior.

You would justify your meal decision by citing important texts or respected secondary commentary. Maybe it is a day of fasting on the religious calendar, so you will not eat anything today. Perhaps you can only eat these foods if they are prepared according to interpretations of religious scripture. Emerging data technology has come to the attention of major religious leaders. The Pope wrote about artificial intelligence in 2022. His Holiness the Dalai Lama has held a regular conference with the Mind Life Institute that reflects on the interconnection between science and religion. A theological approach to data science emphasizes the age-old principles based on the central teachings of a religion.

1.13 Gray Table—Economics

The economists sit near the cash register. Those representing economical rationality believe in getting value for their money. Your meal choice would be determined solely by the economic value for you alone. You might order the cheapest meal on the menu. You might order the meal that offered the biggest portion for the given price. In any event, you would justify your choice by stating how your selection maximized your own wealth or well-being in a way that can be easily quantified.

This philosophy drives most internet economics. The problem is solved with the *cheapest* solution, not necessarily a complete solution. Some algorithms run longer than their useful life because it costs too much to build a new one. Without any skin in the game, organizations may ignore the people suffering under weaker predictive results in order to save money in developing a new one. This philosophy influences the rise of dark patterns. A dark pattern is a design that ensnares someone into doing something that is not in their individual favor but benefits the company.

Wherever you sit in the philosophy cafe, there is a motivating set of principles that determines what you eat and why. Consider how one of these seven positions might motivate the optimization in a data science project familiar to you.

1.14 Optimize Ethical Data Science

Optimization is a critical aspect of measuring progress in academic data science. The prevalence of benchmarks helps data scientists compare the speed of a new algorithm to older ones using the same evaluation data.

Optimization also enacts values and makes algorithms efficient through a series of judgments about the importance of data, populations, comparisons, perspectives, and predictive goals to achieve efficiency. Data scientists are at a disadvantage when they are not aware of other metrics for optimizing a predictive algorithm.

When a journalist exposed the problem of search algorithms that associated negative terms for animals with some population groups, Google simply made it impossible to search for gorillas and orangutans. The problem was no longer visible, but it was not actually solved.

Optimization has its limitations. The real world is not optimized.

Applying mathematical standards of consistency and perfection in human affairs can often go awry. A predictive model optimized for search queries tracked the spread of the 2009 flu epidemic but fell apart under different conditions a few years later (Washington 2016). Harm or unintended consequences in non-optimal situations are inevitable. Because algorithmic optimization prioritizes specific populations and situations, unforeseen cases could spectacularly fail. Even if the secondary outcome is deemed important, an algorithm can only work with what is given (Kleinberg, Ludwig, and Mullainathan 2016). Most people are not accustomed to expressing and sharing all possible values they find important. Everyone may want faster travel lanes on the freeway, but they do not expect to sacrifice road safety to get it. Secondary effects may impact new subpopulations or existing populations in unanticipated ways.

One assumption of optimization is that one goal is preferred over another, meaning that resources will be directed, pooled, and funneled toward that goal. Data science implemented over large systems at scale eventually must consider the secondary effects of optimized outcomes. Even if small in terms of percentage, a large number of people may be impacted. Chapter 6 describes the impacts of failure to secure secondary optimization goals.

Unethical data science optimization overlooks potential for harm in a zeal to deliver a predictive goal. It focuses on only one definition of success, using a singular metric that everyone must meet. Anyone not meeting those assumptions is not considered a deserving population (Rochefort and Cobb 1994). Unforeseen situations are dismissed and might be locked out of the system entirely. This type of thinking that ignores cases becomes extremely problematic when delivering a mandatory social service that is used widely.

1.15   Research Ethics: Risk and Benefit Trade-offs

The entire research ethics review process is an examination of the risks, benefits, and limitations of a research study. Biomedical and social science investigators are asked to justify their design choices and explain how it will affect society or individual participants. Investigators who must do ethical review generally have to get approval for the underlying premise of the study, clarify the potential for harm, and consider possible alternatives to mitigate harm. They also may be asked to substantiate their approach by citing existing literature. The process helps investigators to determine the right balance and will assist in recruiting fully informed prospective participants who can appropriately consent to the study.

The Belmont Report argues that risk should be expressed in terms of possibility of harm and the potential magnitude of harm. The first category describes whether something bad is likely to happen. The second category considers how bad that harm could be. Together this allows for participants to understand economic, social, legal, physical, or psychological impacts of study participation on themselves and their families.

Predictive data science unilaterally deployed often does not describe their trade-offs, but they are balancing advantages and disadvantages nonetheless. The algorithm that admitted students to university in the United Kingdom decided the ultimate benefit of getting students assigned was worth with the risk of misclassifying some subpopulations (Hern, 2020). The COMPAS risk assessment scores balanced the risk of putting innocent people in jail against the benefit of finding violent re-offenders (Washington, 2017). The rewards of Robodebt were only accrued to the organizations commissioning and building the algorithm, while the risks were everyone else's problem. The Michigan applicants for social programs had two risky choices: try to pay back the government and admit fraud, or fight the accusation, ruin their credit, and be labeled a criminal. In these opposing value systems, both sides are represented with quantified data. When an important resource cannot be quantified, it can literally and figuratively be removed from the equation, making it impossible to optimize equally. Would it be possible to put into an equation the importance of a college education to a first-generation student?

Predictive data science generally has some idea of the potential convenience to the organization, to the investigator, or to data subjects. Data science rarely is required to explicitly state how its optimizations may pose a risk. And that inability can completely sidetrack implementation.

Decisions without reasons. Data hoarding without explanations of future plans. People familiar with data science may expect this transfer of power. Some people who already experience diminished authority and control may not. People who exercise inordinate control over policy decisions also may push back. This is why data science projects that ignore this important step of expressing the trade-offs between harms and benefits may get trashed in public opinion.

1.16 Thinking Like a Philosopher to Optimize

Thinking like a philosopher means systematically challenging established views in the interest of more comprehensive interpretation. Data scientists who think like a philosopher cultivate methods for disciplined reflection, especially when interrogating ideas without straightforward answers. Philosophers deliberate fundamental questions about the nature of life. As a broad humanities discipline, philosophy covers a wide range of inquiries into conditions that influence what it means to be human.

Data science could learn from the balance of abstract and rational thinking that philosophers develop. Three branches of philosophy seem particularly relevant to prediction in the public interest: epistemology, logic, and ethics.

Epistemology unpacks how we know what we know. This branch of philosophy develops theories of knowledge or a science of knowing. What counts as knowledge and what is outside that scope? How is new knowledge created, and what methods are acceptable? Data science generates insights that are building blocks for knowledge creation. Understanding how people throughout history defended new knowledge creation could help data scientists better communicate when challenged about the voracity of their methods.

Logic expresses rational inferences. As the science of argument, logic is a disciplined method to convey reasoning and comprehensive explanations. Why are concepts related? How are connections justified? Is this justification rigorous and substantially different from myth and opinion? Deduction is communicated through logical reasoning. Logic indicates relationships, order, and structure. Data science could benefit from using an ordered approach to expressing skepticism and boundary conditions about patterns.

Ethics guides appropriate conduct. Applied ethics is a branch of philosophy that asks what is right and wrong and how to develop moral guidance. For centuries people asked what is the right or best human action. Today ethics asks what is the best action for a machine. Or are we asking what is appropriate action for the people who control machines? The philosophical approaches at the philosophy cafe described in the earlier sections are theories of applied ethics. They justify actions and can explain differing approaches to the same decisions. The applied ethics positions considered earlier were utilitarianism, duty ethics, virtue ethics, social contract theory, feminist ethics, theology, and rational choice economics.

All branches of philosophy seek deeper interpretation through iterative inquiry. Philosophers bring radical skepticism (Maddy 1997) to ascertain whether conclusions match up with the evidence. Thinking like a philosopher means systematically challenging established views in data science in the interest of more comprehensive interpretation.

1.17 Chapter 4 Summary

Algorithms make choices. Each choice for this excludes that. Ethical data science is able to state the reasoning that drives those choices. Hyper focus on only one priority can skew the results for others. Algorithms may default to the financial priorities of the organization over anything else without intentional intervention. Be intentional about priorities while recognizing that algorithms may not be able to cope with all dynamics of human life. This penultimate part of the data supply chain is usually the sole focus of many data science courses. Approaching and leaving the optimization stage requires care and awareness of trade-offs between risks and rewards. The next chapter considers what we do with what we learn from predictions.

1.18 APPENDIX EXERCISES—Chapter 4 Optimize

Points to consider:

- Make resource distribution visible.
- Avoid constraining secondary priorities.
- Justify algorithmic goals.
- Clarify target populations.
- Be aware of entitled populations who may complain.
- Support impacted populations who may not have a voice.
- Articulate guiding principles to share with external stakeholders.

References

Balkin, Jack M. 2017. "The Three Laws of Robotics in the Age of Big Data." *Ohio State Law Journal* 78 (5): 1217–41.

Butler, Octavia E. 1993. *Parable of the Sower*. 1st ed. New York: Penguin Random House.

Combahee River Collective. 1979. "The Combahee River Collective: A Black Feminist Statement." In *Capitalist Patriarchy and the Case for Socialist Feminism*, edited by Zillah R. Eisenstein, 362–72. Women's Studies, Political Science. New York, N.Y.: Monthly Review Press. https://monthlyreview.org/2019/01/01/a-black-feminist-statement/.

Goodman, Ellen P. 2019. "The Challenge of Equitable Algorithmic Change." *Regulatory Review* 8 (1): 1–10

Hern, Alex. 2020. "Ofqual's A-Level Algorithm: Why Did It Fail to Make the Grade?" *The Guardian*, August 21, 2020, sec. Education. http://www.theguardian.com/education/2020/aug/21/ofqual-exams-algorithm-why-did-it-fail-make-grade-a-levels.

hooks, bell. 2015. *Feminist Theory: From Margin to Center*. 3rd ed. New York: Routledge.

Katwala, Amit. 2020. "An Algorithm Determined UK Students' Grades. Chaos Ensued." *Wired UK*, August 15, 2020. https://www.wired.co.uk/article/results-day-exams-bias.

Kleinberg, Jon, Jens Ludwig, and Sendhil Mullainathan. 2016. "A Guide to Solving Social Problems with Machine Learning," December. https://hbr.org/2016/12/a-guide-to-solving-social-problems-with-machine-learning.

Maddy, Penelope. 1997. *Naturalism in Mathematics*. Oxford; New York: Clarendon Press; Oxford University Press.

Murray, Jessica. 2020. "Royal Statistical Society Hits Back at Ofqual in Exams Algorithm Row." *The Guardian*, August 24, 2020, sec. Education. https://www.theguardian.com/

education/2020/aug/24/royal-statistical-society-hits-back-at-ofqual-in-exams-algori thm-row.

Rochefort, David A., and Roger W. Cobb. 1994. "Problem Definition: An Emerging Perspective." In *The Politics of Problem Definition: Shaping the Policy Agenda*, edited by David A. Rochefort and Roger W. Cobb, 1–31. Lawrence, KS: University Press of Kansas.

Taylor, Keeanga-Yamahtta, ed. 2017. *How We Get Free: Black Feminism and the Combahee River Collective*. Chicago: Haymarket Books.

Washington, Anne L. 2016. "Interviewing Data—The Art of Interpretation in Analytics." *Proceedings of the 2016 IConference*, March. https://doi.org/10.9776/16256.

Washington, Anne L. 2017. "How to Argue with an Algorithm: Lessons from the COMPAS ProPublica Debate." *The Colorado Technology Law Journal* 17 (1): 131–60.

Washington, Anne L., and Rachel Kuo. 2020. "Whose Side Are Ethics Codes On? Power, Responsibility and the Social Good." In *Proceedings of the 2020 Conference on Fairness, Accountability, and Transparency*. FAT* '20. New York: Association for Computing Machinery, 230–40. https://doi.org/10.1145/3351095.3372844.

5

Learn

For Good

1. FOR GOOD

The fifth and final stage in the prediction supply chain is learning from the aggregated data processed through optimized algorithms. Data-driven predictions are the result of a continuous cycle of finding digital sources, designing models, identifying patterns, and learning insights. Insights represent new knowledge that connects characteristics or behaviors with specific outcomes.

Data scientists distribute what they discover and what they learn. A core part of education is to share what you know with others. Yoda, the great sage and mentor of a film series, emphasized the importance of sharing failures in *Star Wars: Return of the Jedi* (Marquand 1983). On his deathbed, Yoda commands his student to pass on what he has learned about the Force to others. It is essential for ethical data science to notice who has the privilege to learn from triumphs or from mistakes.

This step determines how new insights are allocated and for whose benefit. A logic of aggregation explains why some populations, but not others, benefit from what data science offers. This basic form of accountability sets the stage for

Ethical Data Science. Anne L. Washington, Oxford University Press. © Oxford University Press 2023.
DOI: 10.1093/oso/9780197693025.003.0007

checking for ethical outcomes. This chapter draws attention to the link between what is collected and what is learned. Thinking about beneficence could build wider distributions of predictive knowledge.

1.1 And the Award Goes To ...

How do you describe the creative talent behind your favorite movie? Is it a Steven Spielberg film because of the director? Is it a Harrison Ford movie because of the actor? Do you know the author of the screenplay? The head of the special effects team?

Each creative industry has its own way of honoring the multiple forms of talent that go into making artistic output. The book industry rewards authors, and not acquisition teams, indexers, publishers, or editors. Similarly, the fashion industry rewards clothing designers and not stylists or seamstresses or textile artists. The fashion designer Lilly Pulitzer became famous for the bold fabric of her simple-cut dresses in the 1960s. The bright colors and innovative patterns were actually the work of the unrecognized, and unnamed, textile artist Suzie Zuzek, who finally had a posthumous exhibition of her work decades later.

Performing industries solve the problem with award shows that make a clear distinction between collaborative contributions. On Broadway, the Tony Awards celebrate individual talent but also award the entire production team. Playwright Michael R. Jackson won the 2022 award for best book of a musical while his entire show, "A Strange Loop," won for best musical. Even those who are not directly nominated benefit from being on a show that has won in an overall category. Everyone who contributed to the show can enjoy its success.

Similarly, data science is a massive collaboration. Choosing who will learn from a prediction is like trying to decide who gets recognized for collaborative work.

People leave digital traces. Organizations pay for prediction supply chains. Data scientists conduct sophisticated analyses. Widely distributed predictive decisions influence entire communities. How will the aggregated data be of service and to whom? At this stage in the prediction supply chain, we account for who originated the data source and to whom new knowledge is distributed.

1.2 What Insights Can Be Learned?

Trends, sequences, and correlations reveal associations that the world has never known. Combining disparate elements into a whole generates novel information. Insights represent new knowledge that connects characteristics or behaviors with specific outcomes.

This stage in the prediction supply chain adds to the careful consideration from previous chapters. The optimizations built from the sources, models, and comparisons generate new knowledge about the predictive goals. Once information is placed in a group, the predictive system will find variance, and produce trends. At the end of this process, we get insights that teach us things we did not know before starting. In statistical terms, these are probabilistic inferences that indicate the likelihood that something will or will not happen.

This chapter introduces a framework for testing whether the final insights are providing benefits for its intended population. We begin by thinking about active inclusion or exclusion of populations from the new knowledge generated by data science. Research ethics refer to this as beneficence.

1.3 Research Ethics: Beneficence

The word "beneficence" has its roots in Latin for doing good. On the surface, doing good is popular in predictive science. Some common phrases for this effort include "data for good," "artificial intelligence for social good," "data science for social impact," and "machine learning fairness."

With all these good intentions, why do we have ethical problems?

Intention cannot be the sole determinant for a data-driven project meeting its beneficent aims. Altruistic purposes drive many interactions that in fact demand subordination. Settlers claiming to want to help people instead spread disease and domination while monopolizing natural resource wealth (Wynter 2003). A common altruistic justification for the Atlantic slave trade was that forced labor under Europeans was better for people stolen from freedom in their homes in Africa (Davis 2010). Efforts intended to do good can overstep boundaries in a single-minded attempt to save the world.

Beneficence can be defined as acts of charity by the rich and powerful. Yet in the Belmont Report on research ethics, it has a more specific meaning (U.S. Department of Health, Education, and Welfare and National Commission for the Protection of Human Subjects of Biomedical and Behavioral Research 1979). As one of the report's core principles, beneficence is an intention to reduce harm and enhance the possibility of an advantage. It invites researchers to move far beyond what is strictly obligated and toward an interest in participant well-being. Under the principle of beneficence, ethical scholars treat research participants with respect.

Beneficent intentions combined with poor treatment of research participants is most obvious in cases of medical experiments. The people being studied often receive no benefit and in fact are harmed to advance medical care that will be given to others. An example of this is James Marion Sims (Washington 2018). Lauded for his contributions to gynecology, Sims gained that professional esteem by experimenting on enslaved Black women who were unable to give consent. Furthermore, Sims's research was designed so that none of the women included in his studies would benefit from it. While the medical field may justify the advances in reproductive health, the cost was the death and pain of the people who gave the field that knowledge.

Particularly striking were the medical experiments on prisoners during the twentieth century. During World War II, physicians caused or ignored harm in the interest of medical attention for dominant populations. This prompted the 1964 Helsinki declaration on medical ethics (World Medical Association 1964), which lay the foundation for research ethics initiatives around the world. Contemporary regulators impose a strict standard before experimental studies can proceed. In the least, researchers must explain how the study does not harm participants.

Data science is rarely held to the standard of medical research. However, predictive systems could pause to reflect about which population groups stand to benefit from new knowledge.

The scholar Annette Markham, in initially writing for the Association of Internet Researchers, called the people who participate in the study "data subjects." The data collected represents something about their own life, their life, what they like, or what they have done. Like human subjects in experimental research studies, these people are studied, evaluated, and tested in the name of gathering new knowledge, but the intervention takes place through computer information technology. Calling them data subjects also invites in the history of ethical research guidelines for handling humans in experiments (U.S. Department of Health, Education, and Welfare and National Commission for the Protection of Human Subjects of Biomedical and Behavioral Research 1979; World Medical Association 1964).

Whose life will be better with the newly discovered aggregated knowledge? If the data subjects are not the beneficiaries, who is? Projects that cannot answer this question with specific populations in mind are likely to unwittingly limit access to those who can pay or who have political power.

The test for beneficence introduced in this chapter spotlights the conflicting logics that justify data science for social good initiatives.

1.4 Google Flu Trends

A popular internet search engine led an early example of data science for social good. In 2008, Google launched the website google.org to publicize a collaboration with the Centers for Disease Control and Prevention (CDC) the US federal agency for public health. Google Flu Trends' extraordinary but short-lived success provides a cautionary tale about data science beneficence.

Predictions of flu outbreaks help officials to anticipate the production of vaccines. The CDC looks for signals of a possible flu outbreak by monitoring hospital records, physicians' reports, and lab results (Helft 2008). Public health officials want to predict a strong possibility of a problem but do not want to cause unnecessary panic. The CDC continuously looks for new ways to make decisions about public health outbreaks. Public health decision-making was called into question when a predicted 1976 flu epidemic never happened (Argyris 1979). The false prediction triggered an overproduction of vaccines that ultimately were wasted when the outbreak never occurred (Neustadt and Fineberg 1978).

Google Flu Trends sought to forecast influenza outbreaks by analyzing search trends. A search trend is a pattern that emerges from identical queries over a specific period of time. For instance, many people searched for Morocco during the 2022 World Cup playoffs, but those queries would have subsided by the semifinals. Search trends could surface an unusual or sudden increase in queries of health-related words. A search query such as "cough syrup" or "what are flu symptoms" could be an early indicator for public health officials. Google never releases queries, so it is not possible to confirm the exact words.

The early success was extraordinary. Google Flu Trends was heralded as preventing a rash public health response to a "swine flu epidemic." The flu trends model predicted outbreaks up to two weeks before the CDC's traditional public health data could pick up a similar signal. In 2009, the search trend algorithm was able to detect a new form of influenza (Ginsberg et al. 2009). The World Health Organization (WHO) joined the project and was able to repeat the success of the CDC. Google Flu Trends modeled the outbreak of flu worldwide using similar public health benchmarks provided by the WHO. At its height of popularity, Google Flu Trends could identify the outbreak of flu at national, regional, city, or other smaller geopolitical levels. From 2008 to 2012, it represented the ideal public service that big data could offer.

Google could not maintain the success of Google Flu Trends. The model began to lose its predictive reliability by 2013. Something began to break down in the assumption that flu-related queries were correlated with a sick searcher. It is possible that the earlier model detected physical responses to winter weather (Lazer et al. 2014). Perhaps additional queries were tied to increased media reports about flu season (Butler 2013; Ginsberg et al. 2009). This was also an important point when Google was intentionally beginning to change the algorithms that processed its queries to build personalized search (Washington 2016). The infrastructure for submitting queries through Google search was also in transition over this period. Google changed its internal policies and began to fully integrate mail, news, and search (Treese 2009). This may have created a feedback loop of suggested queries, advertisements, or recommended news stories that were based on Google's own product evolution. Google Flu Trends stopped publishing estimates by August 2015. The .org website rolled over to .com for a few years until it became the home of Google's Philanthropic Initiatives.

How did a project that intended to do good eventually not only fail but stop trying? The story of Google Flu Trends fits into this large question over benefits, logics, and practical beneficence.

1.5 Who Benefits?

Who gets the greatest benefit from the new knowledge? Is there any benefit for the people who shared their data? Is the organization sponsoring the data analysis getting the most benefit? How does the new knowledge serve the most vulnerable or the most powerful?

This chapter asks why the people who share information sometimes do not get to learn from it. A logic, or interconnected series of beliefs, animates who gets to learn from data. An underlying series of assumptions motivate the distribution of what data science learns.

The sociologists Roger Friedland and Robert R. Alford introduced the concept of institutional logics to explain the different philosophies that drive business (Friedlander and Alford 1991; Lounsbury et al. 2021; Ocasio, Thornton, and Lounsbury 2017). Institutional logics might explain why one family-owned firm is driven by profits, while another emphasizes passing the business to future generations. This chapter draws on this conceptualization from management science to argue that there are distinct constellations of practices, values, beliefs, and rules (Thornton and Ocasio 1999) that reproduce material configurations of insights and orient their symbolic role in social systems. I argue that predictive systems have their own logics that shape, in this case, who can benefit from predictive insights.

1.6 Logics of Aggregation

People learn from data.

Predictions in the public interest should be able to easily trace data subject participation to some advantage. One obvious marker for determining this is if the people who appear in the aggregate data are not the people who will benefit from the research. Ethical data science considers whose life will improve after learning from the data aggregation.

The human relationships that bind together what is collected and what is learned form the logic of aggregation. I offer three ways to think about data aggregation: autopsy logic, warden logic, and butler logic. Each one has a different relationship to the data subject and who benefits. An autopsy logic brings no merit to anyone but researchers and future data subjects. A warden logic brings institutional benefits to related data subjects. A butler logic generates insights that are directly applicable to the data subject. A logic of aggregation explains how and where to apply the inferences generated from combining sources. Data science for social good projects often confuses these logics of aggregations, dashing expectations or frustrating the data subjects.

Data science has a compelling need to articulate its rationale for gathering empirical evidence. Inductive research emphasizes inquiry choices as part of its methodology. Scholars are responsible to explain the many directions of research design from an initial interest all the way through to analysis (Lincoln and Guba 1985). Data science could learn from inductive researchers who are able to relate plans to outcomes. Data scientists, like other researchers, could be trained to defend their reasons for bundling sources in pursuit of specific inferences.

Logics of aggregation is a way of communicating the success of a data science project in providing benefits to broad populations. This chapter illustrates the autopsy, warden, and butler aggregation logics.

1.7 Autopsy Logic of Aggregation

An autopsy examines the effects of disease or injury on the human form. An autopsy report indicates the cause of death and is often required when additional information is needed to understand why someone died. This surgical procedure on a dead body confirms a diagnosis but does not help the patient. Physicians perform autopsies to learn how to prevent others from dying in similar ways.

An autopsy logic of aggregation never benefits people who share data. Research extracted from "othered" communities is autopsy data. This extracted knowledge does not support the data subjects. It does not help the people who are in the experience. Its after-data benefit is only useful to a researcher who is interested in causes and causalities. As post facto information, it cannot be used in the moment to make changes to the data subject's life. What we learn will not help the person we learned it from.

Even though the Black men were living research participants, the information John H. Heller began collecting in 1930 on syphilis was autopsy data. Heller, director of the US Public Health Service, insisted that letting men die without medical care, and actively discouraging them from getting treatment, was ethical (Heller 1972; Washington 2018). The research design did the opposite of what doctors are trained to do. Heller's plan augmented the transmission of disease in the population as it spread between spouses and from parent to child over four decades. What Heller learned in his study, paid with federal money, was intended to benefit White medical patients and not the people of Tuskegee, Alabama. This is not an unusual example. Cornelius P. Rhoads, the first director of the Sloan-Kettering Institute, perfected cancer drugs by designing inhumane experiments on the people of Puerto Rico and American soldiers (Starr 2003). The medical ethicist Harriet A. Washington (2017) argues that some unethical biomedical experiments also reinforced monopoly practices in the pharmaceutical industry.

Experimental biomedical research on vulnerable populations with the intention to benefit a socially powerful population is considered a violation in research ethics. Yet this dynamic happens all the time in digital research.

In 2014, a lecturer at the University of Cambridge paid informal workers $1 or $2 to download an app and take a psychometric test. Unlike classic studies (Christakis and Fowler 2013), the insights from this study were sold to the highest bidder through a company. The company ultimately became Cambridge Analytica, which relied heavily on monetizing an autopsy logic of aggregation.

1.8 Cambridge Analytica: Your Data, Their Money

The Cambridge Prosociality and Well-Being Lab developed an app to collect data for building psychological profiles. The app both administered surveys and downloaded Facebook profiles. In 2014, Facebook announced that it would start to restrict access to its application programming language (API) and therefore the ability to download data.

Aleksandr Kogan, the lab's director, downloaded as much data as possible and started a commercial research company. Kogan, also known as Aleksandr Spectre, had been a lecturer at Cambridge for two years (Briant 2018). A June 2014 contract released to the UK Parliament explicitly states that Kogan had a commercially competitive product because the data sets were no longer available under Facebook's API terms of service (Wylie 2018).

Like many academic researchers, Kogan found participants on an informal employment platform (Paolacci, Chandler, and Ipeirotis 2010). People with stable employment are not often looking to earn small amounts doing micro-task work (Irani and Silberman 2013). These platforms are global and attract people looking to earn extra money from anywhere. The project implicitly gathered information from economically marginal people who could be anywhere in the world.

The study collected enough data to connect demographics, political party affiliations, and Facebook "likes" to psychometric measures. Importantly, the app was able to collect the Facebook profiles of friends of the original research participants. The app, This Is Your Digital Life, gathered data from only

270,000 research participants. Yet the data Kogan sold contained over 90 million Facebook profiles (Cadwalladr 2018).

The data trove was bigger because of network dynamics known as friend of a friend (FOAF) (Washington 2018). In 2014, the average number of friends of a typical Facebook user was 338. The participants in the study became training data for his models. Kogan used the friends of participants to verify his predictive models. The FOAF profiles served as an experimental group to test micro-targeted ads.

Trained in psychology, Kogan evaluated research participants with the empirically validated big five personality traits score (Hotz 2013). Participants answer questions that have specific words associated with each personality trait. The results are analyzed through factor analysis, also known as the Five Factors Model. None of the data subjects learned how their life choices and circumstances related to characteristics like openness, conscientiousness, extraversion, agreeableness, or neuroticism (Briant 2018). The data subjects could not learn if their social network had extroverts who lived in Dunsmuir and drove pickup trucks. The study was not designed for them. New knowledge generated from the aggregated data was only shared with powerful and wealthy clients.

Cambridge Analytica sold their analysis of occasional workers as political strategy. Participants' psychometric patterns enabled successful predictions of how to persuade voters. In collaboration with Strategic Communication Laboratories Group (SLC), SLC election division, Kogan micro-targeted election ads based on personality profiles. Clients were able to implement the predictions because they could also afford to buy the necessary micro-targeted social ads. The study was designed to persuade the wider public toward the views of paying clients. Cambridge Analytica and SLC elections advertised success making a politician seem macho for a Romanian election or persuading opposition voters in Nigeria to stay home according to leaked documents released by the UK Parliament (Briant 2018; Wylie 2018). In our complex communications environment, politicians are wise to seek a social media strategy. However, the tools could also easily be used by powerful people who wanted to control the general voting public. While it is possible to argue that the original data subjects benefited from a nominal payment, they certainly did not know they compromised the privacy of over three hundred of their best friends. None of these insights supported or improved the lives of the original participants.

On May 1, 2018, Cambridge Analytica closed in disgrace after a whistleblower exposed its practices. While the uproar was over stealing Facebook profiles and selling data, it was, without a doubt, that people felt used. Even the few people who downloaded the app, received no benefit. People were infuriated that liking a nephew's photo pulled them into the digital dragnet (Ruderman 2013; Richardson 2022). The Cambridge Analytica data set contained nearly 72 percent of Facebook's 1.23 billion user profiles (Cadwalladr 2018).

What Cambridge Analytica learned from the economically vulnerable was sold to powerful people. None of these insights supported or improved the lives of the data subjects. New knowledge generated from the study was never intended to be shared with the people who generated it. In fact, information gathered from these people as workers were used to manipulate similar people as voters. Worse, people may be left more vulnerable and less powerful than they were before they shared their data.

An autopsy logic of aggregation explicitly exploits anyone who shares data to the benefit of other populations. The information learned is inevitably shared with someone richer, more powerful, more visible, and more influential. The benefiting population may be deemed as the broad public, but often knowledge is merely transferred to groups with higher social status.

1.9   Warden Logic of Aggregation

Wardens hold primary administrative responsibility for an institution. As chief guardian and top official, a warden supervises all activities and is accountable for how things run. The title is often used for the person who oversees a prison. A warden prioritizes operational demands of the institution over individual needs.

A warden logic of aggregation benefits the organization collecting data. Research designed to only fold into organizational strategic goals is warden data. The collection of information from individuals solely serves the needs of whomever is doing the prediction and analysis. Insights help whoever commissioned the predictions without concern for the data subjects. A warden logic drives fears and conformity.

A Stanford researcher became famous for his findings on psychological domination, although the police had to stop the 1971 experiment. Undergraduate volunteers randomly became either prisoners or guards in this week-long study. Philip G. Zimbardo played dual roles as the study's principal investigator and as the simulated prison warden. The notorious Stanford prison study ended after six days in response to pleas to stop the physical and mental abuse. Zimbardo put the undergraduates at risk, wrote a sensational and popular book, and received tenure at Stanford. Experimental social-behavioral studies that disregard participant harms create an imbalance when paired with a researcher's pursuit of professional success. The researcher holds all the advantages while the data subject is ignored.

Data subjects who remain part of the organization may enjoy the general improvements informed by the new knowledge. Those in the majority may find their choices naturally reflected in the organizational changes. The data subject may have an ability to see a presentation of their data or some simple personal trends. However, the choice and variety of aggregated analysis is tightly controlled by the organization. The primary motive is always the safe continuous running of the organization.

Social media platforms frequently are compared to panopticons (Bucher 2012). A panopticon, with its ever-present gaze, was originally a design for prisons. Legal theorist Jeremy Bentham designed a circular room with a tower for the guards at its center. The guard tower is opaque so no one can know if anyone is watching. The presence of the tower makes both inmates and guards feel like they are always under scrutiny. The goal of the panopticon design is not individual comfort but the warden's desire for orderly functioning.

In 2012, a data scientist published the results of a study that manipulated user emotions on a social media platform. The experiment, which greatly benefited the company's core business, illustrates a warden logic of aggregation.

1.10 Testing A, Testing B

Websites constantly try out new designs. It is subtle to the average user, who may not notice that a color changed or that something moved to another part of the page. Some people, group a, may see a blue banner, while others, group b, may see a green banner. A/B testing is prevalent in interface design because it helps website designs to empirically evaluate design choices. It received pronounced scrutiny when Facebook conducted psychometric A/B tests.

Adam Kramer, as an employee and industry data scientist, had access to controlling the status updates of millions of Facebook users. Kramer wanted to know if people became happier around Facebook friends who were happy. The hypothesis builds on years of research in the sociology of medicine. Emotional contagion theory emerged from the analysis of two decades of data from the Framingham Heart Study. Fowler and Christakis (2008) found that happiness spread throughout the social network.

In 2012, Kramer published a paper on the spread of emotion on Facebook. The "ACM Conference on Computer Human Interaction" paper was followed with an experimental study that prompted a note from the journal's editor-in-chief questioning the study's adherence to the common rule in research ethics which asserts the importance of voluntary participation. Kramer, Guillory, and Hancock (2014) manipulated the emotional expressions in the news feeds of nearly 690,000 Facebook users. The experiment included both positive and negative expressions one week in January. One of their findings is that content that lacked emotional valence decreased interaction with Facebook, Kramer's employer. Together these two publications are known as the Facebook contagion study.

Facebook benefited from the new knowledge. The company had new insight into how people interacted with its core product. These insights could help develop the newsfeed so Facebook could be more profitable. Also, Facebook benefited from the prestige of publishing in important scientific journals. The published results could be shown to advertisers as scientific evidence of the validity of the social media platform's reach. Facebook at the time was pivoting to an aggressive strategy of serving ads, and this research would have bolstered their advertising revenue. The Facebook contagion study changed user emotions for the sole purpose of testing the emotional influence of the company's newsfeed algorithms.

The study participants may or may not have benefited from the study because they did not know they were in a study. Facebook never released additional information to explain or to contact people who might have been impacted. There was no additional follow-up or support for anyone who may have been served a preponderance of bad news. In the note from the editors of *Proceedings of the National Academy of Sciences*, Inder M. Verma reminds the authors that informed consent and voluntary participation are the hallmarks of research ethics (Kramer, Guillory, and Hancock 2014).

The Facebook contagion study is an example of a warden logic of aggregation. Anyone who remained on Facebook after the study would benefit from more specific ads and anything else Facebook learned from the study. However, participants did not individually gain at all. For instance, the people whose reality was distorted by only good news never learned of the disasters, deaths, and problems that might have occurred during the week the research occurred. A/B testing always generates data for the organization.

A warden logic of aggregation explicitly and solely supports the organization that commissioned the research. This is why the organization funds data science in the first place. Information trends are invisible to all but those who own the predictions. This monopoly and information asymmetry can lead to intentional misdirection and deception (Akerlof 1970; Shapiro and Varian 1998). While some individual researchers or populations may benefit, the new information directly supports an organization.

What Amazon learns from buyer habits helps them limit search visibility to higher priced, ad-sponsored, or Amazon-brand products. Consumers may end up spending more money because they cannot locate lower priced non-Amazon products. In all cases, warden logic applied to a two-sided marketplace is also seen as an opportunity for antitrust legislation.

1.11 Butler Logic of Aggregation

Butlers cater to individual preferences. As servants known for high service standards and specialized attention, these personal attendants carefully monitor and quietly deliver wishes at the appropriate time. A butler is often the highest ranked staff within a large household and is ultimately responsible for the domestic comfort of the employers. Personal choice rises to the level of ritual but always with the flexibility of intermittent whimsy.

A butler logic of aggregation tailors benefits to the people who share data. It supports superior and timely direct delivery of services. The collection and analysis of information serves the needs of the person it is collected from. The data subject also has complete control of raw values and comparative trends and can merge information with other sources to create their own forms of aggregated analysis. Butler data is not the social conformity that comes with "people who bought this also bought" recommendation engines. This level of service will alert you that your favorite product is on sale at another store. The focus is on you and your habits alone.

The classic image is a British manservant impeccably dressed in formalwear and deftly anticipating the impulses of the upper classes. A gentleman begins a transatlantic cruise by ordering a Scotch and water. The butler returns to the table with the whiskey and two small pitchers. The butler eagerly awaits to see how much chilled water and how much warm water will be poured into the glass. As the butler removes the extra glassware, he murmurs that he will remember that the gentleman prefers his Scotch and water tepid. No questions are asked. With as little interference as possible, the butler determines the desired configuration and makes that the default.

Butlers are eager to determine what pleases yet are always in servitor roles. This is how many services want us to imagine how data serves us. We set something once, and it delivers it directly to us.

Most machine learning and artificial intelligence masquerades as butler data. Few systems share trends immediately, support the individual, and ignore base rates. The artificial intelligence in fiction most closely resembles butler data because there is no commercial function. One artificial intelligence bot in Kim Stanley Robinson's novel *New York 2140* helps someone learn how to become a trader and then slowly make a career change. It is fiction because the bot does not sell anything. It simply gives the user a menu of skills related to the chosen task and then tracks progress.

Consistency, radical transparency, portability, and fiduciary care are the distinctive features of butler logic. What is learned from a butler will directly and immediately give an advantage to the person they learned it from. And it will be done with discretion. It is running in the background remembering what we want, not telling us what other people want. It does not enforce a norm, an average, or a standard. It does not strive to get our attention. It repeats what has happened before until told to change. The aggregate feedback enriches the data subject's life.

Only a few digital services provide this level of service. The following examples come from the world of elite individual sports.

1.12   Customization Is Tradition

Tennis is uniquely a sport of solo athletes and independent circuits. Tennis analytics provides customized data to help players face the best odds of winning based on the opposition at each match and location.

Team sports innovations are dictated by large organizations looking for efficiencies with individual athletes largely not in control of their own biometric material (Karkazis and Fishman 2017). Michael Lewis popularized sports analytics in his book *Moneyball: The Art of Winning an Unfair Game*, which showed how managers used statistics to predict undervalued players for a team sport (Lewis 2003).

Tennis, however, focuses on the skills of two people who happen to be facing each other across the net in the middle of a court. Tennis players, solo or in teams of doubles, volley a ball back and forth. The goal of the racquet sport is to stay in the game until the opponent misses the ball. Part of the strategy in tennis is to serve so that the opposition cannot return a valid volley across the net.

And it is hard to know in advance everyone you might meet on the court. Tennis is played within a multitude of organizing bodies. Tennis players are independent, unlike team sports like baseball, basketball, and football that are managed by regional teams and organized into leagues. Players choose to join circuits such as the Grand Slams and Masters Tournaments and may drop out of events at any time.

Players have to not only be in top form, they must also prepare for a wide variety of conditions. Each match has several variables that change in combination, the most important of which is that players do not know in advance who will play against whom. Even the court's surface changes from clay to grass as athletes fly from Melbourne to Dubai to Wimbledon to Shanghai in an annual rotation of events. Tennis has few pressures to change or standardize, so players are beginning to invest in navigating all these options as a form of digital strategy.

Companies that sell tennis analytics compile detailed measurements, such as tracking the ball from different camera angles and tagging videos of past professional games. Tennis analytics provides detailed information about how one person performs in swinging a racquet to hit a ball across a court. Sensors can track the speed and spin of a ball, where the ball hit the racquet, or the trajectory of the shot. One company charged players $3,500 per game for data and analysis of an opponent's patterns before game day.

Top tennis star Novak Djokovic used data to prepare his strategy. A same-day strategy helps meet an opponent's strength or take advantage of any injury or sudden weakness. One of the few professional players to embrace analytics early, Djokovic used analytics in 2019 to determine how he planned to approach his opponent. Many coaches use data to train more effectively.

Tennis analytics is a form of butler data. It is information tailored to the needs of one person based on their own physical patterns, habits, or responses to environmental conditions. The analytics give an obvious competitive advantage. An athlete can request data on their opponent's habits and have time to consider how to best respond. Having data analytics about your own game helps you know your strengths and how to compensate for your own weaknesses. On the other hand, Roger Federer said that he only focuses on his own game, not worrying about how others might place against him.

Collecting data that directly gives an advantage to individuals who share their data is rare; however, tennis analytics illustrates butler logic of aggregation.

1.13 Multiple Logics of Aggregation

The three logics of aggregation are theoretical bundles and are not always mutually exclusive. Taken together they can also represent the complex feelings and conflicts of interests that data science projects routinely express.

Logics of aggregation may imply a feeling that data subjects experience. A family who visits Disney theme parks receives radio-frequency identification (RFID)-enabled wristbands and other surveillance technology to facilitate payments, long queues, and reservations. The technology is visible and possibly helps families manage what might be a once-in-a-lifetime trip. MagicBands and the MyMagic+ systems are positioned as butler data but actually were established to support park management. Wait times were too long at rides, and Disney needed a better way to track crowd flow (Carr 2015). While all of this information operates and exists to support a warden logic of aggregation, the visitors to the happiest place on earth perceive these systems as tailored just for their needs.

Families that encounter state and local services endure similar surveillance as anyone at a Disney park but with a different experience of the logic of aggregation. No one even pretends that the data could help the people who are experiencing the system. A government agency has the authority to collect but not share information on frequency of meals, housing choices, and waits in long lines. The predictive goal is to identify problems that might lead to the removal of children. Dorothy E. Roberts refers to this as family policing instead of child protective services, foster care, or the child welfare system. Families, particularly Black children of Black parents, are often under forced supervision and, unfortunately, separation. Roberts argues that 84 percent of the children who enter the system for neglect live in homes experiencing poverty. In an analysis of the National Child Abuse and Neglect Data System Files, child protective services investigated 53 percent of Black children in the United States over eleven years (Kim et al. 2017). The patterns serve as warden data, while the people within these systems experience it as a form of autopsy data. Anything learned from their personal case will rarely help them reunite with their family.

Logics of aggregation may be interdependent and change over time. Google Flu Trends seemed to be an effective altruistic endeavor, but a lack of interest in updating it may be an indication of other motivations. Most technology companies launch charitable initiatives similar to A/B testing. They bolster an image of charitable giving, but it also gives the company an advantage in the marketplace and a better understanding of how something works that relates to its core business. Advertising and marketing generally advertise new predictive systems as having butler logics of aggregation but ultimately deliver warden logics, or worse, autopsy logics.

Autopsy, warden, and butler logics set the conditions for true beneficence.

Aggregation that does not serve the data subject but is explicitly created to support a different population group indicates an autopsy logic of aggregation. The data do not serve the data subject at all. This information is useful for the scientists and for people who later suffer from similar conditions but is of no merit to the individual who shares data.

Aggregation primarily in service of the organization reflects a warden logic of aggregation even though some data subjects who remain with the organization may receive benefits. The information is solely for the purpose of the organization and helps it make decisions.

New predictive knowledge that supports every whim through just-in-time delivery emulates a butler. Everything learned from aggregated personal information is immediately available to improve the life of the data subject. The unique data support the lifestyle and choices of one person. The ultimate goal of butler data is to return everything that is good directly to the originating data subject.

The three logics of aggregation could be combined to better understand why projects fail or how to avoid problems in the first place. Practitioners may find that the logics of aggregation provide a means to determine whether good intentions line up with actions.

This chapter asked readers to think about why analysis is shared. The utility of data that connect family members differs across contexts.

1.14 Thinking Like an Architect to Learn

Data scientists who think like architects can build within an existing landscape with an eye toward future uses and a changing environment. Reflecting on what architects do could help to balance elements that seem like opposing forces in data science.

Architects are professionals who make designs for new buildings which may include plans, style, and construction. They are intensely aware of how one structure fits in within its given location and placement. As structures are added over time, each one represents a period in history.

Architecture is both aesthetic and practical. A building may reflect a unique style that can be elevated to a work of art. Architecture relates to questions of culture, society, civilizations, and how humans live. While beauty may be an ultimate goal, the building is expected to remain standing. In the first instance, the structural integrity must be sound.

Architects build for someone who commissions the structure today yet know that it may last for decades if not centuries. A bridge, for instance, is built for the worst possible flood, not an average high tide. The Brooklyn Bridge was built with cables that supported six times the strength necessary at the time it opened in 1883. The money spent on delivering beyond specifications was made up in reputation. The maker of the suspension cables was able to sell the high-quality wire rope at a premium for decades. What if data science had this level of integrity?

Data science could learn from architecture that provides consistent benefits to a range of current and future clients. Architecture invites conversations about utility over time. Perhaps Google Flu Trends could have been maintained and might have indicated the 2019 SARS-2 COVID-19 worldwide pandemic. When will design predictions be robust enough to withstand changing times and tastes?

Predictive systems must recognize that they do not appear in a vacuum. Human systems, governments, and political motives shape how predictions are experienced. Architects are able to keep this duality in mind when designing one building that will also make a positive contribution to the wider location. Architects do not just build one building but add one more point of spatial experience.

Thinking like an architect means holding an awareness of temporal and experiential contexts that shape the delivery of benefits to targeted populations and others in the environment.

1.15   Ethical Data Science Insights

This final action in the ethical prediction supply chain makes sure what you learn is shared so someone can benefit from it.

Unlike an actual autopsy diagnosis, data science inferences could turn around to help the data subject. Instead of finding out how someone died, maybe the predictions could help someone avoid disease in the first place. This reversal of benefit could be one implementation of data justice (Bui and Noble 2020). Matt Bui and Safiya Noble (2020) construct data justice as a radical reimagining of social structures that brings balance not only for individuals but between social groups. Justice in this sense has a visible relation to structures of power that limit who experiences positive benefits of artificial intelligence.

The correlations and cautions we can gleam from data could be of wide interest for many people. Getting information distributed is one of the challenges that often is outside the scope of most data science education. Sadly, predictive insights are typically hoarded for the express purpose of improving the operational efficiency of the organization that paid for them. However, communities are interested in using data to provide tailored specific services for themselves.

Microtask workers on Mechanical Turk (Irani and Silberman 2013) organized themselves to build an alternative data system that serves their activist goals. The butler logic of aggregation applies although no one is an elite or a servant. These systems deliver community-level projects that strive to give attention and meet the needs of underserved populations. Where they could not access corporate data or open government data, the workers made their own that fit their needs. These projects serve as an important model for future public interest data science.

Advocating for secondary uses, sharing information as open data, and actively examining who benefits from data science could pave the way for more butler data.

1.16   Chapter 5 Summary

Patterns in data reveal insights that the world has never known before. Ethical data science considers who has access to the knowledge generated by data aggregation. The goal of these systems is to find variance. And that variance includes how the trends will be put to use. Many data science projects say that the data subject will directly benefit from aggregation, but this chapter provides three tests for determining if that is actually possible. Predictions in the public interest should be able to easily trace data subject participation to some advantage.

References

Akerlof, George A. 1970. "The Market for 'Lemons': Quality Uncertainty and the Market Mechanism." *The Quarterly Journal of Economics* 84 (3): 488–500.

Argyris, Chris. 1979. "Using Qualitative Data to Test Theories—The Swine Flu Affair: Decision Making on a Slippery Disease." *Administrative Science Quarterly* 24 (4): 672–79.

Briant, Emma L. 2018. "Cambridge Analytica Transcripts." UK House of Commons, Digital, Culture, Media and Sport Committee's Fake News Inquiry. https://www.par liament.uk/business/committees/committees-a-z/commons-select/digital-culture-media-and-sport-committee /news/fake-news-briant-evidence-17-19/.

Bucher, Taina. 2012. "Want to Be on the Top? Algorithmic Power and the Threat of Invisibility on Facebook." *New Media & Society* 14 (7): 1164–80. https://doi.org/10.1177/1461444812440159.

Bui, Matthew Le, and Safiya Umoja Noble. 2020. "We're Missing a Moral Framework of Justice in Artificial Intelligence: On the Limits, Failings, and Ethics of Fairness." In *The Oxford Handbook of Ethics of AI*, edited by Markus D. Dubber, Frank Pasquale, and Sunit Das, 161–79. Oxford; New York: Oxford University Press. https://doi.org/10.1093/oxfordhb/9780190067397.013.9.

Butler, Declan. 2013. "When Google Got Flu Wrong." *Nature* 494 (7436): 155–56. https://doi.org/10.1038/494155a.

Cadwalladr, Carole. 2018. "Our Cambridge Analytica Scoop Shocked the World. But the Whole Truth Remains Elusive." *The Guardian*, December 23, 2018, sec. UK news.

Carr, Austin. 2015. "The Messy Business Of Reinventing Happiness," April 15, 2015. https://www.fastcompany.com/3044283/the-messy-business-of-re.

Christakis, Nicholas A., and James H. Fowler. 2013. "Social Contagion Theory: Examining Dynamic Social Networks and Human Behavior." *Statistics in Medicine* 32 (4): 556–77. https://doi.org/10.1002/sim.5408.

Davis, Angela Y. 1971. *Lectures on Liberation.* Los Angeles: Committee to Free Angela Davis. http://archive.org/details/AngelaDavis-LecturesOnLiberation.

Davis, Angela Y. 2010. "Lectures on Liberation." In *Narrative of the Life of Frederick Douglass, an American Slave, Written by Himself: A New Critical Edition*, by Frederick Douglass, edited by Angela Y. Davis. Open Media Series. San Francisco: City Lights Books.

Fowler, J.H., and N.A. Christakis. 2008. "Dynamic Spread of Happiness in a Large Social Network: Longitudinal Analysis over 20 Years in the Framingham Heart Study." *BMJ* 337 (dec04 2): a2338–a2338. https://doi.org/10.1136/bmj.a2338.

Friedlander, Roger, and Robert R. Alford. 1991. "Bringing Society Back in: Symbols, Practices, and Institutional Contradictions." In *The New Institutionalism in Organizational Analysis*, edited by Walter W. Powell and Paul DiMaggio, 232–63. Chicago: University of Chicago Press.

Ginsberg, Jeremy, et al. 2009. "Detecting Influenza Epidemics Using Search Engine Query Data." *Nature* 457: 1012–14.

Helft, Miguel. 2008. "Google Uses Searches to Track Flu's Spread." *The New York Times*, November 11, 2008, sec. Technology. https://www.nytimes.com/2008/11/12/technol ogy/internet/12flu.html.

Heller, Jean. 1972. "Syphilis Victims in U.S. Study Went Untreated for 40 Years." *The New York Times*, July 26, 1972, sec. Archives. https://www.nytimes.com/1972/07/26/archives/syphilis-victims-in-us-study-went-untreated-for-40-years-syphilis.html.

Hotz, Robert Lee. 2013. "When 'Likes' Can Shed Light." *The Wall Street Journal Online*, March 11, 2013, sec. US.

Irani, Lilly C., and M. Six Silberman. 2013. "Turkopticon: Interrupting Worker Invisibility in Amazon Mechanical Turk." In *Proceedings of the SIGCHI Conference on Human Factors in Computing Systems*. CHI '13. New York: ACM, 611–20. https://doi.org/10.1145/2470654.2470742.

Karkazis, Katrina, and Jennifer R. Fishman. 2017. "Tracking U.S. Professional Athletes: The Ethics of Biometric Technologies." *The American Journal of Bioethics* 17 (1): 45–60. https://doi.org/10.1080/15265161.2016.1251633.

Kim, Hyunil, et al. 2017. "Lifetime Prevalence of Investigating Child Maltreatment Among US Children." *American Journal of Public Health* 107 (2): 274–80. https://doi.org/10.2105/AJPH.2016.303545.

Kramer, Adam D.I., Jamie E. Guillory, and Jeffrey T. Hancock. 2014. "Experimental Evidence of Massive-Scale Emotional Contagion through Social Networks." *Proceedings of the National Academy of Sciences* 111 (24): 8788–90. https://doi.org/10.1073/pnas.1320040111.

Lazer, David, et al. 2014. "The Parable of Google Flu: Traps in Big Data Analysis." *Science* 343 (6176): 1203–05. https://doi.org/10.1126/science.1248506.

Lewis, Michael. 2003. *Moneyball: The Art of Winning an Unfair Game*. 1st ed. New York: W.W. Norton.

Lincoln, Yvonna S., and Egon G. Guba. 1985. *Naturalistic Inquiry*. Beverly Hills, CA: Sage Publications. http://www.loc.gov/catdir/enhancements/fy0658/84026295-d.html.

Lounsbury, Michael, et al. 2021. "New Directions in the Study of Institutional Logics: From Tools to Phenomena." *Annual Review of Sociology* 47 (1): null. https://doi.org/10.1146/annurev-soc-090320-111734.

Marquand, Richard, dir. 1983. *Star Wars: Episode VI—Return of the Jedi*. https://www.imdb.com/title/tt0086190/.

Neustadt, Richard E., and Harvey V. Fineberg. 1978. *The Swine Flu Affair: Decision-Making on a Slippery Disease*. Washington DC: National Academies Press. http://www.ncbi.nlm.nih.gov/books/NBK219606/.

Ocasio, William, Patricia H. Thornton, and Michael Lounsbury. 2017. "Advances to the Institutional Logics Perspective." In *The SAGE Handbook of Organizational Institutionalism*, by Royston Greenwood, et al., 509–31. London: SAGE Publications Ltd. https://doi.org/10.4135/9781446280669.n20.

Paolacci, Gabriele, Jesse Chandler, and Panagiotis G. Ipeirotis. 2010. "Running Experiments on Amazon Mechanical Turk." *Judgment and Decision Making* 5 (5): 411–19. https://doi.org/10.1017/S1930297500002205.

Richardson, Rashida. 2022. "Racial Segregation and the Data-Driven Society: How Our Failure to Reckon with Root Causes Perpetuates Separate and Unequal Realities." *Berkeley Technology Law Journal* 36 (3): 1051–90. https://doi.org/10.15779/Z38PN8XG3V..

Ruderman, Wendy. 2013. "For Troubled Teenagers in New York City, a New Tack: Forced Outreach." *The New York Times*, March 3, 2013. https://www.nytimes.com/2013/03/04/nyregion/to-stem-juvenile-robberies-police-trail-youths-before-the-crime.html?pagewanted=all.

Shapiro, Carl, and Hal R. Varian. 1998. *Information Rules: A Strategic Guide to the Network Economy*. Boston, MA: Harvard Business School Press. http://www.inforules.com/.

Starr, Douglas. 2003. "Revisiting a 1930s Scandal, AACR to Rename a Prize." *Science* 300 (5619): 573–74. https://doi.org/10.1126/science.300.5619.573.

Thornton, Patricia H., and William Ocasio. 1999. "Institutional Logics and the Historical Contingency of Power in Organizations: Executive Succession in the Higher Education Publishing Industry, 1958–1990." *American Journal of Sociology* 105 (3): 801–43. https://doi.org/10.1086/ajs.1999.105.issue-3.

Treese, Win. 2009. "Is Google Too Big to Fail?" *NetWorker* 13 (2): 11. https://doi.org/10.1145/1540392.1540396.

U.S. Department of Health, Education, and Welfare, and National Commission for the Protection of Human Subjects of Biomedical and Behavioral Research. 1979. "The Belmont Report. Ethical Principles and Guidelines for the Protection of Human Subjects of Research."

Washington, Anne L. 2016. "The Interoperability of US Federal Government Information: Interoperability." In *Managing Big Data Integration in the Public Sector*, edited by Anil Aggarwal, 1–19. Hershey, PA: IGI Global. https://doi.org/DOI:%20 10.4018/978-1-4666-9649-5.ch001.

Washington, Anne L. 2018. "Facebook Math: How 270,000 Became Millions." *Points: Data & Society* (blog). April 11, 2018. https://medium.com/p/bd8cf1009b32.

Washington, Anne L., and David Morar. 2017. "Open Government Data and File Formats: Constraints on Collaboration." In *Proceedings of the 18th Annual International Conference on Digital Government Research*. Dg.o '17. New York: ACM, 155–59. https://doi.org/10.1145/3085228.3085232.

World Medical Association. 1964. "Declaration of Helsinki—Ethical Principles for Medical Research Involving Human Subjects." 1964. https://www.wma.net/policies-post/wma-declaration-of-helsinki-ethical-principles-for-medical-research-involving-human-subjects/.

Wylie, Chris. 2018. "Cambridge Analytica Leaked Documents." UK House of Commons, Digital, Culture, Media and Sport Committee's Fake News Inquiry. https:// www.par liament.uk/documents/commons-committees/culture-media-and-sport /Chris%20 Wylie%20Background%20papers.pdf.

Wynter, Sylvia. 2003. "Unsettling the Coloniality of Being/Power/Truth/ Freedom: Towards the Human, After Man, Its Overrepresentation—An Argument." *CR: The New Centennial Review* 3 (3): 257–337. https://doi.org/10.1353/ncr.2004.0015.

6

Predict

Show Us Your Work or Someone Gets Hurt

1. SHOW US YOUR WORK OR SOMEONE GETS HURT

Although the prediction supply chain comes to a conclusion, data science has implications for those living with its insights. Just as a factory can have downstream environmental consequences, the prediction supply chain changes its surrounding context. Technology implementation always has an impact. In the movie *Jurassic Park*, an amusement park applies genetic advances to bring back extinct dinosaurs with devastating results. Dr. Ian Malcolm accuses the team of abusing scientific power because they released technology they did not have the discipline to develop themselves (Spielberg 1993). Organizations and the answers they need to make decisions cannot solely justify all data science, especially when the technology places an additional burden on individuals who identify predictive errors. Implementation requires determining how the automated system engages with social worlds and physical environments.

Predictive technology possesses not only scientific authority but it also holds significant social power. The distance between production and distribution on any supply chain means problems can fester given the power asymmetries between those two points. Streamlining for ideal cases may place additional burdens on people who have to live with algorithmic accusations. Data science that does not show its work does not allow transparency into its inner functions. Not showing the work of automated systems can hurt people who

Ethical Data Science. Anne L. Washington, Oxford University Press. © Oxford University Press 2023.
DOI: 10.1093/oso/9780197693025.003.0008

represent unanticipated situations. Ethical data science knows that predictions that shape society benefit from clarity about research methods. This chapter offers mechanisms for more precise feedback that acknowledges the attention that predictive data science demands from the humans around it.

1.1 Efficiency Comes at a Cost

In March 2019, Derek Jacobs pulled his van to a shoulder lane in Derbyshire, England, perhaps unaware that the road was part of Smart Motorways, a new traffic efficiency scheme in the United Kingdom. The government viewed the shoulder as a wasted lane in a modern era with reliable cars, and they turned the hard shoulder into a dynamic travel lane. The British Smart Motorways system is an extreme example of what goes wrong when pursuing one-dimensional optimization in predictive systems.

Authorized to provide efficient infrastructure, Highways England prioritized traffic flow and built dynamic road signs to indicate changing speed limits, lane closures, and lane openings. Even if the truck driver had seen Mr. Jacobs's van in time, there was nowhere for either of them to go. The government built places for emergency stops, but none were visible from the site of this fatal accident. Removing the redundant lane during popular driving times increased the chances that someone needing a safe place to stop would encounter someone rushing home. Claims of efficient traffic management made by the organization were stifled by the obvious burden of compliance placed on each driver.

The new digital signage required each driver's full attention to respond to the fluctuations, which were often based on calculated traffic flows. The reasoning behind Smart Motorways adjustments were not perceptible to drivers nor obviously consistent across times of day. The constantly changing instructions provided little rational explanation but required total submission. Instead of penalties or fines, drivers had to bear far worse. Failure to respond to the normative controls calculated by Highway England could literally kill. Demanding the minute-by-minute concentration of drivers improved the overall traffic but also created infrastructure affordances that, on one Derbyshire road alone, led to multiple fatalities. The people controlling the single goal of continuous traffic flow demanded absolute compliance even when they failed to consider earlier and universally shared expectations, such as road safety.

Facing lawsuits for corporate manslaughter, the Smart Motorways scheme ended operations in late 2019 after several deaths along the M1 highway. Highways England chief executive Jim O'Sullivan defended the technology to the House of Commons Transport Select Committee by explaining that motorists did not understand the new system. The Automobile Association raised concerns, however, noting that twenty-six cars a day, on average, require a breakdown lane on a hard shoulder. The British government decided that the efficiency of Smart Motorways traffic flow came at too high a cost.

Digital transformation, especially in government, often promises to sustain its mission to serve all. Yet the structural nature of streamlining majority cases for efficiency may limit equivalent participation from other groups (Collins 1993). Efficiency streamlines certainty for the majority and leaves others open to disaster or the vagaries of chance. Predictions for everyone include as much as they exclude.

Many people will enjoy a positive experience when automation speeds up predictable cases. On the other hand, some people who are not accurately depicted or represented may clash with the organization and its predictive data systems. Those who are disadvantaged by systems deemed efficient may be penalized in the extreme. Predictive data science makes participation and interpretation more complicated for outsiders or anyone who only casually engages with the system.

The goal of predictive data science often is to cut down on red tape or bureaucratic issues that prevent efficiency (Bozeman and Scott 1996). The other side of efficiency is friction. Friction could be applied intentionally to achieve desirable effects such as human values or fair competition (Ohm and Frankle 2019). Slowing things down could also serve as a form of political opposition (Madsen, Mikkelsen, and Moynihan 2021) or administrative burden (Herd and Moynihan 2019). All forms of friction, however, open up mechanisms for evaluating the hidden individual burdens of organizational efficiency.

How do data scientists get feedback and whose gaze dominates that process? This chapter reflects on how to spot unethical data science by identifying when claims of organizational efficiency actually impose demands on multiple people. Organizational clerical responsibilities will subtly shift to individual administrative burdens. Using efficiency claims to justify automated systems could be counterbalanced with the procedural burden of attention to correcting decisions. This mechanism reveals new forms of accountability that could systematically handle predictive errors that occur at scale.

1.2 Research Ethics: Accountability

Accountability endorses repercussions for bad behavior. Research ethics is not just about doing things well but enforcing penalties for deception or actions that cause suffering. The 1994 Menlo Report on research ethics explicitly called for accountability as a core principle for information technology studies. The Menlo Report acknowledges the possibilities of malicious actors intentionally breaking laws and the need to mitigate harms no matter why or how they occurred (U.S. Department of Homeland Security et al. 2012). Extending the earlier 1979 Belmont Report, this document on digital research ethics urged clear compliance and transparency in an attempt to mitigate practices that perpetuate harm (U.S. Department of Health, Education, and Welfare and National Commission for the Protection of Human Subjects of Biomedical and Behavioral Research 1979). For biomedical and social science researchers, these obligations are triggered in the planning process. Data scientists are not restricted in planning predictive research but may have additional responsibilities when predictive systems are broadly integrated into social systems.

Research participants must not be unduly influenced by restrictions, controls, or advantages. Traditional research ethics limits study participation by designating special rules for some groups, described as vulnerable populations. Research ethics guidelines on vulnerable populations, such as children or imprisoned people, are highly proscribed to avoid coercion. It is important to note that vulnerable people can take autonomous actions. A child can refuse to answer the questions. An incarcerated person can go on a hunger strike. Vulnerable populations may demonstrate free will within a fairly constrained system, yet someone else controls the shape of their daily lives and may be held responsible for their well-being.

The US research regulations define a vulnerable population as a group of people with diminished autonomy. A truly autonomous research participant is not coerced. Rewards are not given to show preferences. One difficulty in avoiding rewards and preferences is that participants are often given an experimental treatment. The literature on ethics stresses the need for blind or double-blind experiments to bypass social coercion between the researcher and participants.

Coercion on digital systems looks different. Digital systems can easily mask ethical problems, including who is the primary actor, who receives the harmful action, and when actions occur. Harms with digital technology cut across a wide range of areas, including privacy, intellectual property rights, human rights, identity theft, nonconsensual photos, deep fakes, and other forms of digital deception (Citron 2022). In this sense, everyone on digital platforms has the potential for some exposure to vulnerability. Vulnerable populations cannot be isolated as they are in research studies.

The digital environment changes a fundamental aspect of accountability. The predictive system may not be able to monitor itself appropriately and only the organization who created it truly knows everyone impacted. If something goes very wrong, the organization may not have an incentive to acknowledge problems. While some intentionally avoid responsibility, many people may not be able to see the data science prediction's faults. They simply do not notice the problems or register them as important. The small numbers negatively impacted, the social status of people pleased with the results, or simply the relief of some success gives false assurance. Worse, the people within the system may become so objectified and stigmatized that their feedback could be summarily dismissed.

Predictive data science accountability often comes from those outside the system. Getting feedback from everyone, even stigmatized users, becomes crucial to identify patterns between individual sufferers. Understanding accountability in predictive supply chains requires an enhanced awareness of whose views are present in the production process. It is only through collective action or publicity that the scope of the problem becomes visible.

1.3 Fighting the System with Attention

Local news anchor Anne McCloy knew how to get the attention of the New York State unemployment office and helped her town register for benefits online in 2020. It started with one news segment about the difficulties of filing for unemployment and ballooned into processing over thirty-five hundred digital applications. The COVID-19 pandemic stopped the economy, revealing the importance of social safety nets and their digital fragility. Means-testing social welfare programs create more paperwork than universal programs in which everyone is automatically enrolled. US means-tested unemployment applications jumped in March 2020, yet states paid out only 14 percent of claims by the end of the month. The number stretched to 47 percent of claims by April but still far below the obvious need (Christensen et al. 2020). The disparity in who has the support to file means-tested paperwork gives the advantage to those with high social capital (Christensen et al. 2020). But not everyone has a friendly local television personality to help people fill out vague digital forms.

Applicants seeking public services have full responsibility for appropriately navigating a system that may seem mysterious and could intentionally be difficult. Dorothy E. Roberts in her 2022 book *Torn Apart: How the Child Welfare System Destroys Black Families—And How Abolition Can Build a Safer World* describes how forms reduce and objectify families who must interact with child protective services or social welfare systems. Participants are forced to embrace the system's restricted representation of themselves to receive benefits. Applicants being evaluated in person for a social program had to curb behavior, speech, and other mannerisms to demonstrate compliance. The shallow normative assessments necessary to receive welfare benefits are now transferred into many interactions with the digital state.

Automated digital systems may not be fully explained, and predictive dependencies can be hard to find. Each stage in navigating a government algorithm embeds possibly high-risk choices that may not be clear to the applicant. For example, a dual-citizenship family who completed the US Department of State digital entry system successfully for fifteen years of vacation visits changed one field and suddenly was barred entry to the country. Not only did the non-US citizen miss the funeral, but the delay to get an answer to possibly enter the country again lasted two years. Just like going against a large bureaucracy, confronting an algorithm requires equal tenacity and courage.

Civic tech advocates and data scientists need to be aware that technology may be a tool to intentionally place additional testing on some populations for political purposes. Governments have an incentive to reduce access to programs because the money saved will increase budgets (Herd and Moynihan 2019). The civic tech firm Civilla simplified Michigan State paper applications into a single digital form for multiple social programs. The project saved the time of both applicants and government officials. This seemed ideal, but no one asked why the original paper forms contained intrusive questions, such as the date of conception for each child, as well as an explanation for choosing that date.

Predictive data science introduces a new type of subordination, one that revolves around symbolic interpretation.

Patricia Hill Collins developed a theory of oppression that expresses how subordination is continually enacted through domination. Oppression is based on three structural dimensions: the institutional, the symbolic, and the individual (Collins 1993). Institutional structures dominate by controlling the range of possible actions. Symbolic structures control through descriptions and attributes. Individual people engage in inhabited and embodied acts of interpersonal oppression. Collins's framework is useful for understanding epistemological problems in predictive algorithms that considers how knowledge is created. Central to this conceptualization is the role of symbols in administering penalties or privileges. Like the families in crisis that Roberts (2022) describes being forced into submissive behaviors, all users of digital systems must be sensitive to how algorithms might negatively categorize them.

Algorithms mix math with moral through quantitative and cultural symbols. Predictive systems contain symbolic representations that are deeply embedded within institutional definitions (Solow-Niederman, Choi, and Van den Broeck 2019) that demand certain performative responses (Gilliard 2020). Algorithmic performances shape the legitimacy of the feedback given to the system. In the case of the Australian Robodebt system, the input from people accused of fraud was dismissed as inconsequential complaints. Only people who were deemed as legitimate applicants were allowed to give negative feedback about the system.

The automated administrative state implements its statutory duty by leveraging algorithms, large-scale digital resources, machine learning, and data science to digitize public policy (Calo and Citron 2021). Predictive data science can shift the balance between augmenting human decisions and thwarting decisions (Bader and Kaiser 2019). For decades executive decision-making relied on information systems technology that would describe, select, arrange, or predict in relation to defined goals using internal and mostly structured data sources (Stohr and Viswanathan 1999). Items could be readily compared (Espeland and Stevens 1998) because these closed systems contained consistent symbolic interpretations. Management information systems eventually blossomed into automated decision systems that mix internal data with third-party sources leading to more elusive meaning-making. More people have to understand and interpret the meaning of predictive data systems.

1.4 Feedback Failures

Predictive data systems need feedback but often fail to get information they need when people drop out of the system altogether. A failure to notice or fix these situations condemns predictive systems to survival bias. In statistical analysis, survival or survivorship bias is the problem of evaluating success based on the cases that were able to make it through the system while overlooking the cases that did not last as long.

Facial recognition as identity solidifies this type of feedback failure. Research has demonstrated that facial technologies only work on one section of the population, leaving most people with inaccurate or unreadable results (Buolamwini and Gebru 2018).

The state of California implemented a new unemployment system that verified claimants by matching a selfie to a driver's license photo. A first-time unemployment claimant had all the documentation to file but never got past the initial authentication step because the selfie photo taken at home was rejected and could not be matched to the government-issued photo (Sato 2021). JB, an artist in Los Angeles, lost a retail job during the pandemic and was unable to get unemployment benefits. The photo identification system did not recognize JB. The predictive algorithm did not consider that people may significantly change hair and facial characteristics over three years. The procedures necessary to compensate for a predictive data failure can be laborious. JB eventually gave up seeking a resolution when confronted with multiple failed authentications, long waits for phone assistance, and no response to filed paperwork. Many people using the same facial analytics technology for government verification ended up stymied. The ID.me system, which was implemented widely during the 2020 pandemic crisis, claims that they do not discriminate. If asked, it is unlikely that the California government would proclaim that the system was only for normative gender-conforming people with consistent hair styles and facial features, yet in effect the system seemed to function seamlessly for that group.

Efficient systems handle frequently occurring cases with minimal effort. The cars move fast with an extra lane. A mobile phone selfie speeds authentication without an office visit. If efficiency expedites most cases, by definition, a subset cannot be handled as quickly. A car has mechanical problems during rush hour. An informal snapshot does not match a photo taken with bureaucratic precision. While these situations cannot be handled as quickly as the others, was it necessary to have them lead to complete rejection or catastrophe?

How the automated administrative state handles exceptional cases reveals its ability to protect the public interest. Most technology is skewed toward efficiency that streamlines outcomes for predictable cases. Public sector systems have a unique challenge to make services available to all, unlike the private sector, which creates and caters to specific markets (Margetts, 6, and Hood 2010). Despite examples demonstrating the potential for harms, the automated administrative state purports to continue its mission to serve everyone with advanced digital systems.

Understanding when efficiency fails is one way to isolate and solve problems within predictive data science. Predictive systems so easily shift the organization's administrative work onto individual users, especially those who have an atypical situation. Poorly conceived predictions and inadequate explanations are often viewed as technical failures when actually they are epistemological failures. The system cannot explain how it produces new knowledge, which in this case, would be predictive insights. Scholars have made similar observations of how bureaucratic systems function.

1.5 Administrative Burden

Extremely rigid administrative systems can exact a cost on people forced to engage with them. The public administration literature calls this administrative burden (Christensen et al. 2020; Herd and Moynihan 2019; Moynihan, Herd, and Harvey 2015).

Predictive data systems that claim organizational efficiency often actually levy administrative burdens on individuals en masse. Responsibility for solving a mistake or finding systemic errors shifts from the organization to the individual whose reputation is at stake. Predictive system burdens may consistently fall on subpopulations that are not the efficiency ideal, which, taken together with other social conditions, can exacerbate inequality at scale.

Pamela Herd and Donald Moynihan, in their research on administrative burden, identified trends in the procedures for applying for social services such as unemployment, public health benefits, and food assistance across multiple states and regions in the United States (Herd and Moynihan 2019; Moynihan, Herd, and Harvey 2015). US social policy exacted three types of costs to applicants: learning, psychological, and compliance (Moynihan, Herd, and Harvey 2015). The initial burden was to simply learn about the program, its eligibility requirements, and access methods. Participation in these programs might also come with the psychological costs of stigma for seeking assistance, and stress from the uncertainty of receiving it. Finally, participants face penalties for failure to comply to state-sanctioned regulation of personal behavior.

Political pressure or agency discretion create extra layers of work that in essence reduce access to social programs. For instance, one estimate is that only 10 percent of eligible unemployed people in North Carolina receive any benefits (Herd and Moynihan 2019). These numbers are not unusual. Tennessee routinely drops Medicaid-enrolled children from the program via an onerous recertification process. The state handles social service renewals solely on paper forms delivered through the postal service. Mail-in forms often do not reach target populations, mostly because poorer families move frequently. Those families who failed to complete the forty-seven-page form, mailed it late, or made errors lost benefits. Subsequently, one out of ten Tennessee children enrolled in Medicaid in 2018 lost their benefits after the first year (Herd and Moynihan 2019). Researchers observed that food insecurity and uncertain employment, along with the stress of engaging with the agencies, devastated people when they have the lowest ability to use executive functioning (Christensen et al. 2020).

Politicians can claim to champion the social safety net, despite restricting access through stringent eligibility tests. Administrative burdens give politicians a means to insert partisan decisions within procedural systems to explicitly avoid political debate (Stohr and Viswanathan 1999). Scholars note that these administrative tricks are deliberate cost-saving features intended to save money since few people can meet the demands for program enrollment (Bader and Kaiser 2019; Elyounes 2021; Rose, Persson, and Heeager 2015). Administrative burdens serve two opposing political benefits: popular social policy and limited government spending.

Algorithmic systems allow for a new form of political distance from policy decisions. Data science may computerize or strengthen public policy designed to coerce populations or exploit confusion. Sometimes it is not that the technology does not work, it is that the predictive system prioritizes previously hidden political agendas.

People struggling against predictive systems face the pernicious problem of finding out how the algorithms establish calculated claims. This is especially difficult because it requires understanding how and why the organization generates knowledge. While predictive systems initially promise to support applicants, they actually can increase an applicant's learning burden. In addition to mastering the rules, applicants for social programs now also have to become proficient in how the organization implements access or eligibility through algorithms.

The tendency to create endless bureaucratic loops is not limited to government. Research on dark patterns emphasizes the labyrinth of procedures that the private sector deploys so customers are kept on email lists, pay subscription fees, or are registered for unwanted rewards programs. Like the changing road signs on the smart motorways, we are all now required to pay close attention to organizational whimsy just to stay alive.

1.6 Automated Burdens

Predictive data science automates administrative burdens. Driven solely by financial motives, predictive algorithms often fail when confronting other value systems such as fairness or due process. Governments are particularly susceptible to this when, in an attempt to save money, they automate while ignoring less quantifiable aspects of the social contract.

Australia's welfare system, nicknamed Robodebt, automatically charged indigent people with fraud, sending them into further poverty when they could not challenge the automated system. Accused applicants had to prove they were innocent, without any clear knowledge of how they were determined to be guilty (Royal Commission 2023). The government ruined the credit of anyone who received overpayments and also gave them a criminal record (Parliament of Australia 2021). The algorithm indulged in circular reasoning. Some applicants who were accused of and eventually classified as a criminal did nothing more than accept the system's estimate of their payment (Henriques-Gomes 2020). The algorithm predicted welfare fraud but in many cases also created the circumstances of the overpayment in the first place. In order to disprove a data-generated claim, each person had to learn the organization's symbolic language embedded in the algorithm. In legislative hearings, it became clear that people accused of fraud could not estimate their two-week income accurately within the window calculated by the algorithm.

While the Australian government wanted to claim technological efficiency, it would be hard to dismiss the extreme friction experienced by the over seven hundred thousand people accused of fraud. To try to clear their name, people had to wait in long queues, hire lawyers, and file additional paperwork. The Robodebt program might have been an honest mistake in implementing a new system, but the politicians made it clear they wanted to blemish people who rely on social services. The predictive system enabled the subordination of entire subpopulations at scale.

Robodebt is not alone among government systems attempting to automate fraud detection in social welfare systems. In the United States, Michigan created an automated welfare payment system which attempted to identify fraud. The algorithm made several general assumptions about income that routinely overpaid welfare benefits. The state then required that the people on welfare pay the state back, with interest.

The Dutch automated family welfare system fell into a similar trap. The government in the Netherlands reimburses parents for family care. In the wake of a scandal where a non-Dutch company scammed the system, the government wanted to automatically detect similar corruption. One private childcare provider set up its system in a way that was later flagged as inappropriate. Parents had no control over whether their childcare provider subsequently fell out of favor with the government's model for legitimacy, yet any parent who sent their child to that childcare service was accused of fraud. Furthermore, an accusation of attempting to defraud the government ruined families and their finances. Parents had to reimburse the government, while the private firm with the dubious reputation kept any government money received.

The organization's gaze was dominant in the predictive data systems in the Netherlands, Michigan, and Australia. And money was the only thing these predictive systems could see. Fiscal motives are often the primary cause for the administrative state to transition to predictive data science. The outside vendors who developed the systems received a percentage of the money recovered, creating additional financial incentives to find overpayments and to recover funds. The quality of the source data in Australia may have caused some of the confusion, but because finance was the dominant value system, numbers were trusted over people. Money dominated every priority, from creating the system, to motivating the algorithm designers and enacting the prediction.

Fiscal efficiency alone can result in poorly designed systems that often cost more than the money they save. Think again about how the Australian government spent US$1.8 billion to compensate for the imperfect predictions in the Robodebt scandal. Or the state of Michigan generating $60 million in revenue from accusations of fraud from its unemployment system but having to pay $100 million in damages. And how the Netherlands sanctioned families for enrolling with a state-sanctioned provider instead of the suspicious company itself. All three examples show how financial efficiency is insufficient for understanding how social programs interact with government budget practices and political incentives.

Organizations rely on predictive algorithms to minimize operational effort and maximize organizational results. Efficiency dominates the logic in government systems (Rose, Persson, and Heeager 2015). While new technology offers enhanced legitimacy for organizations, it can stigmatize anyone who does not meet its, often unknown, normative standard. It may take significant amounts of time to appeal an algorithm's accusation. Poorly designed predictive systems claim organizational efficiency while shifting risk and administrative labor to the users by exacting extreme procedural penalties. The additional work placed on these people can be explained by understanding how the attention economy intersects with administrative burdens to produce algorithms that fail at efficiency, and in fact create new forms of harms.

Automated burdens are implemented solely from the perspective of the organization with little consideration for people, especially anyone disgraced by the algorithm. An adjustment from the organization's gaze to an individual's gaze may begin to address automated burdens.

1.7 Whose Gaze?

Whose gaze dominates responses to the predictive systems?

There is power in an ability to direct attention and concentrate focus. A gaze can limit the agency of a person being predominantly valued for only one aspect of their humanity. A gaze can objectify a person creating an "other" as much as it also distorts the experience of the in-group with its unilateral perspective.

Predictive systems focus on serving the majority. And rightly so. This is the goal of efficient and functioning systems. Attention on this group is essential for successful implementation. However, there may be a high price to pay for that success if other perspectives are not taken into consideration. Ethical data science focuses attention on the power asymmetries in claims of success for predictive systems.

Predictions are implemented and are interpreted within social worlds that may have important feedback. Responses to the predictive system may emphasize due process, fairness, or accountability over financial costs. An ability to seek feedback and diversify sources for input could significantly improve operations and accountability.

1.8 Procedural Attention

Giving feedback to predictive data systems has an inherent cost. In situations where the predictive decision has a systemic blind spot, it pressures perhaps thousands of people to contend with a broken system individually. This occasional inefficiency stands in stark contrast to promised productivity gains. It forces anyone interacting with the automated system to bear the psychological costs of stigma when it does not work for them. Furthermore, people also confront high compliance penalties in the face of algorithmic accusations. It takes time away from earning income, leisure, or caring for family. Individuals end up serving the organization instead of focusing and giving attention to their personal lives. Unlike an economic penalty that focuses on the exchange of goods and services with a price mechanism, predictive data technology fails by exacting an unmanageable time and effort cost, which I call "procedural attention."

Procedural attention is an administrative burden placed on users to successfully interact with a predictive system. Here, attention is directed toward the organization and its symbolic structures (Collins 1993). Diverting attention from participation in personal, civic, or economic life, procedural attention instead prioritizes an individual's adherence to symbols defined by the organization.

These failures generate a flurry of possible responses. One response is frustration and avoidance, as in the case of an unemployment claimant who gave up because California's software could not authenticate their face. Capitulation is another choice, such as the welfare recipients who paid the state of Michigan when it accused them of fraud. Another reaction is to resist using nonpredictive systems, such as the thousands of phone calls about Robodebt that overloaded staff, breaking all government claims to efficiency. Many others resist by studying the symbolic systems embedded in the algorithms and sharing how the predictive system creates knowledge. The thousands of solo civil suits as well as class action lawsuits against governments in Australia, Michigan, and the Netherlands show yet another response.

The goal of procedural attention is to shift responsibility and the weight of administrative tasks onto those who do not understand the policy and who have no insight into the algorithmic structure. It is a form of information asymmetry. Building on the conceptualization of the attention economy, concentration is seen as valuable. Timothy Wu (2016) noted that the extraction of advertising when people are compelled to be somewhere is a form of attentional theft. Procedural attention is closely aligned with this form of captive attention but is not confined to advertising.

Behavioral economists are aware of the interplay between incentives and procedures. Nudge, popularized by Cass Sunstein and Richard H. Thaler, is often illustrated with automatic retirement plan enrollment that encourages action (Sunstein 2018, 2020; Thaler 2018). They complement the concept of nudge with sludge to address both positive and negative incentives. While nudge removes procedural institutional barriers, sludge inserts friction (Sunstein 2018). Sludge does not consider deliberate misdirection or coercive power. Procedural attention attempts to move beyond intentions and incentives to focus on the system itself.

Most inimical are systems that sublimate human attention at a time of great need, which is why people are likely reaching toward external resources, such as unemployment benefits. The COVID-19 pandemic technology solutions from the private sector provide another stark example of this. Procedural attention becomes a net deficit when these people are subsequently less visible and valuable in the advertising attention economy.

The automated administrative state provides opportunities to systematically study abuses of power within predictive data science. Corporations and nonprofits have less transparency, so most of the examples here are based on parliamentary inquiries into public sector systems. Yet procedural attention describes harms extracted by both the public and private sectors.

While these cases focus on governments, the same could be said for any organizational system that offloads administrative burdens to individuals. The literature on dark patterns explores how corporations use similar tricks. Dark patterns extract attention through deception that intrudes and then locks people into behaviors that divert them from their personal goals. It is an intentional assault on free will, usurping individual priorities in favor of goals of the organization controlling the system. Procedural attention is why dark patterns are dangerous.

Predictive systems that fail to adequately prepare for unexpected cases undermine their own self-governance. This dynamic is particularly acute when a data science system predicts illegal or socially shameful behavior and immediately sanctions anyone who fails to meet its definitions. Because this is often the only feedback these systems receive and it is likely from stigmatized subpopulations seeking remedies, many organizations will dismiss the information. This blocks opportunities to improve the system during implementation. It is also a vicious cycle that can prop up poorly constructed automated systems.

An emphasis on feedback and resilience is one mechanism for establishing something other than price as the observable criteria in analyzing harms that happen at scale. Understanding predictive data science as not merely a tool of organizational efficiency but as a potential carrier of mass administrative burdens opens new avenues for evaluation. Abuse of state power could be tracked though transfer of government administrative burdens. Procedural attention could be a test of abuse of market power in antitrust law.

Algorithmic predictions rely on symbolic interpretation more than math, which make them particularly challenging to contradict. Procedural attention, or the administrative burden to deconstruct the algorithm's symbolic system, is most acute when trying to prove an algorithm wrong. Data science in the public interest must contend with less common situations to ensure digital service for everyone.

1.9   Ethical Data Science Feedback

What is the method for getting feedback on your prediction supply chain? This final stage is the critical link in deployment because it directly connects the commissioning organization to the individuals living with the organization's predictions.

First, feedback can give an independent evaluation of whether the system is functional. The people sponsoring the algorithm and the people who build the algorithm both have incentives to hide problems with their predictive systems. Professional independent assessments can run thorough quality assurance routines such as a privacy impact statement (Bamberger and Mulligan 2008). Assessors who are employed by the commissioning organization could be compromised through that business relationship. Feedback directly from the people experiencing the algorithm is ideal, although crowdsourced feedback can be more difficult to manage. Strive for some methodology to incorporate responses during implementation to determine if there is a previously undetected pattern.

Second, before launching the system, the organization commissioning the prediction should get some ethical feedback. An ethical evaluation may point to the success rate of the algorithm across multiple subpopulations (O'Neil 2016). This will allow the organization to be aware of who may be consistently experiencing suboptimal results and mitigate for those situations. In the case of Ofqual's 2020 college admissions scandal, the organization realized that high-performing students from low-performing schools would be unusually burdened by their predictive algorithm (Specia 2020). If Ofqual could have taken clear steps to mitigate the issues with that important subpopulation, it might have avoided the many subsequent problems it had with implementation.

Finally, consider how risk will be mitigated in the prediction supply chain. All supply chains are exposed to disasters or disruptions in coordination (Kleindorfer and Saad 2005). Few prediction supply chains actively engage in risk management. Predictive systems that rely on data must expect other shocks as definitions and contexts change. Data-driven predictions calculate the likelihood of continuing trends and are most efficient for determining typical outcomes in stable digital environments. Efficient systems can easily fail when trying to operate outside of original or known conditions (Petroski 2012). The case of Google Flu Trends illustrates the struggles to maintain valid predictions over time (Lazer et al. 2014). Organizations may be tempted to "sweat the asset," which in business circles means keeping something in production, possibly even past its useful life. A predictive system is simply not the same as a printer or other equipment. Replacement and updates of automated digital systems are not straightforward. Another aspect of risk is to understand when an established predictive system becomes too unstable to keep it in operation (Maguire and Hardy 2013). Predictive technologies should be able to know their tipping point. Deferred maintenance can increase liability exposure. Determine which symbolic, process, or industry signals may indicate potential upcoming problems and know how to incorporate that feedback to improve the system.

Independent assessments can provide functional and ethical feedback that can lead to improvements. Ethical prediction supply chains have sufficient internal oversight and management that data scientists have the ability to incrementally improve their work.

1.10 Paperwork Reduction Act for Algorithms

The prediction supply chain can have aftereffects like other industrial systems. A new factory could poison the water. A new mine can lead to erosion and landslides. Predictive data science that leaves over one million people trying to individually solve mistakes is not only inefficiency at its best, it leads to broad violations of human rights law with little access to evidence. A formal way of observing collective errors as quickly as they occur is rare. The myth of the paperless office may still be debated, but digital bureaucracies always require electronic questionnaires. This section proposes a methodology to evaluating predictive algorithms similar to the 1974 Paperwork Reduction Act (PRA). The irony of including both algorithms and paperwork in the same idea underscores the inefficiencies of some data science systems.

Other proposals include post hoc analysis of predictive systems with regulatory penalties, audits (O'Neil 2016), or ethical evaluations (Bender et al. 2021). A proactive approach might include implementing human-centered design, privacy impact assessments, and compliance checklists. Yet audits and post hoc evaluations are like using forensic analysis of poisonous hot dogs instead of food regulations that prevent harm in the first place.

Since 1974, the US federal government requires every agency to estimate the amount of time it takes to complete a government form in an attempt to reduce the amount of paperwork. While not always popular, the PRA provides a benchmark. A similar evaluation may be able to assess how predictive systems handle feedback. It would not be necessary to solely rely on the credibility of the person making the critique.

A PRA for algorithms would provide observable evidence for standardized feedback. How many steps are necessary to dispute a claim of unemployment fraud? How many pages does it take to report harassment? How many clicks are necessary to turn off a subscription service? Answering these empirical questions may begin to provide some clarity and balance to promotional zeal about predictive systems that save organizations money. If we could specify that addressing an algorithm's accusation required two hours, five steps, and twenty-eight pages of forms, we would begin to capture the actual costs of predictive data technology. This proposed regulatory rule needs additional research. Scholars could develop methodologies that better estimate postprediction administrative burdens.

The tools used to limit public expenditures are also used to maintain profits. The dark patterns in the private sector are as onerous as the administrative burdens of the public sector. These estimates could either analyze a mobile app subscription or evaluate a social service application.

It is time to systematically address the demands for procedural attention extracted by organizations. With better evidence, administrative burdens could become more visible and a positive force for improving predictive systems. This mechanism could establish a new standard to evaluate commercial and government predictive systems.

1.11   Thinking Like a Detective

Data scientists who think like detectives understand when they are leaving behind clues that will help or distract someone from solving the case. Most people receiving an algorithmic accusation will have to become detectives to save their reputation. People will want to understand how the data science works, what it prioritizes, and why it left behind these clues and not others.

Detectives investigate crimes by looking at what happened after the fact. Solving crimes means weighing possible motives against forensic evidence. Most liberal arts colleges do not have a department for detectives, but they do have language arts and rhetoric scholars.

The art of using symbols as traces of meaning has always been with us. Rhetoric is often connected to classical scholarship. Data science creates its own grammar, discourse, and symbols that can be as impenetrable to the uninitiated as Aristotle's Greek. Predictions are communicated and should make sense within existing human systems of beliefs, attitudes, morals, and values. Understanding the rhetoric of data science is as important as scientific and mathematical skills.

Thinking like a detective means sharing sufficient information for someone else to interpret and understand the symbolic origins of data science predictions.

1.12   Chapter 6 Summary

This chapter argues that ethical data science requires redefining efficiency. Predictive algorithms cannot only render services for the mainstream and ignore everyone else. Otherwise, predictive data science operates under adverse inclusion, where some people may participate only with high expenditures of time and attention. Automated decision systems carry mass administrative burdens under the veneer of organizational efficiency. Understanding this shift to procedural attention opens new avenues for balancing costs and benefits. Data science in the public interest must contend with less common situations to ensure digital service for everyone.

References

Bader, Verena, and Stephan Kaiser. 2019. "Algorithmic Decision-Making? The User Interface and Its Role for Human Involvement in Decisions Supported by Artificial Intelligence." *Organization* 26 (5): 655–72. https://doi.org/10.1177/1350508419855714.

Bamberger, Kenneth A., and Deirdre K. Mulligan. 2008. "Privacy Decisionmaking in Administrative Agencies." *University of Chicago Law Review* 75 (1): 75–108. https://www.jstor.org/stable/20141901.

Bender, Emily M., et al. 2021. "On the Dangers of Stochastic Parrots: Can Language Models Be Too Big?" In *Proceedings of the 2021 ACM Conference on Fairness, Accountability, and Transparency*. Virtual Event Canada: ACM, 610–23. https://doi.org/10.1145/3442188.3445922.

Bozeman, Barry, and Patrick Scott. 1996. "Bureaucratic Red Tape and Formalization: Untangling Conceptual Knots." *The American Review of Public Administration* 26 (1): 1–17. https://doi.org/10.1177/027507409602600101.

Buolamwini, Joy, and Timnit Gebru. 2018. "Gender Shades: Intersectional Accuracy Disparities in Commercial Gender Classification." *Proceedings of Machine Learning Research* 81 (February): 77–91.

Calo, Ryan, and Danielle Citron. 2021. "The Automated Administrative State: A Crisis of Legitimacy." *Emory Law Journal* 70 (4): 797.

Christensen, Julian, et al. 2020. "Human Capital and Administrative Burden: The Role of Cognitive Resources in Citizen-State Interactions." *Public Administration Review* 80 (1): 127–36. https://doi.org/10.1111/puar.13134.

Citron, Danielle Keats. 2022. *The Fight for Privacy: Protecting Dignity, Identity, and Love in the Digital Age*. 1st ed. New York: W.W. Norton & Company, Inc.

Collins, Patricia Hill. 1993. "Toward a New Vision: Race, Class, and Gender as Categories of Analysis and Connection." *Race, Sex & Class* 1 (1): 25–45.

Elyounes, Doaa. 2021. "'Computer Says No!': The Impact of Automation on the Discretionary Power of Public Officers." *Vanderbilt Journal of Entertainment & Technology Law* 23 (3): 451.

Espeland, Wendy Nelson, and Mitchell L. Stevens. 1998. "Commensuration as a Social Process." *Annual Review of Sociology* 24 (1): 313–43. https://doi.org/10.1146/annurev.soc.24.1.313.

Gilliard, Chris. 2020. "The Two Faces of the Smart City." *Fast Company*, January 20, 2020. https://www.fastcompany.com/90453305/the-two-faces-of-the-smart-city.

Henriques-Gomes, Luke. 2020. "All Centrelink Debts Raised Using Income Averaging Unlawful, Christian Porter Concedes." *The Guardian*, May 31, 2020, sec. Australia news. https://www.theguardian.com/australia-news/2020/may/31/all-centrelink-debts-raised-using-income-averaging-unlawful-christian-porter-concedes.

Herd, Pamela, and Donald P. Moynihan. 2019. *Administrative Burden*. New York: Russell Sage Foundation.

Kleindorfer, P.R., and G.H. Saad. 2005. "Managing Disruption Risks in Supply Chains." *Production and Operations Management* 14 (1): 53–68.

Lazer, David, et al. 2014. "The Parable of Google Flu: Traps in Big Data Analysis." *Science* 343 (6176): 1203–05. https://doi.org/10.1126/science.1248506.

Madsen, Jonas K., Kim S. Mikkelsen, and Donald P. Moynihan. 2021. "Burdens, Sludge, Ordeals, Red Tape, Oh My!: A User's Guide to the Study of Frictions." *Public Administration* 100 (2): 375–93.. https://doi.org/10.1111/padm.12717.

Maguire, Steve, and Cynthia Hardy. 2013. "Organizing Processes and the Construction of Risk: A Discursive Approach." *Academy of Management Journal* 56 (1): 231. https://doi.org/10.5465/amj.2010.0714.

Margetts, Helen, Perri 6, and Christopher Hood. 2010. *Paradoxes of Modernization: Unintended Consequences of Public Policy Reform*. Oxford; New York: Oxford University Press.

Moynihan, Donald, Pamela Herd, and Hope Harvey. 2015. "Administrative Burden: Learning, Psychological, and Compliance Costs in Citizen-State Interactions." *Journal of Public Administration Research and Theory* 25 (1): 43–69. https://doi.org/10.1093/jopart/muu009.

Ohm, Paul, and Jonathan Frankle. 2019. "Desirable Inefficiency." *Florida Law Review* 70 (4): 777.

O'Neil, Cathy. 2016. *Weapons of Math Destruction: How Big Data Increases Inequality and Threatens Democracy*. New York: Crown.

Parliament of Australia. 2021. "Centrelink's Compliance Program." Parliamentary Inquiry. Canberra, Australia: Senate. Australia. https://www.aph.gov.au/Parliamentary_Business/Committees/Senate/Community_Affairs/Centrelinkcompliance.

Petroski, Henry. 2012. *To Forgive Design: Understanding Failure*. Cambridge, MA: Belknap Press of Harvard University Press.

Roberts, Dorothy E. 2022. *Torn Apart: How the Child Welfare System Destroys Black Families—And How Abolition Can Build a Safer World*. 1st ed. New York: Basic Books.

Rose, Jeremy, John Stouby Persson, and Lise Tordrup Heeager. 2015. "How E-Government Managers Prioritise Rival Value Positions: The Efficiency Imperative." *Information Polity* 20 (1): 35–59. https://doi.org/10.3233/IP-150349.

Royal Commission. 2023. "Royal Commission into the Robodebt Scheme." https://robodebt.royalcommission.gov.au/publications/report.

Sato, Mia. 2021. "The Pandemic Is Testing the Limits of Face Recognition." *MIT Technology Review*, September 28, 2021. https://www.technologyreview.com/2021/09/28/1036279/pandemic-unemployment-government-face-recognition/.

Solow-Niederman, Alicia, YooJung Choi, and Guy Van den Broeck. 2019. "The Institutional Life of Algorithmic Risk Assessment." *Berkeley Technology Law Journal* 34 (3): 705–44.

Specia, Megan. 2020. "Parents, Students and Teachers Give Britain a Failing Grade over Exam Results." *The New York Times*, August 17, 2020, sec. World. https://www.nytimes.com/2020/08/14/world/europe/england-a-level-results.html.

Spielberg, Steven, dir. 1993. *Jurassic Park*. https://www.imdb.com/title/tt0107290/.

Stohr, Edward A., and Sivakumar Viswanathan. 1999. "Recommendation Systems: Decision Support for the Information Economy." In *Classics of Organization*

Theory, edited by Jay M. Shafritz and J. Steven Ott. 5th ed., 520–35. Belmont, CA: Wadsworth/Harcourt College Publishers.

Sunstein, Cass R. 2018. "Sludge and Ordeals." *Duke Law Journal* 68 (8): 1843–83. https://doi.org/10.2139/ssrn.3288192.

Thaler, Richard H. 2018. "Nudge, Not Sludge." *Science*, August. https://doi.org/10.1126/science.aau9241.

U.S. Department of Health, Education, and Welfare,. 1979. "The Belmont Report. Ethical Principles and Guidelines for the Protection of Human Subjects of Research." National Commission for the Protection of Human Subjects of Biomedical and Behavioral Research.   https://www.hhs.gov/ohrp/regulations-and-policy/belmont-report/index.html.

U.S. Department of Homeland Security, et al. 2012. "The Menlo Report: Ethical Principles Guiding Information and Communication Technology Research." Cyber Security Division, U.S. Department of Homeland Security Science and Technology Directorate. https://www.dhs.gov/sites/default/files/publications/CSD-MenloPrinciplesCORE-20120803_1.pdf.

Wu, Tim. 2016. *The Attention Merchants: The Epic Scramble to Get Inside Our Heads.* 1st ed. New York: Alfred A. Knopf.

7

Conclusion

Prediction in the Public Interest

1. PREDICTION IN THE PUBLIC INTEREST

The prediction supply chain became popular as a closed system run by powerful organizations, but it does not have to stay this way. As one character in the film *Enemy of the State* (Scott 1998) says, big organizations are slow and exposed, while smaller groups are mobile and hidden.

It is a reminder that David can beat Goliath even in the digital world. All positions on the field hold some unique form of strength and leadership. While massive proprietary data infrastructures seem insurmountable, they are not invincible. Community-driven and locally focused organizations have a different form of power exactly because they are more nimble. Every data science mashup requires curation that unleashes possibilities for alternatives, change, or even pure magic.

The future of prediction is heading in the direction of social engineering, as seen in the "Selfish Ledger," a leaked video purported to come from Google (Savov 2018). History shows the danger in trying to nudge populations to the will of a few, even if well meaning. An alternative future for prediction could build on the algorithms that adjudicate contentious moral choices, such as the allocation of organs for kidney transplants (Robinson 2022).

Data science contributes to a long procession of tools intended to absorb information for human consumption through history. Yet human knowledge systems change as often as they are standardized. As algorithmic predictions become the dominant tool of institutions, social construction (Berger and Luckmann 1990) may be stagnated. Algorithms may be helpful for society but

Ethical Data Science. Anne L. Washington, Oxford University Press. © Oxford University Press 2023.
DOI: 10.1093/oso/9780197693025.003.0009

only in conjunction with institutional processes and procedures (Lawrence 2008) that allow for dynamic social change over time.

This concluding chapter provides two points of departure by situating predictive science as one step in the long chronicle of written human knowledge. First, library history suggests a path toward accepting the tension between financial interests and public memory. Second, advocacy for intellectual freedom may liberate the restrictions placed on who can learn from predictive science. In conclusion, outliers who resist domination by controlling their own digital material hold promise for the emergence of a radical tradition in data science.

1.1 History of the Data

The history of the book is what bibliographic scholars and historians call the steady dissemination of knowledge through the circulation of tablets, parchment, scrolls, or printed text. Future scholars who wish to establish how predictive findings contributed to the production of human knowledge may have far fewer artifacts to examine. Although often compared to a natural resource or physical labor, predictive science creates capital by producing new ideas to solve problems. Most data science is tightly held commercial property. In this section, I imagine what policies are necessary today to make robust future scholarship possible on the "history of the data."

The commercialization of knowledge is not new. Medieval books were more likely to be personal objects than communal ones (Sharpe 2019) just as books today are targeted to individual buyers. The publishing industry thrived and still flourishes by selling to private collectors and readers. Rich learned men wanted to amass their own set of knowledge, and booksellers were happy to sell to each aspiring scientist. Somehow, booksellers and libraries manage to coexist for centuries because of changing dynamics in commercial markets and political freedom.

Early book collectors commissioned editions for their own pleasure. The medieval book economy in the United Kingdom was geared toward serving the wealthy (Sharpe 2019). The estates of the first collectors transformed the book trade into one that valued historic publications. Booksellers in the fifteenth century began to sell previously owned volumes, creating the first rare book market (McKitterick 2018).

Political events intervened to make owning books that represented the wrong ideas undesirable. The momentary disruption in the individual book trade during the English Reformation facilitated the creation of communal collections, like libraries (McKitterick 2018). King Henry the VIII, in a disagreement with the Pope, sought to purge all books related to Catholicism. The dissolution of

Catholic monasteries sparked a great transfer of material from private to shared collections (Sharpe 2022). Book lovers avoided having their collections burned by donating to institutions such as universities. In 1598, Thomas Bodley donated his books and encouraged other gifts to a collection which became the Bodleian library at the University of Oxford (Clapinson 2020). Bodley also built the collection through mandatory deposits.

Booksellers and libraries both survived despite the inherent friction in giving access to marketable objects at no cost. Books, unlike unique valuable oil paintings, may appear in many parallel collections. Libraries in the United States are protected by "right of first sale," according to 17 U.S.C. 106(3), which allows them to loan and digitize books they own. Publishers handle the situation by sometimes charging a higher library price to offset long-term shared use. The 2020 pandemic lockdowns exacerbated unresolved controversy between publishers and libraries over price hikes, privacy, and restrictions on lending digital material (Gross 2021). Institutional and private sales, however, are both an expected part of today's book economy.

Catalogs and estate notices made it possible for modern bibliographers to piece together an intricate understanding of the English medieval book trade. History of the data scholars may not be as fortunate as historians of the medieval period. This period of commercial data collection has produced few resources available for study. Data science predictions, like early books, are commissioned by the wealthy and powerful and not available to the wider public. While only one person could own an illuminated manuscript, digital information is a nonrival resource that everyone can share simultaneously. Organizations that have paid to amass knowledge through prediction do not have any incentive to share what they have learned. Other mechanisms for sharing data science knowledge are necessary.

Books deposited for copyright now help to build national collections like the British Library or the Library of Congress. If we could use the copyright deposit process for sharing data sources, public data repositories could start to grow. Just as the death of the first book collectors started the rare book market, there could be formal ways to ensure that corporate collections do not go missing forever once those organizations fail. Perhaps data collections could be donated to public repositories when companies are sold, go bankrupt, or suffer some other institutional closing event. Sharing data is still a complicated task for scientific researchers (Darch and Knox 2017) and governments (Washington 2020), however, attempts to accumulate predictive digital evidence is essential for the progression of science and society.

A long-term perspective on data science taken today will be essential for future scholars to grasp what happened. While dismantling existing prediction supply chains may be appropriate in some cases, this chapter offers an alternative path where public interest supply chains exist in parallel or in opposition to commercial interests.

1.2 Freedom to Learn

Few people have the right to learn from predictive information. The Mechanical Turk workers who gave their data to Cambridge Analytica never gained insight into their own lives and friends. Australian welfare applicants never learned how the Robodebt algorithm calculated the fraud accusations they received. People whose data generated these insights rarely learn from them. Worse, predictions severely limit the range of options some populations have to act. Many social patterns that are generated through algorithms remain tightly held information.

Only a small group of politicians, executives, and technologists learn from the knowledge generated from predictive data science, and some exploit it to their advantage. Uber charged higher prices when they predicted that a phone with low battery strength would lose its charge before the end of the ride (Calo and Rosenblat 2017). A reliance on information asymmetry not only can be seen as a tool of coercion, it stifles intellectual freedom.

Intellectual freedom as championed by the American Library Association (ALA) is the right to learn information on an equitable basis. Neither the seeker nor the information itself is restricted in any way. Privacy was the core obligation of early professionalization as stated in the 1939 ALA Code of Ethics for Librarians (American Library Association 2017). The Enlightenment may have transformed Europe, but it was based on knowledge accumulated by a few wealthy book buyers. The librarian ethos of intellectual freedom and freedom of information is a response, in part, to the hoarding of knowledge by the powerful.

The accumulation of knowledge has always been contested as a source of power. Books have been banned, collectors jailed, and authors imprisoned (Battles 2015). Writing that advances non-Western or non-White perspectives represent too great a challenge for some. Book challenges in public and school libraries over critical race theory echo (Jaeger et al. 2023) earlier times when some information was deemed too dangerous to share. Banned books often reflect communities with less political power (Knox 2015). Libraries, always resourceful, still manage to make information available (Ovenden 2020). The Russian Communist Party in the mid twentieth century banned prominent authors overnight, causing mayhem for library catalogs. Soviet librarians were rumored to simply memorize shelf locations to avoid the never-ending task of purging books by enemies of the state.

Despite intellectual freedom being the hallmark of librarianship, libraries were not always open to all. Rome provided some of the earliest free libraries, yet access was denied to enslaved populations. The Baths of Trajan, essentially a public recreation center, contained a section for everyday Roman citizens to read scrolls, as long as they were male heads of households (Casson 2002). Similarly, anti-literacy laws in the United States criminalized reading for Black populations, making books effectively illegal (Ingram-Willis 2023). Even as Andrew Carnegie built public libraries as palaces for the people, Black Americans were denied access to library services (Gleason 1945). Access to the public library was part of civil rights efforts to desegregate schools starting as early as a 1929 case in Kanawha, West Virginia (Bailey 2009). The restrictions on gaining entry to collections of written knowledge demonstrates its importance in the balance of power.

An open forum of all ideas, without promotion or exclusion, is the moral center of modern librarianship in the United States (Knox 2023). Generating the digital cultural record solely through the private sector challenges the ability to maintain written knowledge systems across generations. The privatization of information through the consolidation of a few internet technology firms challenges this well-established norm in the production of human knowledge. The underlying premise is that through public access, knowledge can grow and expand.

To achieve intellectual freedom, data science must recognize its contributions to society and its origins as a commercial product. Data science is not a typewriter that remains blameless for the words it produces. It is an accumulation of user-generated content that represents a collective past through the rationale of the hosting platform. To contribute to the body of human knowledge, data science needs what the political theorist Joy James calls a "Revolutionary Love" that releases control over change (James 2022). Without relinquishing control, data science will sink into a pseudoscience for elites interested in justifying coercive speculation.

Once coveted weather information is openly available from most government agencies. No longer is the next rainstorm only shared with the politician's favorite industry or the technologist's best friends. Everyone can learn about weather predictions. Atmospheric data can still be repackaged in successful commercial systems, such as the Rain Parrot app that predicts within thirty minutes hyperlocal rainstorms in Australia. Prediction cannot be in the public interest if new patterns about society and the environment are not widely shared, debated, and challenged.

1.3 Deviant Data Science

Hackers who define themselves as whistleblowers release data with the goal of doing good (Manning 2014; Khatchadourian 2010). Other hack systems of expectations as a form of political discourse such as the 2019 Ally AI artwork that is a voice-assistant parody (Richardson and American Artist 2019). Artists, whistleblowers, and exasperated outliers are building technology that better represents their lived experience.

Creative responses to poorly constructed data science exposes the limited thinking behind some predictive goals. The New York City Police Department visualized arrest data as a crime heat map with bright colors to indicate more arrests, which they equated to high crime. Scholars analyzing city open data quickly noticed that the arrest rates and the conviction rates were not the same, arguing that the maps actually just represented police targeting of citizens in low-income neighborhoods (Goel, Rao, and Shroff 2016). The excellent scholarship and statistical analysis was still not as compelling as a white-collar crime heat map. The artists Brian Clifton, Sam Lavigne, and Francis Tseng extended the NYPD's same flawed logic to produce a map showing the concentration of Wall Street firms and bankers' homes to show the probability of financial fraud (Clifton, Lavigne, and Tseng 2017). Lighthearted subversive responses show analyzing data can go both ways. Digital traces can track both the powerful and the disempowered. Authorities looking down at the masses through surveillance can also be observed by a public looking up through sousveillance of the elite.

Art also illustrates the range of possible outcomes and underscores uncertainty that often eludes a desire for scientific precision. DNA may conjure up certainty at the end of a thriller, but it remains a field built on probability. One swab of DNA inspired an art installation of over two dozen portraits showing a range of skin hues, facial characteristics, and eye colors (Dewey-Hagborg and Manning 2017). Bioengineer and artist Heather Dewey-Hagborg created 3D portraits in collaboration with Chelsea E. Manning during her incarceration for releasing material that would become known as WikiLeaks. Data scientists have also confirmed the importance of interpretation in what is essentially an abductive science. More research that reveals the probabilistic nature of data science may better mark the line between real prediction and speculation.

Dignity of work motivates other alternative approaches to prediction. Digitally enabled as gig work, the informal economy in the United States maintains extreme information asymmetry with high stakes over people's livelihoods. Dashboards allow managers to observe workers but limit what workers can understand about the circumstances of their job (Nguyen 2021). Mechanical Turk workers organized to better understand how systems were manipulating their work life (Irani and Silberman 2013). Uber drivers have forums where they discuss how to get the algorithmic system to do what they need (Calo and Rosenblat 2017). Taxi drivers in New York City and San Diego formed new collectives so they can digitize based on their front-line expertise which will improve working conditions and passenger experiences, such as being able to work repeatedly in areas near their homes (Tandon et al. 2022).

Small-scale groups with no financial resources and little incentive to dominate others use data to self-organize. Decentralized autonomous organizations are a recent attempt to use emerging digital tools to create autonomy. Unlike extractive cryptocurrency scams, blockchain technology is supporting artists and creative talent looking to benefit from the long-term valuation of their work. A movement at the Open Data Institute called for investigations of community-led data-gathering efforts. Data sovereignty is starting the conversation about centering the knowledge of aboriginal, First Nation, and other peoples removed from their lands by settlers. From the aptly named Weather Underground to the Western Australia Rain Parrot app, communities are using their collective interests to make hyperlocal predictions. The Zooniverse citizen science project allows those with extra time to document galaxies. The Smithsonian Transcription Center asks volunteers to help transcribe items in museum collections, such as records from the Virginia Freedmen's Bureau. These "bottom-up" data institutions steward digital material that is essential to regional cultures, locations, or communities that can then be used for data analytics.

Some data scientists are building on the Black radical tradition that questions institutional structures that are designed to subordinate populations (Birhane et al. 2022). In these spaces, technology starts from the margins not the center, flipping existing narratives in search of solutions (Benjamin 2019). Informed by Afrofuturism, others imagine a destiny that starts with freedom and liberation from a dominant gaze (LaFleur 2019; Nelson 2002; Winchester 2018). In this way, stories and novels convey imaginaries of resistance.

Finally, activists and abolitionists point toward dismantling current systems altogether. In October 2022, the social media company Twitter made it possible to buy a verified account for a nominal fee. Immediately, parody accounts took over. The chemical conglomerate Eli Lilly for many years ran a Twitter account called @LillyPad, so the impostures made an account @EliLillyOfficial and promptly tweeted that insulin would be free. The tweet went viral and the price of the company to drop 4 percent, wiping off $400 million within a short period of time (Harwell 2022). The punk rock ethos behind these digital protests derail conversations about incremental improvements of the status quo. In doing so, they radically rescript ethical imaginaries for everyone.

If deviance is defined as being outside of traditional lines of power, then data science can certainly be deviant. Organizations that push society too far with predictions will unleash radical, subversive, and punk data responses. Reimagining predictive data science without coercive control is a possible step toward building prediction in the public interest.

1.4 Summary

Data science could be tailored to help individual people make decisions as much as it helps organizations function. Procedural fairness, rule of law, autonomy, conflict of interest, and other values are equally as important as technical, financial, and political considerations. Solutions to complex social issues could take into account the inherent political and commercial aspects of the prediction supply chain at each incremental stage in data science analysis: source, model, compare, optimize, learn. This book seeks to improve existing predictive systems while opening the possibility of resistance and renewal through data science done differently.

The governments and businesses that control predictive data science are driven by their own incentives. They have no moral or ethical obligation to provide a social good, especially one outside their core mandate. Predictive data technology was created to serve technocratic administrative needs, yet it has great possibility to serve everyone. Some argue that data science will never be useful, while others suggest that data science is the optimal solution. Advocates and opponents working together could counterbalance the organizational motives that currently tip the data science scales.

Speculation masquerading as prediction drives too much of contemporary data science. A new vision for data science would reflect noncommercial interests. Just as book publishers and libraries found ways to coexist, organizations could share some of their holdings as open data to provide for the public good. People whose detailed information become data could learn from the knowledge generated from their contribution to the aggregated analysis.

Prediction in the public interest is possible by acknowledging the moral choices embedded in data science, centering vulnerable populations, and being responsive to a broad range of humanity. And then perhaps, the outliers shall inherit the earth.

References

American Library Association. 2017. "ALA's Code of Ethics." May 19, 2017. https://www.ala.org/tools/ethics.

Bailey, Kenneth R. 2009. "The Other Brown v. Board of Education." *West Virginia History, New Series* 3 (2): 53–73. https://www.jstor.org/stable/43265122.

Battles, Matthew. 2015. *Library: An Unquiet History*. New York: W.W. Norton & Company.

Benjamin, Ruha. 2019. *Captivating Technology: Race, Carceral Technoscience, and Liberatory Imagination in Everyday Life*. Durham, NC; London UK: Duke University Press. doi.org/10.1515/9781478004493.

Berger, Peter L., and Thomas Luckmann. 1990. *The Social Construction of Reality: A Treatise in the Sociology of Knowledge*. New York: Anchor Books.

Birhane, Abeba et al. 2022. "Power to the People? Opportunities and Challenges for Participatory AI." In *EAAMO '22: Equity and Access in Algorithms, Mechanisms, and Optimization*, 1–8. Arlington, VA: ACM. https://doi.org/10.1145/3551624.3555290.

Calo, Ryan, and Alex Rosenblat. 2017. "The Taking Economy: Uber, Information, and Power." *Columbia Law Review* 117 (March): 1623–90. https://doi.org/10.2139/ssrn.2929643.

Casson, Lionel. 2002. *Libraries in the Ancient World*. Yale Nota Bene. New Haven, CT: Yale University Press. https://yalebooks.yale.edu/book/9780300097214/libraries-in-the-ancient-world/.

Clapinson, Mary. 2020. *A Brief History of the Bodleian Library*. Revised Edition. Chicago, IL: Bodleian Library Publishing. University of Chicago Press.

Clifton, Brian, Sam Lavigne, and Francis Tseng. 2017. "White Collar Crime Risk Zones." *The New Inquiry* (59-Abolish) March 2017. https://whitecollar.thenewinquiry.com/.

Darch, Peter T., and Emily J.M. Knox. 2017. "Ethical Perspectives on Data and Software Sharing in the Sciences: A Research Agenda." *Library & Information Science Research* 39 (4): 295–302. https://doi.org/10.1016/j.lisr.2017.11.008.

Dewey-Hagborg, Heather, and Chelsea E. Manning. 2017. *A Becoming Resemblance. Fridman Gallery, New York, NY. August 2–September 5, 2017*. 3D-printed portraits. https://www.fridmangallery.com/product-page/a-becoming-resemblance.

Gleason, Eliza Atkins. 1945. "Facing the Dilemma of Public Library Service for Negroes." *The Library Quarterly* 15 (4): 339–44. https://doi.org/10.1086/617176.

Goel, Sharad, Justin M. Rao, and Ravi Shroff. 2016. "Precinct or Prejudice? Understanding Racial Disparities in New York City's Stop-and-Frisk Policy." *The Annals of Applied Statistics* 10 (1). https://doi.org/10.1214/15-AOAS897.

Gross, Daniel A. 2021. "The Surprisingly Big Business of Library E-Books." *The New Yorker*, September 2, 2021. https://www.newyorker.com/news/annals-of-communications/an-app-called-libby-and-the-surprisingly-big-business-of-library-e-books.

Harwell, Drew. 2022. "A Fake Tweet Sparked Panic at Eli Lilly and May Have Cost Twitter Millions." *Washington Post*, November 14, 2022. https://www.washingtonpost.com/technology/2022/11/14/twitter-fake-eli-lilly/.

Irani, Lilly C., and M. Six Silberman. 2013. "Turkopticon: Interrupting Worker Invisibility in Amazon Mechanical Turk." In *Proceedings of the SIGCHI Conference on Human Factors in Computing Systems*. CHI '13. New York, USA: ACM, 611–20. https://doi.org/10.1145/2470654.2470742.

Jaeger, Paul T. et al. 2023. "The Urge to Censor: Raw Power, Social Control, and the Criminalization of Librarianship." *The Political Librarian* 6 (1): 1–20. https://journals.library.wustl.edu/pollib/article/id/8711/.

James, Joy. 2022. *In Pursuit of Revolutionary Love*. Winstone: Divided Publishing.

Khatchadourian, Raffi. 2010. "What Does Julian Assange Want?" *The New Yorker*, May 31, 2010. https://www.newyorker.com/magazine/2010/06/07/no-secrets.

Knox, Emily J.M. 2015. *Book Banning in 21st-Century America*. Lanham, MD: Rowman & Littlefield Publishers.

Knox, Emily J.M. 2023. *Foundations of Intellectual Freedom*. Chicago: ALA Neal-Schuman. https://www.alastore.ala.org/iffoundations.

LaFleur, Ingrid. 2019. "Ingrid LaFleur—There Are Black People in the Future." *Furtherfield* (blog). September 30, 2019. https://www.furtherfield.org/ingrid-lafleur-there-are-black-people-in-the-future/.

Lawrence, Thomas B. 2008. "Power, Institutions and Organizations." In *The SAGE Handbook of Organizational Institutionalism*, 170–97. London: SAGE Publications Ltd. https://doi.org/10.4135/9781849200387.

Manning, Chelsea E. 2014. "The Fog Machine of War." *The New York Times*, June 14, 2014, sec. Opinion. https://www.nytimes.com/2014/06/15/opinion/sunday/chelsea-mann ing-the-us-militarys-campaign-against-media-freedom.html.

McKitterick, David. 2018. *The Invention of Rare Books: Private Interest and Public Memory, 1600–1840*. 1st ed. Cambridgeshire; New York: Cambridge University Press. https://doi.org/10.1017/9781108584265.

Nelson, Alondra. 2002. "Afrofuturism Introduction FUTURE TEXTS." *Social Text* 20 (2 (71)): 1–15. https://doi.org/10.1215/01642472-20-2_71-1.

Nguyen, Aiha. 2021. "The Constant Boss : Labor Under Digital Surveillance." Report. New York: Data & Society Research Institute. https://datasociety.net/library/the-const ant-boss/.

Ovenden, Richard. 2020. *Burning the Books: A History of Knowledge under Attack*. London: John Murray.

Rain Parrot. 2023. "Rain Parrot—Weather When You Need It." 2023. https://www.rainpar rot.com/.

Richardson, Rashida, and American Artist. n.d. *Ally AI*. https://www.artsy.net/article/artsy-editorial-artwork-satirical-siri-check-white-peoples-biases.

Robinson, David G. 2022. *Voices in the Code: A Story about People, Their Values, and the Algorithm They Made*. New York: Russell Sage Foundation. https://www.russellsage.org/publications/voices-code.

Savov, Vlad. 2018. "Google's Selfish Ledger Ideas Can Also Be Found in Its Patent Applications." *The Verge*, May 19, 2018. https://www.theverge.com/2018/5/19/17246 152/google-selfish-ledger-patent-applications.

Scott, Tony, dir. 1998. *Enemy of the State*.

Sharpe, Richard. 2019. "Medieval Libraries of Great Britain." Presented at the Lyell Lectures. Bodleian Library. University of Oxford, Oxford, UK, April. https://podcasts.ox.ac.uk/medieval-libraries-great-britain-lyell-lectures-2019-1.

Sharpe, Richard. 2022. "Dissolution and Dispersion in Sixteenth-Century England: Understanding the Remains." In *How the Secularization of Religious Houses Transformed the Libraries of Europe*, edited by Cristina Dondi, Dorit Raines, and Richard Sharpe, 39–66. Bibliologia 63. Turnhout: Brepols Publishers. https://doi.org/10.1484/M.BIB-EB.5.128477.

Smithsonian Institution. n.d. *Transcribing the Freedmen's Bureau Paper*. https://transcript ion.si.edu/instructions-freedmens-bureau.

Tandon, Udayan et al. 2022. "Hostile Ecologies: Navigating the Barriers to Community-Led Innovation." *Proceedings of the ACM on Human-Computer Interaction* 6 (CSCW2, Article 443). https://dl.acm.org/doi/abs/10.1145/3555544.

Washington, Anne L. 2020. "Uncertain Risk: Assessing Open Data Signals." *Transforming Government: People, Process and Policy* 14 (4): 623–37. https://doi.org/10.1108/TG-09-2019-0086.

Willis, Arlette Ingram. 2023. *Anti-Black Literacy Laws and Policies*. New York: Routledge. https://doi.org/10.4324/9781003296188.

Winchester, Woodrow W. 2018. "Afrofuturism, Inclusion, and the Design Imagination." *Interactions* 25 (2): 41–45. https://doi.org/10.1145/3182655.

References

Ajunwa, Ifeoma. 2016. "The Paradox of Automation as Anti-Bias Intervention." *Cardozo Law Review* 41 (March): 1671–1742. http://dx.doi.org/10.2139/ssrn.2746078.

American Library Association. 2017. "ALA's Code of Ethics." May 19, 2017. https://www.ala.org/tools/ethics.

Amnesty International. 2021. "Xenophobic Machines: Discrimination through Unregulated Use of Algorithms in the Dutch Childcare Benefits Scandal." EUR 35/4686/2021. Amnesty International. https://www.amnesty.org/en/documents/eur35/4686/2021/en/.

Anthopoulos, Leonidas, et al. 2016. "Why E-Government Projects Fail? An Analysis of the Healthcare.Gov Website." *Government Information Quarterly* 33 (1): 161–73. https://doi.org/10.1016/j.giq.2015.07.003.

Arcas, Blaise Aguera, Alexander Todorov, and Margaret Mitchell. 2018. "Do Algorithms Reveal Sexual Orientation or Just Expose Our Stereotypes?" *Medium Microsoft Research* (blog). January 18, 2018. https://medium.com/@blaisea/do-algorithms-reveal-sexual-orientation-or-just-expose-our-stereotypes-d998fafdf477.

Aristotle, and William David Ross. 1963. *The Nicomachean Ethics of Aristotle—The Internet Classics Archive*. London: Oxford University Press.

Bader, Verena, and Stephan Kaiser. 2019. "Algorithmic Decision-Making? The User Interface and Its Role for Human Involvement in Decisions Supported by Artificial Intelligence." *Organization* 26 (5): 655–72. https://doi.org/10.1177/1350508419855714.

Balkin, Jack M. 2017. "The Three Laws of Robotics in the Age of Big Data." *Ohio State Law Journal* 78 (5): 1217–41.

Bamberger, Kenneth A. 2009. "Technologies of Compliance: Risk and Regulation in a Digital Age." *Texas Law Review* 88: 669.

Bamberger, Kenneth A., and Deirdre K. Mulligan. 2008. "Privacy Decisionmaking in Administrative Agencies." *University of Chicago Law Review* 75 (1): 75–108. https://www.jstor.org/stable/20141901.

Battles, Matthew. 2015. *Library: An Unquiet History*. New York: W.W. Norton & Company.

BBC. 2020. "A-Levels: Wales' Education Minister 'Truly Sorry' for Exam Results Handling." *BBC News*, August 18, 2020, sec. Wales. https://www.bbc.co.uk/news/uk-wales-53817855.

BBC News. 2019. "Smart Motorways 'Too Confusing', Says Highways Boss." *BBC News*, October 23, 2019, sec. England. https://www.bbc.com/news/uk-england-50159162.

Beamon, Benita M. 1998. "Supply Chain Design and Analysis: Models and Methods." *International Journal of Production Economics* 55 (3): 281–94. https://doi.org/10.1016/S0925-5273(98)00079-6.

Belot, Henry. 2017. "Government Knew of Potential Problems with Centrelink System." *ABC News*, January 12, 2017. https://www.abc.net.au/news/2017-01-12/government-knew-of-potential-problems-with-centrelink-system/8177988.

Bender, Emily M., et al. 2021. "On the Dangers of Stochastic Parrots: Can Language Models Be Too Big?" In *Proceedings of the 2021 ACM Conference on Fairness,*

Accountability, and Transparency. Virtual Event Canada: ACM, 610–23. https://doi.org/10.1145/3442188.3445922.

Benjamin, Ruha. 2019a. *Captivating Technology: Race, Carceral Technoscience, and Liberatory Imagination in Everyday Life.* Place of publication not identified: Duke University Press. doi.org/10.1515/9781478004493.

Benjamin, Ruha. 2019b. "Assessing Risk, Automating Racism." *Science* 366 (6464): 421–22. https://doi.org/10.1126/science.aaz3873.

Birhane, Abeba, and Fred Cummins. 2019. "Algorithmic Injustices: Towards a Relational Ethics." http://arxiv.org/abs/1912.07376.

Birhane, Abeba, et al. 2022. "Power to the People? Opportunities and Challenges for Participatory AI." In *EAAMO '22: Equity and Access in Algorithms, Mechanisms, and Optimization* . Arlington, VA: ACM, 1–8. https://doi.org/10.1145/3551624.3555290.

Birhane, Abeba, Vinay Uday Prabhu, and Emmanuel Kahembwe. 2021. "Multimodal Datasets: Misogyny, Pornography, and Malignant Stereotypes." http://arxiv.org/abs/2110.01963.

Borgman, Christine L. 2000. *From Gutenberg to the Global Information Infrastructure: Access to Information in the Networked World.* Cambridge, MA: MIT Press.

Borgman, Christine L. 2015. *Big Data, Little Data, No Data: Scholarship in the Networked World.* Cambridge, MA: MIT Press.

Bowersox, Donald J. 2013. *Supply Chain Logistics Management.* 4th ed. New York: McGraw-Hill. http://www.mhhe.com/bowersox4e.

Bowker, Geoffrey C., and Susan Leigh Star. 1999. *Sorting Things Out: Classification and Its Consequences.* Cambridge, MA: MIT Press. https://mitpress.mit.edu/books/sorting-things-out.

Bozeman, Barry, and Patrick Scott. 1996. "Bureaucratic Red Tape and Formalization: Untangling Conceptual Knots." *The American Review of Public Administration* 26 (1): 1–17. https://doi.org/10.1177/027507409602600101.

Briant, Emma L. 2018. "Cambridge Analytica Transcripts." UK House of Commons, Digital, Culture, Media and Sport Committee's Fake News Inquiry. https://www.parliament.uk/business/committees/committees-a-z/commons-select/digital-culture-media-and-sport-committee/news/fake-news-briant-evidence-17-19/.

Brown, Tom B., et al. 2020. "Language Models Are Few-Shot Learners." *arXiv:2005.14165 [Cs],* July. http://arxiv.org/abs/2005.14165.

Bui, Matthew Le, and Safiya Umoja Noble. 2020. "We're Missing a Moral Framework of Justice in Artificial Intelligence: On the Limits, Failings, and Ethics of Fairness." In *The Oxford Handbook of Ethics of AI,* edited by Markus D. Dubber, Frank Pasquale, and Sunit Das, 161–79. Oxford; New York: Oxford University Press. https://doi.org/10.1093/oxfordhb/9780190067397.013.9.

Buolamwini, Joy, and Timnit Gebru. 2018. "Gender Shades: Intersectional Accuracy Disparities in Commercial Gender Classification." *Proceedings of Machine Learning Research* 81 (February): 77–91.

Bush, Vannevar. 1945. "As We May Think." *The Atlantic Monthly,* 1945.

Butler, Octavia E. 1993. *Parable of the Sower.* 1st ed. New York: Penguin Random House.

Calo, Ryan, and Danielle Citron. 2021. "The Automated Administrative State: A Crisis of Legitimacy." *Emory Law Journal* 70 (4): 797.

Carr, Austin. 2015. "The Messy Business of Reinventing Happiness," April 15, 2015. https://www.fastcompany.com/3044283/the-messy-business-of-re.

Casson, Lionel. 2002. *Libraries in the Ancient World*. Yale Nota Bene. New Haven, CT: Yale University Press. https://yalebooks.yale.edu/book/9780300097214/libraries-in-the-ancient-world/.

Cespedes, Frank V., and H. Jeff Smith. 1993. "Database Marketing: New Rules for Policy and Practice." *Sloan Management Review* 34: 7–22.

Christakis, Nicholas A., and James H. Fowler. 2013. "Social Contagion Theory: Examining Dynamic Social Networks and Human Behavior." *Statistics in Medicine* 32 (4): 556–77. https://doi.org/10.1002/sim.5408.

Christensen, Julian, et al. 2020. "Human Capital and Administrative Burden: The Role of Cognitive Resources in Citizen-State Interactions." *Public Administration Review* 80 (1): 127–36. https://doi.org/10.1111/puar.13134.

Christensen, Julian, et al. 2020. "Human Capital and Administrative Burden: The Role of Cognitive Resources in Citizen-State Interactions." *Public Administration Review* 80 (1): 127–36. https://doi.org/10.1111/puar.13134.

Citron, Danielle Keats. 2008. "Technological Due Process." *Washington University Law Review* 85 (6): 1249–313.

Citron, Danielle Keats. 2022. *The Fight for Privacy: Protecting Dignity, Identity, and Love in the Digital Age*. 1st ed. New York: W.W. Norton & Company, Inc.

Clifton, Brian, Sam Lavigne, and Francis Tseng. 2017. "White Collar Crime Risk Zones." *The New Inquiry*, March 2017. https://whitecollar.thenewinquiry.com/.

Cohen, Julie E. 2019. "The Regulatory State in the Information Age." In *Between Truth and Power: The Legal Constructions of Informational Capitalism*, 170–201. Oxford; New York: Oxford University Press. DOI:10.1093/oso/9780190246693.003.0007.

Collins, Patricia Hill. 1993. "Toward a New Vision: Race, Class, and Gender as Categories of Analysis and Connection." *Race, Sex & Class* 1 (1): 25–45.

Combahee River Collective. 1979. "The Combahee River Collective: A Black Feminist Statement." In *Capitalist Patriarchy and the Case for Socialist Feminism*, edited by Zillah R. Eisenstein, 362–72. Women's Studies, Political Science. New York: Monthly Review Pr.

Criado-Perez, Caroline. 2019. "The Deadly Truth about a World Built for Men—From Stab Vests to Car Crashes." *The Guardian*, February 23, 2019, sec. US news. http://www.theguardian.com/lifeandstyle/2019/feb/23/truth-world-built-for-men-car-crashes.

Curtiz, Michael, dir. 1942. *Casablanca*. https://www.imdb.com/title/tt0034583/.

Dewey-Hagborg, Heather, and Chelsea E. Manning. 2017. *A Becoming Resemblance*. Fridman Gallery, New York. August 2–September 5, 2017. 3D-printed portraits. https://www.fridmangallery.com/product-page/a-becoming-resemblance.

Diakopoulos, Nicholas. 2014. "Algorithmic Accountability: Journalistic Investigation of Computational Power Structures." *Digital Journalism* 3 (3): 398–415. https://doi.org/10.1080/21670811.2014.976411.

Donovan, Joan, Emily Dreyfuss, and Brian Friedberg. 2022. *Meme Wars: The Untold Story of the Online Battles Upending Democracy in America*. New York: Bloomsbury Publishing.

Elyounes, Doa. 2021. "'Computer Says No!': The Impact of Automation on the Discretionary Power of Public Officers." *Vanderbilt Journal of Entertainment & Technology Law* 23 (3): 451.

Espeland, Wendy Nelson, and Mitchell L. Stevens. 1998. "Commensuration as a Social Process." *Annual Review of Sociology* 24 (1): 313–43. https://doi.org/10.1146/annurev.soc.24.1.313.

Eubanks, Virginia. 2018. "A Child Abuse Prediction Model Fails Poor Families." *Wired*, January 15, 2018. https://www.wired.com/story/excerpt-from-automating-ine quality/.

Evans, Sophie Jane. 2019. "Smart Motorways Killed My Husband—More People Will Die Unless They're Banned." *The Sun*, October 17, 2019. https://www.thesun.co.uk/news/ 10130630/smart-motorways-safe-husband-killed/.

Feathers, Todd. 2021. "Facial Recognition Failures Are Locking People Out of Unemployment Systems." *Vice* (blog). June 18, 2021. https://www.vice.com/en/arti cle/5dbywn/facial-recognition-failures-are-locking-people-out-of-unemployment-systems.

"Former Director for Tuskegee Syphilis Study Believes Work Was 'Completely Ethical.'" 1972. *All Things Considered*. Washington DC: National Public Radio. https://www.npr. org/2020/03/03/808621619/former-director-for-tuskegee-syphilis-study-believes-work-was-completely-ethical.

Fourcade, Marion, and Kieran Healy. 2017. "Seeing Like a Market." *Socio-Economic Review* 15 (1): 9–29. https://doi.org/10.1093/ser/mww033.

Fowler, J.H., and N.A. Christakis. 2008. "Dynamic Spread of Happiness in a Large Social Network: Longitudinal Analysis over 20 Years in the Framingham Heart Study." *BMJ* 337 (dec04 2): a2338–a2338. https://doi.org/10.1136/bmj.a2338.

GAO. 2012. "Electronic Government Act: Agencies Have Implemented Most Provisions, but Key Areas of Attention Remain." GAO-12-782. Washington DC: Government Accountability Office. http://gao.gov/products/GAO-12-782.

Gilliard, Chris. 2020. "Caught in the Spotlight." *Urban Omnibus—A Publication of the Architectural League of New York*, January. https://urbanomnibus.net/2020/01/caught-in-the-spotlight/.

Gilligan, Carol. 1982. *In a Different Voice: Psychological Theory and Women's Development*. Cambridge, MA: Harvard University Press.

Ginsberg, Jeremy, et al. 2009. "Detecting Influenza Epidemics Using Search Engine Query Data." *Nature* 457: 1012–14.

Gleason, Eliza Atkins. 1945. "Facing the Dilemma of Public Library Service for Negroes." *The Library Quarterly* 15 (4): 339–44. https://doi.org/10.1086/617176.

Goodman, Ellen P. 2019. "The Challenge of Equitable Algorithmic Change." *Regulatory Review* 8 (1): 1–10.

Gunn, James, dir. 2014. *Guardians of the Galaxy*. https://www.imdb.com/title/tt2015381/.

Hacking, Ian. 2006. "Making Up People." *London Review of Books*, August 17, 2006.

Halevy, Alon, Peter Norvig, and Fernando Pereira. 2009. "The Unreasonable Effectiveness of Data." *IEEE Intelligent Systems* 24 (2): 8–12. https://doi.org/10.1109/MIS.2009.36.

Hall, Stuart. 1980. "Cultural Studies and the Centre: Some Problematics and Problems." In *Culture, Media, Language: Working Papers in Cultural Studies, 1972-79*, edited by Stuart Hall, Doothy Hobson, Andrew Lowe, and Paul Willis, 1st ed., 1–33. London: Routledge. https://doi.org/10.4324/9780203381182.

Harvey, Penny, Madeleine Reeves, and Evelyn Ruppert. 2013. "Anticipating Failure: Transparency Devices and Their Effects." *Journal of Cultural Economy* 6 (3): 294–312.

Henriques-Gomes, Luke. 2019. "Robodebt Scheme Costs Government Almost as Much as It Recovers." *The Guardian*, February 21, 2019, sec. Australia news. https://www.theg uardian.com/australia-news/2019/feb/22/robodebt-scheme-costs-government-alm ost-as-much-as-it-recovers.

Henriques-Gomes, Luke. 2020. "Disability Pensioners Were Increasingly Drawn into Robodebt While Scheme Was under Scrutiny." *The Guardian*, February 9, 2020, sec. Australia news. https://www.theguardian.com/australia-news/2020/feb/10/disability-pensioners-were-increasingly-drawn-into-robodebt-while-scheme-was-under-scrutiny.

Herd, Pamela, and Donald P. Moynihan. 2019. *Administrative Burden*. New York: Russell Sage Foundation.

Hern, Alex. 2020. "Ofqual's A-Level Algorithm: Why Did It Fail to Make the Grade?" *The Guardian*, August 21, 2020, sec. Education. http://www.theguardian.com/education/2020/aug/21/ofqual-exams-algorithm-why-did-it-fail-make-grade-a-levels.

Hood, Christopher. 1999. *Regulation Inside Government: Waste Watchers, Quality Police, and Sleaze-Busters*. Oxford; New York: Oxford University Press.

Hoofnagle, Chris Jay. 2016. *Federal Trade Commission Privacy Law and Policy*. Cambridge; New York: Cambridge University Press.

hooks, bell. 2000. *Feminism Is for Everybody: Passionate Politics*. Cambridge, MA: South End Press.

hooks, bell. 2015. *Feminist Theory: From Margin to Center*. 3rd ed. New York: Routledge.

Hotz, Robert Lee. 2013. "When 'Likes' Can Shed Light." *The Wall Street Journal Online*, March 11, 2013, sec. US.

Ingold, David, and Spencer Soper. 2016. "Amazon Doesn't Consider the Race of Its Customers. Should It?" *Bloomberg*, 2016. http://www.bloomberg.com/graphics/2016-amazon-same-day/.

Irani, Lilly C., and M. Six Silberman. 2013. "Turkopticon: Interrupting Worker Invisibility in Amazon Mechanical Turk." In *Proceedings of the SIGCHI Conference on Human Factors in Computing Systems*. CHI '13. New York: ACM, 611–20. https://doi.org/10.1145/2470654.2470742.

James, Joy. 2022. *In Pursuit of Revolutionary Love*. Winstone: Divided Publishing.

Jasanoff, Sheila. 2007. "Technologies of Humility." *Nature* 450 (7166): 33. http://dx.doi.org/10.1038/450033a.

Johnson, Khari. 2021. "Twitter's Photo Crop Algorithm Favors White Faces and Women." *Wired*, May 21, 2021. https://www.wired.com/story/twitter-photo-crop-algorithm-favors-white-faces-women/.

Johnson, Robert, and Adam Cureton. 2018. "Kant's Moral Philosophy." In *The Stanford Encyclopedia of Philosophy*, edited by Edward N. Zalta, Spring 2018. Stanford, CA: Metaphysics Research Lab, Stanford University. https://plato.stanford.edu/archives/spr2018/entries/kant-moral/.

Kant, Immanuel, and Louis Infield. 1963. *Lectures on Ethics*. New York: Harper & Row.

Karp, Paul, and Christopher Knaus. 2018. "Centrelink Robo-Debt Program Accused of Enforcing 'Illegal' Debts." *The Guardian*, April 4, 2018, sec. Australia news. https://www.theguardian.com/australia-news/2018/apr/04/centrelink-robo-debt-program-accused-of-enforcing-illegal-debts.

Katwala, Amit. 2020. "An Algorithm Determined UK Students' Grades. Chaos Ensued." *Wired UK*, August 15, 2020. https://www.wired.co.uk/article/results-day-exams-bias.

Khan, Lina M. 2017. "Amazon's Antitrust Paradox." *Yale Law Review* 126 (January): 710.

Kim, Hyunil, et al. 2017. "Lifetime Prevalence of Investigating Child Maltreatment Among US Children." *American Journal of Public Health* 107 (2): 274–80. https://doi.org/10.2105/AJPH.2016.303545.

Kleinberg, Jon, Jens Ludwig, and Sendhil Mullainathan. 2016. "A Guide to Solving Social Problems with Machine Learning." *Harvard Business Review*, December. https://hbr.org/2016/12/a-guide-to-solving-social-problems-with-machine-learning.

Kleindorfer, Paul R., and Germaine H. Saad. 2005. "Managing Disruption Risks in Supply Chains." *Production and Operations Management* 14 (1): 53–68. https://doi.org/10.1111/j.1937-5956.2005.tb00009.x.

Knaus, Christopher. 2017. "Government Knew about Discrepancies in Data-Matching System before Reducing Human Oversight." *The Guardian*, January 11, 2017, sec. Australia news. https://www.theguardian.com/australia-news/2017/jan/12/centrelink-human-oversight-slashed-after-cost-benefit-analysis.

Kooragayala, Shiva, and Tanaya Srini. 2016. "Pokémon GO Is Changing How Cities Use Public Space, but Could It Be More Inclusive?" *Urban Wire: The Blog of the Urban Institute*. August 1, 2016. https://www.urban.org/urban-wire/pokemon-go-changing-how-cities-use-public-space-could-it-be-more-inclusive.

Kraut, Richard. 2018. "Aristotle's Ethics." In *The Stanford Encyclopedia of Philosophy*, edited by Edward N. Zalta, Summer 2018. Stanford, CA: Metaphysics Research Lab, Stanford University. https://plato.stanford.edu/archives/sum2018/entries/aristotle-ethics/.

Lanham, Richard A. 2006. *The Economics of Attention: Style and Substance in the Age of Information*. Chicago: University of Chicago Press. http://www.loc.gov/catdir/enhancements/fy0666/2005022857-d.html.

Lazer, David, et al. 2014. "The Parable of Google Flu: Traps in Big Data Analysis." *Science* 343 (6176): 1203–05. https://doi.org/10.1126/science.1248506.

Leslie, David, et al. 2022. "Advancing Data Justice Research and Practice: An Integrated Literature Review." https://doi.org/10.5281/zenodo.6408304.

Lewis, Michael. 2003. *Moneyball: The Art of Winning an Unfair Game*. 1st ed. New York: W.W. Norton.

Lincoln, Yvonna S., and Egon G. Guba. 1985. *Naturalistic Inquiry*. Beverly Hills, CA: Sage Publications.

"Local TV Anchor Helps Thousands Fighting for Unemployment Benefits | CNN Business." 2020. https://www.cnn.com/videos/business/2020/12/13/local-tv-anchor-helps-thousands-fighting-for-unemployment-benefits.cnn.

Lounsbury, Michael, et al. 2021. "New Directions in the Study of Institutional Logics: From Tools to Phenomena." *Annual Review of Sociology* 47 (1): null. https://doi.org/10.1146/annurev-soc-090320-111734.

Maddy, Penelope. 1997. *Naturalism in Mathematics*. Oxford; New York: Clarendon Press; Oxford University Press.

Madsen, Jonas K., Kim S. Mikkelsen, and Donald P. Moynihan. 2021. "Burdens, Sludge, Ordeals, Red Tape, Oh My!: A User's Guide to the Study of Frictions." *Public Administration* 100 (2): 375–93. https://doi.org/10.1111/padm.12717.

Maguire, Steve, and Cynthia Hardy. 2013. "Organizing Processes and the Construction of Risk: A Discursive Approach." *Academy of Management Journal* 56 (1): 231. https://doi.org/10.5465/amj.2010.0714.

Majchrzak, Ann, and M. Lynne Markus. 2013. *Methods for Policy Research: Taking Socially Responsible Action*. 2nd ed. Thousand Oaks, CA: SAGE Publications Ltd.

Maloni, Michael J., and Michael E. Brown. 2006. "Corporate Social Responsibility in the Supply Chain: An Application in the Food Industry." *Journal of Business Ethics* 68 (1): 35–52. https://doi.org/10.1007/s10551-006-9038-0.

Margetts, Helen, Perri 6, and Christopher Hood. 2010. *Paradoxes of Modernization: Unintended Consequences of Public Policy Reform.* Oxford; New York: Oxford University Press. http://lccn.loc.gov/2010285948.

Markus, M. Lynne. 2014. "Maybe Not the King, but an Invaluable Subordinate: A Commentary on Avison and Malaurent's Advocacy of 'Theory Light' IS Research." *Journal of Information Technology* 29 (4): 341–45. https://doi.org/10.1057/jit.2014.19.

Marquand, Richard, dir. 1983. *Star Wars: Episode VI—Return of the Jedi.* https://www.imdb.com/title/tt0086190/.

McKitterick, David. 2018. *The Invention of Rare Books: Private Interest and Public Memory, 1600–1840.* 1st ed. Cambridge; New York: Cambridge University Press. https://doi.org/10.1017/9781108584265.

Mehrabi, Ninareh, et al. 2021. "A Survey on Bias and Fairness in Machine Learning." *ACM Computing Surveys (CSUR)* 54 (6): 1–35. https://doi.org/10.1145/3457607.

Michigan State. 2016. "Michigan Integrated Data Automated System (MiDAS)/." Michigan Office of the Auditor General. https://audgen.michigan.gov/complete-projects/michigan-integrated-data-automated-system-midas/.

Mill, John Stuart. 1863. *Utilitarianism.* Project Gutenberg. https://archive.org/details/a592840000milluoft.

Mitchell, Shira, et al. 2021. "Algorithmic Fairness: Choices, Assumptions, and Definitions." *Annual Review of Statistics and Its Application* 8 (1): 141–63. https://doi.org/10.1146/annurev-statistics-042720-125902.

Mohamed, Shakir, Marie-Therese Png, and William Isaac. 2020. "Decolonial AI: Decolonial Theory as Sociotechnical Foresight in Artificial Intelligence." *Philosophy & Technology*, July. https://doi.org/10.1007/s13347-020-00405-8.

Moor, James H. 1985. "What Is Computer Ethics?" *Metaphilosophy* 16 (4): 266–75.

Moynihan, Donald, Pamela Herd, and Hope Harvey. 2015. "Administrative Burden: Learning, Psychological, and Compliance Costs in Citizen-State Interactions." *Journal of Public Administration Research and Theory* 25 (1): 43–69. https://doi.org/10.1093/jopart/muu009.

Mulligan, Deirdre K., and Kenneth A. Bamberger. 2019. "Procurement as Policy: Administrative Process for Machine Learning." *Berkeley Technology Law Journal* 34 (3): 773–852.

Murray, Jessica. 2020. "Royal Statistical Society Hits Back at Ofqual in Exams Algorithm Row." *The Guardian*, August 24, 2020, sec. Education. https://www.theguardian.com/education/2020/aug/24/royal-statistical-society-hits-back-at-ofqual-in-exams-algorithm-row.

Noble, Safiya Umoja. 2018. *Algorithms of Oppression: How Search Engines Reinforce Racism.* New York: New York University Press.

Nosrat, Samin. 2017. *Salt, Fat, Acid, Heat: Mastering the Elements of Good Cooking.* Simon & Schuster Nonfiction Original Hardcover. New York: Simon & Schuster.

Obermeyer, Ziad, et al. 2019. "Dissecting Racial Bias in an Algorithm Used to Manage the Health of Populations." *Science* 366 (6464): 447–53. https://doi.org/10.1126/science.aax2342.

Ocasio, William. 2011. "Attention to Attention." *Organization Science* 22 (5): 1286–96.

Ocasio, William, Patricia H. Thornton, and Michael Lounsbury. 2017. "Advances to the Institutional Logics Perspective." In *The SAGE Handbook of Organizational Institutionalism*, by Royston Greenwood, et al., 509–31. London: SAGE Publications Ltd. https://doi.org/10.4135/9781446280669.n20.

OECD. 2013. "The Organisation for Economic Co-Operation and Development Due Diligence Guidance for Responsible Supply Chains of Minerals from Conflict-Affected and High-Risk Areas." 2nd ed. http://www.oecd.org/corporate/mne/mining.htm.

Ohm, Paul, and Jonathan Frankle. 2019. "Desirable Inefficiency." *Florida Law Review* 70 (4): 777.

O'Neil, Cathy. 2016. *Weapons of Math Destruction: How Big Data Increases Inequality and Threatens Democracy*. 1st ed. New York: Crown.

Onuoha, Mimi. 2016. *The Library of Missing Datasets*. Mixed Media Installation. https://github.com/MimiOnuoha/missing-datasets.

O'Rourke, Dara. 2014. "The Science of Sustainable Supply Chains." *Science* 344 (6188): 1124–27. https://doi.org/10.1126/science.1248526.

Ovenden, Richard. 2020. *Burning the Books: A History of Knowledge under Attack*. London: John Murray.

Oyer, Paul E. 2014. *Everything I Ever Needed to Know about Economics I Learned from Online Dating*. Boston, MA: Harvard Business Review Press.

Painter, Ann F. 1974. "Classification: Theory and Practice." *Drexel Library Quarterly* 10 (4): 1–4.

Paolacci, Gabriele, Jesse Chandler, and Panagiotis G. Ipeirotis. 2010. "Running Experiments on Amazon Mechanical Turk." *Judgment and Decision Making* 5 (5): 411–19. https://doi.org/10.1017/S1930297500002205.

Parliament of Australia. 2017. "Better Management of the Social Welfare System Initiative Report of the Community Affairs References Committee." Parliament Report. Australia. https://www.aph.gov.au/Parliamentary_Business/Committees/Senate/Community_Affairs/SocialWelfareSystem/Report.

Parliament of Australia, Canberra. 2021. "Centrelink's Compliance Program." Australia. https://www.aph.gov.au/Parliamentary_Business/Committees/Senate/Community_Affairs/Centrelinkcompliance.

Parliament of Netherlands. 2020. "Unprecedented Injustice—Childcare Allowance Parliamentary Inquiry." CDL-REF(2021)073-e. https://www.houseofrepresentatives.nl/members_of_parliament/committees/pok.

Pasquale, Frank A., and Danielle Keats Citron. 2014. "Promoting Innovation While Preventing Discrimination: Policy Goals for the Scored Society." *Washington Law Review* 89: 1413–24.

Petroski, Henry. 2012. *To Forgive Design: Understanding Failure*. Cambridge, MA: Belknap Press of Harvard University Press.

Provost, Foster, and Tom Fawcett. 2013. *Data Science for Business: What You Need to Know about Data Mining and Data-Analytic Thinking*. Sebastopol, CA: O'Reilly.

Raji, Inioluwa Deborah. 2022. "From Algorithmic Audits to Actual Accountability: Overcoming Practical Roadblocks on the Path to Meaningful Audit Interventions for AI Governance." In *Proceedings of AIES '22: AAAI/ACM Conference on AI, Ethics, and Society*, 5–10. Oxford, UK: ACM. https://doi.org/10.1145/3514094.3539566.

Raji, Inioluwa Deborah, and Joy Buolamwini. 2019. "Actionable Auditing: Investigating the Impact of Publicly Naming Biased Performance Results of Commercial AI Products." In *Proceedings of AIES '19: AAAI/ACM Conference on AI, Ethics, and Society*, 429–35.Honolulu, HI: ACM. https://doi.org/10.1145/3306618.3314244.

Rawls, John. 2000. *A Theory of Justice*. Revised. Oxford, UK: Oxford University Press.

Rhue, Lauren, and Anne L. Washington. 2020. "AI's Wide Open: Premature Artificial Intelligence and Public Policy." *Boston University Journal of Science and Technology Law* 26 (2): 353–78. https://ssrn.com/abstract=3720944.

Richardson, Rashida. 2022. "Racial Segregation and the Data-Driven Society: How Our Failure to Reckon with Root Causes Perpetuates Separate and Unequal Realities." *Berkeley Technology Law Journal* 36 (3): 1051–90. https://papers.ssrn.com/abstract=3850317.

Richardson, Rashida, and American Artist. n.d. *Ally AI.* https://www.artsy.net/article/artsy-editorial-artwork-satirical-siri-check-white-peoples-biases.

Roberts, Dorothy E. 2022. *Torn Apart: How the Child Welfare System Destroys Black Families—And How Abolition Can Build a Safer World.* 1st ed. New York: Basic Books.

Robey, Daniel, and William Taggart. 1982. "Human Information Processing in Information and Decision Support Systems." *MIS Quarterly* 6 (2): 61.

Rochefort, David A., and Roger W. Cobb. 1994. "Problem Definition: An Emerging Perspective." In *The Politics of Problem Definition: Shaping the Policy Agenda*, edited by David A. Rochefort and Roger W. Cobb, 1–31. Lawrence, KS: University Press of Kansas.

Rose, Jeremy, John Stouby Persson, and Lise Tordrup Heeager. 2015. "How E-Government Managers Prioritise Rival Value Positions: The Efficiency Imperative." *Information Polity* 20 (1): 35–59. https://doi.org/10.3233/IP-150349.

Roth, Lorna. 2009. "Looking at Shirley, the Ultimate Norm: Colour Balance, Image Technologies, and Cognitive Equity." *Canadian Journal of Communication* 34 (1): 111–36. https://doi.org/10.22230/cjc.2009v34n1a2196.

Rousseau, Jean-Jacques, and G.D.H. Cole. 1963. *The Social Contract and Discourses.* London; New York: Dent; Dutton.

Ruderman, Wendy. 2013. "For Troubled Teenagers in New York City, a New Tack: Forced Outreach." *The New York Times*, March 3, 2013. https://www.nytimes.com/2013/03/04/nyregion/to-stem-juvenile-robberies-police-trail-youths-before-the-crime.html?pagewanted=all.

Ruggles, Steven, Catherine A. Fitch, and Evan Roberts. 2018. "Historical Census Record Linkage." *Annual Review of Sociology* 44 (1): 19–37. https://doi.org/10.1146/annurev-soc-073117-041447.

Satariano, Adam. 2020. "British Grading Debacle Shows Pitfalls of Automating Government." *The New York Times*, August 20, 2020, sec. World. https://www.nytimes.com/2020/08/20/world/europe/uk-england-grading-algorithm.html.

Sato, Mia. 2021. "The Pandemic Is Testing the Limits of Face Recognition." *MIT Technology Review*, September 28, 2021. https://www.technologyreview.com/2021/09/28/1036279/pandemic-unemployment-government-face-recognition/.

Savov, Vlad. 2018. "Google's Selfish Ledger Ideas Can Also Be Found in Its Patent Applications." *The Verge*, May 19, 2018. https://www.theverge.com/2018/5/19/17246152/google-selfish-ledger-patent-applications.

Scism, Leslie, and Mark Maremont. 2010. "Insurers Test Data Profiles to Identify Risky Clients." *Wall Street Journal*, November 19, 2010, sec. Tech. http://www.wsj.com/articles/SB10001424052748704648604575620750998072986.

Scott, James C. 1998. *Seeing Like a State: How Certain Schemes to Improve the Human Condition Have Failed.* New Haven, CT; London: Yale University Press.

Scott, Tony, dir. 1999. *Enemy of the State.* https://www.imdb.com/title/tt0120660/.

Sexton, Anna, et al. 2018. "The Role and Nature of Consent in Government Administrative Data." *Big Data & Society* 5 (2): 2053951718819560. https://doi.org/10.1177/20539 51718819560.

Sharpe, Richard. 2019. "Medieval Libraries of Great Britain." Presented at the Lyell Lectures. Bodleian Library. University of Oxford, Oxford, UK, April. https://podcasts. ox.ac.uk/medieval-libraries-great-britain-lyell-lectures-2019-1.

Sharpe, Richard. 2022. "Dissolution and Dispersion in Sixteenth-Century England: Understanding the Remains." In *How the Secularization of Religious Houses Transformed the Libraries of Europe*, edited by Cristina Dondi and Dorit Raines. Bibliologia 63. Turnhout: Brepols. https://doi.org/10.1484/M.BIB-EB.5.128477.

Shelby, Tommie. 2004. "Race and Ethnicity, Race and Social Justice: Rawlsian Considerations." *Fordham Law Review* 72 (5): 1697. https://ir.lawnet.fordham.edu/flr/ vol72/iss5/15.

Shuster, Evelyne. 1998. "The Nuremberg Code: Hippocratic Ethics and Human Rights." *The Lancet* 351 (9107): 974–77. https://doi.org/10.1016/S0140-6736(05)60641-1.

Silbey, Susan S. 2011. "The Sociological Citizen: Pragmatic and Relational Regulation in Law and Organizations." *Regulation & Governance* 5 (1): 1–13. https://doi.org/10.1111/ j.1748-5991.2011.01106.x.

Simon, Herbert Alexander. 1996. *The Sciences of the Artificial.* Vol. 3. Cambridge, MA: MIT Press.

Smith, Bayeté Ross. 2010. *Our Kind of People.* Photographs. http://www.bayeterosssmith. com/our-kind-of-people.

Snow, John. 1856. "On the Mode of Communication of Cholera." *Edinburgh Medical Journal* 1 (7): 668–70. https://www.ncbi.nlm.nih.gov/pmc/articles/PMC5307547/.

Solow-Niederman, Alicia, YooJung Choi, and Guy Van den Broeck. 2019. "The Institutional Life of Algorithmic Risk Assessment." *Berkeley Technology Law Journal* 34 (3): 705–44.

Spielberg, Steven, dir. 1993. *Jurassic Park.* https://www.imdb.com/title/tt0107290/.

Starr, Douglas. 2003. "Revisiting a 1930s Scandal, AACR to Rename a Prize." *Science* 300 (5619): 573–74. https://doi.org/10.1126/science.300.5619.573.

State of Michigan. 2018. "MDHHS Re:Forms Assistance Application to Be More User Friendly; New Document Is Less than Half the Size of Previous Version." 2018. https://www.michigan.gov/mdhhs/inside-mdhhs/newsroom/2018/02/01/ mdhhs-reforms-assistance-application-to-be-more-user-friendly-new-docum ent-is-less-than-half-the-si.

Stearns, Peter N. 1998. "Why Study History?" 1998. https://www.historians.org/about- aha-and-membership/aha-history-and-archives/historical-archives/why-study-hist ory-(1998).

Stearns, Peter N. 2020. "Why Study History? Revisited." *Perspectives on History* (blog). September 18, 2020. https://www.historians.org/research-and-publications/perspecti ves-on-history/september-2020/why-study-history-revisited.

Stevens, Robin, et al. 2019. "Sex, Drugs, and Alcohol in the Digital Neighborhood: A Multi-Method Analysis of Online Discourse amongst Black and Hispanic Youth." In *Proceedings of Hawaii International Conference on System Sciences*, 2152–63. https:// doi.org/10.24251/HICSS.2019.261.

Stohr, Edward A., and Sivakumar Viswanathan. 1999. "Recommendation Systems: Decision Support for the Information Economy." In *Classics of Organization Theory*, edited by Jay M. Shafritz and J. Steven Ott. Vol. 5, 520–35. Belmont, CA: Wadsworth/ Harcourt College Publishers.

Stone, Deborah. 2020. *Counting: How We Use Numbers to Decide What Matters*. 1st ed. New York: Liveright Publishing Corporation, a division of W.W. Norton & Company Inc.

Suchman, Lucille Alice. 2007. *Human-Machine Reconfigurations: Plans and Situated Actions*. Vol. 2. Cambridge; New York: Cambridge University Press.

Sunstein, Cass R. 2018. "Sludge and Ordeals." *Duke Law Journal* 68 (8): 1843–83. https://doi.org/10.2139/ssrn.3288192.

Sunstein, Cass R. 2020. "Sludge Audits." *Behavioural Public Policy* First View (January): 1–20. https://doi.org/10.1017/bpp.2019.32.

Sutherland, Tonia. 2019. "The Carceral Archive: Documentary Records, Narrative Construction, and Predictive Risk Assessment." *Journal of Cultural Analytics* 4 (1): 1–21. https://doi.org/10.22148/16.039.

Sweeney, Latanya. 1997. "Weaving Technology and Policy Together to Maintain Confidentiality." *Journal of Law, Medicine & Ethics* 25 (2–3): 98–110. https://doi.org/10.1111/j.1748-720X.1997.tb01885.x.

Taleb, Nassim Nicholas. 2007. *The Black Swan: The Impact of the Highly Improbable*. 1st ed. New York: Random House.

Taleb, Nassim Nicholas. 2019. *Skin in the Game: Hidden Asymmetries in Daily Life*. London: Penguin Books.

Taylor, Keeanga-Yamahtta, ed. 2017. *How We Get Free: Black Feminism and the Combahee River Collective*. Chicago: Haymarket Books.

Thaler, Richard H. 2015. "The Power of Nudges, for Good and Bad." *The New York Times*, October 31, 2015, sec. The Upshot.

Thaler, Richard H. 2018. "Nudge, Not Sludge." *Science* 361(6401): 431. https://doi.org/10.1126/science.aau9241.

The New Inquiry. 2017. "Abolish," 59 (March 9). https://thenewinquiry.com/magazine/abolish/.

Thornton, Patricia H., and William Ocasio. 1999. "Institutional Logics and the Historical Contingency of Power in Organizations: Executive Succession in the Higher Education Publishing Industry, 1958–1990." *American Journal of Sociology* 105 (3): 801–43. https://doi.org/10.1086/ajs.1999.105.issue-3.

Tulchinsky, Theodore. 2017. "John Snow, Cholera, the Broad Street Pump; Waterborne Diseases Then and Now." In *Case Studies in Public Health*, 1st ed., 77–99. Boston, MA: Elsevier.

Tong, Rosemarie, and Nancy Williams. 2018. "Feminist Ethics." In *The Stanford Encyclopedia of Philosophy*, edited by Edward N. Zalta, Winter 2018. Stanford, CA: Metaphysics Research Lab, Stanford University. https://plato.stanford.edu/archives/win2018/entries/feminism-ethics/.

U.S. Department of Health, Education, and Welfare, and National Commission for the Protection of Human Subjects of Biomedical and Behavioral Research. 1979. "The Belmont Report. Ethical Principles and Guidelines for the Protection of Human Subjects of Research." National Commission for the Protection of Human Subjects of Biomedical and Behavioral Research. https://www.hhs.gov/ohrp/regulations-and-policy/belmont-report/index.html.

U.S. Department of Homeland Security, et al. 2012. "The Menlo Report: Ethical Principles Guiding Information and Communication Technology Research." Cyber Security Division, U.S. Department of Homeland Security Science and Technology Directorate.

https://www.dhs.gov/sites/default/files/publications/CSD-MenloPrinciplesCORE-20120803_1.pdf.

Vaidhyanathan, Siva. 2011. *The Googlization of Everything: And Why We Should Worry.* Berkeley, CA: University of California Press.

Van Doren, Charles Lincoln. 1991. *A History of Knowledge: Past, Present, and Future.* New York: Random House Books—Carol Pub. Group.

Varian, Hal R., and Hyunyoung Choi. 2009. "Predicting the Present with Google Trends." http://googleresearch.blogspot.com/2009/04/predicting-present-with-google-trends.html.

Verhoeven, Paul, dir. 1987. *RoboCop.* https://www.imdb.com/title/tt0093870/.

Vidal, Carlos J., and Marc Goetschalckx. 1997. "Strategic Production-Distribution Models: A Critical Review with Emphasis on Global Supply Chain Models." *European Journal of Operational Research* 98 (1): 1–18. https://doi.org/10.1016/S0377-2217(97)80080-X.

Vincent, James. 2020. "What a Machine Learning Tool That Turns Obama White Can (and Can't) Tell Us about AI Bias." *The Verge*, June 23, 2020. https://www.theverge.com/21298762/face-depixelizer-ai-machine-learning-tool-pulse-stylegan-obama-bias.

Wachowski, Lana, and Lilly Wachowski, dirs. 1999. *The Matrix.* https://www.imdb.com/title/tt0133093/.

Wagner, Wendy E. 2010. "Administrative Law, Filter Failure, and Information Capture." *Duke Law Journal* 59 (7): 1321–1432.

Washington, Anne L. 2016. "Interviewing Data—The Art of Interpretation in Analytics." *Proceedings of the 2016 IConference*, March. https://doi.org/10.9776/16256.

Washington, Anne L. 2017. "How to Argue with an Algorithm: Lessons from the COMPAS ProPublica Debate." *The Colorado Technology Law Journal* 17 (1): 131–60.

Washington, Anne L. 2018. "Facebook Math: How 270,000 Became Millions." *Points: Data & Society* (blog). April 11, 2018. https://medium.com/p/bd8cf1009b32.

Washington, Anne L., and Rachel Kuo. 2020. "Whose Side Are Ethics Codes On? Power, Responsibility and the Social Good." In *Proceedings of the 2020 Conference on Fairness, Accountability, and Transparency.* FAT* '20. New York: Association for Computing Machinery, 230–40. https://doi.org/10.1145/3351095.3372844.

Washington, Anne, et al. 2022. "Uncoupling Inequality: Reflections on the Ethics of Benchmarks for Digital Media." In *Proceedings of Hawaii International Conference on System Sciences.* https://doi.org/10.24251/HICSS.2022.352.

Washington, Harriet A. 2006. *Medical Apartheid: The Dark History of Medical Experimentation on Black Americans from Colonial Times to the Present.* 1st ed. New York: Doubleday.

Wedell-Wedellsborg, Thomas. 2017. "Are You Solving the Right Problems?" *Harvard Business Review* 90 (February): 76–83. https://doi.org/10.1109/EMR.2016.7792409.

Westbrook, Ian. 2020. "GCSEs: What's Different with This Year's Exams?" *BBC News*, August 20, 2020, sec. Family & Education. https://www.bbc.com/news/education-53682466.

Wexler, Rebecca. 2021. "Privacy Asymmetries: Access to Data in Criminal Defense Investigations." *U.C.L.A. Law Review* 68 (1): 212–87. https://www.uclalawreview.org/privacy-asymmetries-access-to-data-in-criminal-defense-investigations/.

Wible, Brad, Jeffrey Mervis, and Nicholas S. Wigginton. 2014. "Rethinking the Global Supply Chain." *Science* 344 (6188): 1100–03. https://doi.org/10.1126/science.344.6188.1100.

Williams, Brooks, and Shmargad. 2018. "How Algorithms Discriminate Based on Data They Lack: Challenges, Solutions, and Policy Implications." *Journal of Information Policy* 8: 78–115. https://doi.org/10.5325/jinfopoli.8.2018.0078.

Wright, Christine M., Michael E. Smith, and Brian G. Wright. 2007. "Hidden Costs Associated with Stakeholders in Supply Management." *Academy of Management Perspectives* 21 (3): 64–82. https://doi.org/10.5465/AMP.2007.26421239.

Wu, Tim. 2016. *The Attention Merchants: The Epic Scramble to Get Inside Our Heads.* 1st ed. New York: Alfred A. Knopf.

Wu, Tim. 2019. "Blind Spot: The Attention Economy and the Law." *Antitrust Law Journal* 82 (January): 771.

Wu, Xiaolin, and Xi Zhang. 2017. "Automated Inference on Criminality Using Face Images." arXiv. https://doi.org/10.48550/arXiv.1611.04135.

Wylie, Chris. 2018. "Cambridge Analytica Leaked Documents." UK House of Commons, Digital, Culture, Media and Sport Committee's Fake News Inquiry. https://www.parliament.uk/documents/commons-committees/culture-media-and-sport/Chris%20Wylie%20Background%20papers.pdf.

Yeung, Karen. 2018. "Algorithmic Regulation: A Critical Interrogation." *Regulation & Governance* 12 (4): 505–23. https://doi.org/10.1111/rego.12158.

Young, Amber G., Ariel D. Wigdor, and Gerald C. Kane. 2020. "The Gender Bias Tug-of-War in a Co-Creation Community: Core-Periphery Tension on Wikipedia." *Journal of Management Information Systems* 37 (4): 1047–72. https://doi.org/10.1080/07421222.2020.1831773.

Zeide, Elana. 2014. "The Proverbial Permanent Record." SSRN Scholarly Paper ID 2507326. Social Science Research Network. https://papers.ssrn.com/abstract=2507326.

Zemeckis, Robert, dir. 1988. *Who Framed Roger Rabbit.* https://www.imdb.com/title/tt0096438/.

Index

For the benefit of digital users, indexed terms that span two pages (e.g., 52–53) may, on occasion, appear on only one of those pages.